MUZZY

MY STORY

MY STORY

Sport Media

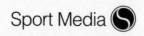

Sport Media

Muzzy Izzet:
My Story

© Muzzy Izzet

Written with Lee Marlow.

First Edition
Published in Great Britain in 2015.

Published and produced by: Trinity Mirror Sport Media,
PO Box 48, Old Hall Street, Liverpool L69 3EB.

Managing Director: Steve Hanrahan
Commercial Director: Will Beedles
Executive Editor: Paul Dove
Executive Art Editor: Rick Cooke
Senior Marketing Executive: Claire Brown
Sales and Marketing Manager: Elizabeth Morgan
Editing & Production: James Cleary

ISBN: 978-1-910335-25-3

Front cover & design: Lee Ashun
Photographic acknowledgements:
PA Photos, Leicester Mercury, Muzzy Izzet collection,
Will 'Warm Hands' Johnston.

Printed and bound by CPI Group (UK) Ltd,
Croydon, CR0 4YY.

CONTENTS

Thanks...

So then – a book, a biography. Eighteen chapters and a few extras, some pictures old and new, more than 90,000 words. Who'd have thought it? Well, not me, that's for sure. I wasn't sure I had it in me. I really hope you think it's all right.

We didn't rush this. We took our time. My memory isn't always the best so we checked everything, and then checked it again. Good luck to you if you find a mistake in here. All I can say is that this was the way it seemed to me, the way I remember it. It's my story, after all. I can only apologise if my version of events doesn't quite tally with yours.

I'd like to say a special thanks to my mum and dad, Jackie and Mehmet. All kinds of good people helped me to become a professional footballer, but no-one did more than my mum and dad. They had patience, they took me everywhere and they never complained. They always believed in me, even – especially – during the toughest times.

My brother, Kem, was dragged all over London and beyond to watch me play football but he never complained. Kem was a very good player himself. He has a lovely family, wife Rachel and three kids (my nephews Thomas, Jack and my niece, Isabella). I'm proud of the man he is today and the career he carved out for himself. I love you, bro! I'd also like to thank...

My old East End mates, Danny and Stu. They're my two oldest friends from East London. We don't see each other as often as we'd all like, but when we do it all falls back into shape. They both did so much to help me and I can't thank them enough.

Steve Plews, my oldest mate in Leicester. Steve was there

when I did my knee at Birmingham. He took me for my scans. He took me to the pub when I was feeling sorry for myself. I was grateful for that. "It went round a corner mate!"

My grandad George for all his love. He made the best stew, even if he wasn't the best pigeon racer! I miss those Saturday afternoons we spent together.

Nene and Dede, the most loving grandparents. I loved Sunday afternoons eating Turkish food at their house.

A huge thank you to all my lovely aunts and uncles – they were all a big part of my childhood: Serif, Ayse and Ian, Ulus and Kim, Metin and Brenda, Hassain and Denise, Muzen and Sulleyman and Tina.

The mother-in-law Christine (Sylvia). Thanks for all your love and support over the years.

Thanks to Martin O'Neill for fishing me out of Chelsea reserves all those years ago, for believing in me, for giving me the opportunity to progress as a footballer. He was a brilliant manager who created a special team at Leicester. I was blessed to be a part of that.

All the good players and good men I played with in my career – and there were a lot of them – but especially Neil Lennon, who made me a better player simply by playing next to me and seeing the game so well. I learned so much from him. Steve Walsh, my business partner, ex-team-mate and loyal friend; Steve Guppy, who always makes the effort to stay in touch when life can sometimes make that difficult. He's a top man. Robbo and Wal – both great coaches, and their old school mentality helped to make us better footballers at Leicester and they also kept our feet on the ground.

My Uncle Paul, my mum's brother, Paul Newman of Bethnal

Green. He took me to my first ever football game. He was 6ft 9ins tall and he used to put me on his shoulders. I never grew tired of that.

Paul was desperate to go to the Middlesbrough League Cup final, but he had to go into hospital for an operation. I wasn't aware of how serious that op was. It was kept from me so I could concentrate on the game. He died on the operating table. I was devastated. Paul was a big part of my childhood.

Thanks to my old mate and co-writer, Lee Marlow. We met every month or so and we'd have a drink and something to eat and we'd just chat. Each time, he went away and turned it into something better. Somehow, three years later, here we are. A proper book. It was his dedication which saw us through. *Magniff*, son. We did it.

Finally, I'd like to thank my beautiful wife Carly, not just for being my wife, but my partner, my soul mate and the one who keeps it all together. She's been so loyal to me over the years. She makes it work. Carly sacrificed everything so I could concentrate on playing football and, to this day, I know that without her, it wouldn't work. She keeps the show on the road.

And my three wonderful children – Ella, Dylan and Lyla. I feel lucky to have three happy, healthy, good kids and each of them makes me immensely proud. That's what it's all about for me, now – being a dad to them. It's the best job in the world.

Muzzy Izzet, 2015

Introduction: Lee Marlow

I interviewed Muzzy Izzet for the first time at the end of 2003/04 season. It was for a *Leicester Mercury* feature, looking back on City's relegation campaign. He doesn't remember it. I'm not offended by that. He barely remembers his own name. But I do. I remember it.

I wanted to ask him about that Wolves game, when City were 3-0 up at half-time before somehow conspiring to lose 4-3.

We spoke, on the phone. It was half-an-hour, 40 minutes maybe. He was a bit wary at first, I remember. A bit guarded. Gradually, as the interview continued, he seemed to thaw out. He was funny. There were no platitudes or cliches. He was honest. I liked him. He seemed decent. I was relieved about that. Muzzy was my favourite player at City. I was pleased he seemed like a decent bloke.

Believe me, it's not always like that.

I interviewed him a few more times after that. He was always good value. We met once in a pub. He was retired, wondering what to do next and we had a longer chat.

"You should do a book," I said.

"Nah," he replied. "No-one wants to read that."

I tried to persuade him that they would but he wouldn't have it and that's how we left it really. I'd see him occasionally, we'd have a chat, I'd always say: "What about that book then?" and he'd always laugh and shake his head. "No-one wants to read about me, saaaaahn." And that was that.

Until one day, in the summer of 2012, he rang me up at work. "About that book," he said. "I've been having a think…"

Three years later, and here we are.

About halfway through writing this book, I read a wise piece of advice to aspiring authors which said you should never write a biography of someone with living children. I read that and sighed. Ah… whoever said that had a point.

What you have here is not a warts-and-all exposé of who did what to who at Chelsea, Leicester City and Birmingham City because Muzzy Izzet is really not that kind of bloke – although he still has loads of interesting and amusing stories to tell.

I haven't worked out how many people he played with during his career. There must be hundreds of them. Muzzy only had a bad word to say about two of them (I'll leave you to find out who). Everyone else – the lads he played with at his three professional clubs, his friends, neighbours, old school mates, work colleagues, the Turkey players he didn't understand… they were all right, he says. That tells you all you need to know about the man.

So this is his story.

A skinny East End kid from a Turkish family who, against all odds, made it. A World Cup semi-final. Premier League. Cup finals. Europe.

People bandy the word 'legend' around so much now that it's lost some of its meaning. But Muzzy Izzet was a Leicester legend. A proper Leicester legend.

I'd like to say a big thanks to long-suffering wife Jo, and kids Ellie and Lucas, for their endless patience and understanding over the past three years or so.

"Where's Dad, Mum?"

"He's upstairs working on 'The Book', of course."

So hello again kids – you've got your dad back.

Thanks also to my brother Richard Marlow, for good advice and encouragement and listening to me banging on about it every time we got together; colleagues and ex-colleagues – Adam Wakelin, Martin Crowson, Jeremy Clay, Dave Wardale and top photographer Will 'Warm Hands' Johnston; Cumbria sports writer Jon Colman for good early advice; Dean Eldredge at Soar Media; my oldest mate Dave Ward, who had to hear about the book's slow progress every time we went out for a pint; wise words from the *Daily Telegraph's* Henry Winter, which stuck with me all the way through the writing process; LCFC's Andrew Neville and the keen-eye of *Mercury* super sub-editor Kevin Hughes.

Thanks to all the Leicester City players who gave their time and their anecdotes – what you have in this book are the printable ones – and their memories of one of the finest periods in Leicester City's history.

Thanks to Muzzy, too. He was always my favourite player during the O'Neill era and it's been a privilege to hear his stories and tell them here. *Magniff*, pal.

Thanks to my old dad for taking me to my first game – Leicester City versus Notts County, September 9, 1978, we lost 0-1 – my Uncle Judd, who took me to City often and my mum, who was in the middle of all this mayhem and never complained.

Special thanks, though, to my grandad George Tracey, and my uncle Terry Tracey. They took me to Filbert Street, week in, week out, when I was a lad. I didn't appreciate at the time what a fine schooling that was. And I never got the chance to say thanks, either. So thank you. I wish you could have been here to read it. X.

Lee Marlow, 2015

Preface by Martin O'Neill

The date: Saturday, March 30th, 1996.
The venue: Filbert Street, Leicester, LE2.
The time: About 4.25pm in the afternoon.

The boos and jeers reverberate around the stadium. Sheffield United, the visitors, are about to inflict a painful defeat on Leicester City and the home supporters are not happy. They are letting the beleaguered manager know in no uncertain terms how seriously upset they are. I am that manager.

An hour or so into the game, I introduce a young, professional footballer. Muzzy Izzet, on loan from Chelsea, arrived from Stamford Bridge less than 48 hours earlier. This is his very first taste of League football and, as I look at the lad, he must be wondering what on earth he has let himself in for.

His talent is unknown to the supporters – but not to me. I have seen him play many, many times at Kingstonian, West London, where Chelsea host their reserve games on Monday evenings. I know he can play. I also know he would prefer a less hostile atmosphere in which to start his league career.

Within minutes of taking the field, he does something that, momentarily, stifles the jeers. Controlling a very difficult pass played to him on a treacherous surface (that's what Filbert Street was always like, back then), he feigns to go one way, twists his body in another direction, leaves his opponent mesmerised and skips away from the tackle.

Passing years can sometimes cloud the memory, but Muzzy's little piece of magic – something he will repeat many times in the coming seasons – remains implanted in my brain. It's one of the fews crumbs of comfort for me over the bleak weekend which lies ahead. He is unable to alter the scoreline but, given the attendant furore this particular afternoon, he will not forget his own introduction to the Football League.

A few days later, he starts in the match against Charlton Athletic at The Valley. He plays brilliantly, too, in a wonderful victory that launches a career that will establish him as one of the finest midfield players ever to don a Leicester City shirt – and there have been quite a number of exceptional midfielders in the club's proud history.

Muzzy Izzet's impact on the club is as breathtaking as it is immediate, helping to guide the team to the First Division play-offs with the winning goal at Vicarage Road against Watford on the final day of the normal season (did I say "normal"?).

A semi-final two-legged win over Stoke City, followed by a now folklore victory over Crystal Palace in the Wembley final paves the way for the players to prove themselves in the Premier League. And it is on the biggest stage where Muzzy's talent shines through. In the coming seasons he not only makes his mark as a top-class midfielder, but he becomes an integral part of the club's success.

Muzzy Izzet was a wonderful footballer. His slim build belied a steely inner-strength capable of withstanding the toughest of challenges. Two-footed and always beautifully balanced, he possessed an uncanny ability to extricate himself from difficult positions and then glide past opponents. He was also an exceptionally good header of the ball under pressure but, perhaps his most endearing quality was his courage, both physical and moral, always the hallmark of a top-class player.

He had a pretty high pain threshold, too, hence the large number of games he played each season. We were always a better team when he was in it.

Popular in the dressing room, I believe, and popular with this particular manager, I know for certain.

Some time ago, a disgruntled player knocked on my office door and demanded to know why he wasn't in the team. When I explained to him my reasons for not selecting him, he shot back: "Well, you've got your favourites," the implicit assumption being that he wasn't in that category.

"You're right," I confessed. "I do have favourites. They are usually the best players."

It would be true to say that Muzzy Izzet was one of my favourites. In truth, he was everyone's favourite. He had, through his consistently brilliant performances, earned that right.

Martin O'Neill, 2015

TURKISH DELIGHT

It's June 25, 2002, late evening in Japan, lunch time in the UK.

The second half of the World Cup semi-final is inching towards its predictable close. Brazil are beating Turkey 1-0 in the Saitama Stadium, Japan's biggest football ground. A capacity 61,058 crowd are inside. An estimated 600 million are watching at home.

Sitting on the bench, wearing the number 13 shirt, is Muzzy Izzet. The number 13 is considered lucky in Turkey. It doesn't feel that way for Izzet. Turkey's number 13 doesn't know what's going on.

He has spent every game of the World Cup sitting on the bench. He doesn't know why he's not playing, only that he isn't. He has been away from his family for nearly two months. He doesn't speak Turkish. No-one speaks English. Two months is a long time when no-one speaks your language and you can't speak theirs.

This is football's biggest stage, one game away from a World Cup final. The number 13, though, he's just about had enough.

I have a series of stock answers I reel out when people ask me about the World Cup in 2002.

'Aw, yeah mate, it was great.'

'Aw, yeah, the crowds... the atmosphere... it was all brilliant.'

'That Brazil team – they were good. The best I've played against.'

And I tell them about me on the right, Roberto Carlos, the world's finest full-back, on the left. A World Cup semi-final. One game away from 'The Big One', the World Cup final.

I tell them how proud I felt running on to the pitch in the red of Turkey and the crowd and the expectation, and how the game passed by in the blink of an eye, a flash of brilliant gold and blue.

And that's all true.

It was a decent World Cup. The crowds in South Korea and later Japan, where we played the quarters and semi-finals, were awesome. They really were. People are usually happy enough to hear that. They don't want to know more. So I don't tell them.

The truth is that I didn't feel that at the time. I feel that through the warm glow of nostalgia. At the time, as the tournament wore on and I sat on the bench – watching, waiting, not getting a look in – I just wanted to come home.

I've never really suffered from home sickness. Playing football means spending huge amounts of time away from home. You travel. You sit on coaches and the world passes by but you laugh and joke; you play cards or, as we did at Leicester, you open a can and have a drink, and the time flies by. It's fine. It's all fine.

The World Cup in 2002 wasn't like that.

It might have looked like it was. We stayed at the finest hotels. We travelled first class. We had everything we wanted. I was treated like a Turkish prince for the best part of two months.

Every day there would be a knock on my door and someone would hand me a new mobile phone or a top-of-the-range camera, a DVD player, a camcorder or a laptop. They were gifts from the sponsors. They handed them out like party prizes. My hotel room looked like a ransacked Currys store.

When I finally got home, I had my suitcase and a bag full of brand new electrical items. The customs officer at Heathrow looked at me as though I'd ram-raided a shop. "I've been to the World Cup," I shrugged. "They gave me all of this."

I paid a bit of tax on it and they waved me through. I got home and gave it all away, not because I wasn't grateful. I just didn't need it. I had a phone. I had a camera. I didn't need two of them. I just thought other people might like them more than me. I had everything in the summer of 2002. I wanted for nothing. And yet, I'd never been so lonely in my life.

You need to know how this started. I was born in Mile End Hospital, East London. The sound of Bow Bells greeted my birth on October 31, 1974. I am a proper East Ender.

I lived in a two bedroom flat off the Vallance Road in the heart of East London with my Turkish Cypriot dad Mehmet, my English mum Jacqueline and my younger brother Kemal.

I was born in England. But I had a Turkish name. I ate pie and mash and watched *Only Fools and Horses* but I also ate dolma, rolled vine leaves pickled in brine, stuffed with mince meat.

We had big Turkish gatherings, where it seemed I was related to every single person in the room. People would sing and dance at these gatherings and I loved every minute of every one of them. But I supported West Ham and when Gary Lineker scored for England I cheered as loudly as my English friends.

I was one half English, one half Turkish. What did I consider myself, this little East End boy with the Cockney accent called Mustafa? A bit of both. Why not? That's what I was.

Dad came to London in 1959. He was three years old. He came on a boat with his mum, my grandmother. To this day, his first memory is that boat trip, his mum being so sick all the way here that she couldn't leave her cabin.

He was brought up here. All of his friends are English. He's a roofer from Mile End. He lives in Leicestershire now, not far from me and his grandkids, but he sounds like Ray Winstone. His dad, my grandad Ali, was a military police officer in the British Army in Cyprus.

"Pack your bags and go to England, Mr Izzet," an army general told him in 1959. Things were changing there, he said. The British were pulling out. It would be better if he left. Cyprus wasn't torn apart by civil war for another 15 years but they knew, even then, what was brewing.

By then Ali, my grandmother Vedia, my dad and his brothers and sisters were in London. They left their old life by the Mediterranean in Larnaca, Cyprus, and started a new one in London – in north London first, and then Bow.

Ali became a cobbler. It was tough for them in north London. But he worked hard and he made a life for his family. London was my dad's home. He doesn't remember anything of Cyprus. London was my home, too. It was all either of us knew.

Family was important to my father. We would get together with his four brothers and two sisters, and their children, and we would laugh and joke and sing Turkish songs celebrating a homeland we had heard all about but never knew. I liked all of that, though. It was nice.

When I was six years old, I was circumcised. To this day, that's one of my earliest memories – and it's not a pleasant one. They call it a *Sunet* in Turkey and it's marked, naturally, with a party; a Sunet party. They like to celebrate, the Turks. Even the removal of a terrified six-year-old boy's foreskin is an excuse for a party. I liked the party element. I was less keen on the circumcision, I have to say.

My nan paid for it. She insisted every good Turkish boy needed to be circumcised. I wasn't really old enough to know why this was so, but I was old enough to ask why it was necessary and I was old enough to know that it sounded excruciating. "Will it be painful, Dad?" I remember asking my father, as he ruffled my hair and tried to pretend that it wouldn't hurt and that, instead, it was something that would make a man of me. I knew, though. I knew he wasn't telling me the truth. He couldn't hide it. I knew it wouldn't be nice.

It wasn't nice, either. It was fucking horrendous. I went private, a small clinic on the outskirts of London. They gave me an anaesthetic, thankfully, but I remember vividly lying on the operating table with a huge screen so I couldn't see what they were doing to my little chap.

They cut off my foreskin and then dressed my poor, besmirched six-year-old Turkish penis in a bandage the size of a baked-bean can. You might think you can imagine how painful that was but you can't. You can't imagine it. Not really. It was agony, an agony that lasted for days. I had a bath every night that week. Eventually, the bandages peeled away and it was over and there I was – a good Turkish boy.

They saved my foreskin. My mum kept it in a little jar. I have no idea why. We lost it when we moved house. I wasn't too upset about that. I don't know if being circumcised has ever made a difference to me. I doubt it.

When I first played for Turkey I remember the other players gathering around me in the changing room, pointing and staring, wanting to know if I'd had it done, if I was 'a good Turkish boy.'

So I showed them. They nodded their approval. And that was that. I can safely say that I've never shown my penis before, or since, to a group of approving young men but, if nothing else, it seemed to help the bonding process.

I have a young son today. He will know all about his Turkish background and where his family are from. He will be a good Turkish/English boy – but he won't go through that.

Let's fast forward a few years. I'm at Leicester City, playing in a midfield that's well-drilled, competitive and surprisingly better than most of our opponents gave us credit for.

I always enjoyed it when other teams underestimated us. I thought, eventually, these teams would work us out. I thought they would work harder. But they never seemed to work harder than us. So there we are. We're playing well. I'm playing well. I don't remember when Martin O'Neill first said it, I just remember feeling embarrassed when he did.

'Izzet for England, says O'Neill' was the back page of the *Leicester Mercury*. He said it a few times. He thought I was ready, that I was one of the best midfielders in the country. Frankly, I wasn't sure if I was. I was flattered and I'd wonder, sometimes, if I was, but then I'd wake up and realise I wasn't. Who was I? I was just this young kid who hadn't made it at Chelsea.

I wasn't ready for England. You have to earn your stripes to get a place in the England squad. I hadn't done that. I was still earning my stripes at Leicester. I felt like that for the lion's share of my career. I never, ever took it for granted. O'Neill never spoke to me about his honestly-held opinion that I should be in the England squad. He just kept saying it. It made me blush.

I came from the hinterland of Chelsea reserves. The manager who wouldn't give me a chance in the first team? Glenn Hoddle – who had become the England manager in 1996. If he didn't fancy me at Chelsea, why would he fancy me at England? He wouldn't, would he? It would have made him look stupid. Letting me go at Chelsea – but picking me for England? It wouldn't happen with most managers. I knew for certain it wouldn't happen with Hoddle.

But things got better and better – better for Leicester, better for me. We won things. We started to get the respect we deserved at Leicester. We weren't just a team of cloggers and long-ball merchants. We could play a bit, too. We always knew that. It just took everyone else a bit longer to realise it.

In 1999, Hoddle quit the England job after making some ill-judged comments about disabled people with Kevin Keegan taking over. O'Neill still carried on with his one man 'Muzzy-for-England' campaign. I still didn't really believe him. But, by now, I wasn't blushing. I was earning my stripes at the top level. It didn't sound quite so ridiculous.

A reporter from the *Daily Telegraph* told me once that both Hoddle and Keegan had given me the once over; that they'd had me watched at Leicester and entertained thoughts of picking me. They never did – but I know why.

It wasn't a great time to be trying to force your way into the England midfield. It wasn't as if they were short on quality:

Gazza, Scholes, Beckham, Ince, Batty, Redknapp, Butt, McManaman, Anderton and two young lads called Gerrard and Lampard, who were coming through and making their mark. It wasn't bad, was it?

This was the start of the so-called Golden Generation. I wondered where a scrawny little half Turkish/half English midfielder might fit in. My agent had a discreet word with Keegan. Was I close? Was I on the verge? Keegan was apprehensive. He ran through his options: Scholes, Beckham, Butt, Redknapp. I wasn't close, no. Not really.

But then as one door closes, another door opens. Just as England were saying 'no', Turkey were saying 'yes'. On February 2, 2000, we beat Aston Villa 1-0 in the second leg of the semi-final of the Worthington Cup. It was one of those magical nights at Filbert Street and, amidst all the jubilation and celebration, someone threw a Turkish flag onto the pitch.

I saw it straight away. I picked it up and draped it over my shoulders. I held it aloft. I waved it. I danced with it. I tied it round my neck. I had it for two or three minutes, no more, and then we were down the tunnel and away, the celebrations carrying on in a nearby pub. But footage of that celebration made its way on to Turkish TV. And that's when it all started.

I wasn't widely known in Turkey. I'd like to pretend that it was my outstanding performances in the Leicester City midfield that changed all that. In reality, it was the flag, me jigging around the pitch with the Turkish flag.

I know all countries are proud of their flag and what it represents but it is especially so in Turkey. The flag is the bloodline of the nation. I was always told growing up that the red flag represented the blood of the nation, the men who fought for Turkey's liberty, that the star and the crescent moon were reflections in a pool of blood spilled by her warriors, fighting for freedom. It's grim, but proud and rousing and that's why it's such a big thing – a representation of the sacrifice of the few for the liberty of the many.

A scout from the Turkish FA wanted to know if I would be interested in playing for Turkey. I said I would. His English was good. I thought they would all speak English. I would come to regret this assumption.

After an away game at Watford – February 12, 2000, we drew 1-1 – I drove to the Turkish Embassy in London where we would meet. They had lots of questions they wanted to ask me. I had lots of questions for them. It was like a date. *Was I right for them? Were they right for me?* Tonight, we would sort it out. I knew already. I was ready. If they wanted me, I would say 'yes'.

Inside the Embassy, there were Turkish TV cameras, a crowd of reporters, TV lights and questions, lots and lots of questions. I'd been warned there might be a photographer, that there might be a small amount of media interest. I didn't expect this.

The feed, I was told, was being transmitted live on a Turkish sports channel. Across my father's homeland, families were tucking into their supper and watching this naive young Turk blinking into the lights of a dozen cameras. Did I consider myself Turkish or English? (Both, but if this is going out on Turkish TV then, yes, Turkish with a bit of English thrown in.)

The truth was I had been to Turkey only once. I went to Bodrum on holiday in 1996, with some of my mates. Leicester had just been promoted. We watched the European Championships in the bars, all of us cheering for Terry Venables' England. I didn't tell them that.

Would I want to play in the European Championships? (I would, yes.) Did I rate the Turkish team? (I did, yes, they had some very good players.) And when would I be completing my mandatory two years' national service?

My what?

Your national service, the reporter said again.

Silence.

In Turkey, every male between the ages of 20 and 41 has to complete two years of mandatory National Service. I looked around. The officials looked around. I wasn't going to do two years' national service. Not. A. Chance. I was playing for Leicester City. I was living my dream. I wasn't going to give that up to serve in the Turkish army. And then, with no explanation, the lights faded and the cameras were switched off.

One of the officials looked at the TV reporter and shook his head. He'd pulled the plug. He took the reporter into a corner. "There will be no national service," he said. "But it's okay. He wants to play. We want him to play. Everything is fine."

There were no more questions. A day later I was given my Turkish passport. That summer, I was picked to play for Turkey in the European Championships. I made my debut in the second group game, against Sweden. I missed the first match, a 2-0 defeat to Italy and the coach, Mustafa Denizil, who had arranged to leave to take the manager's position at Fenerbahce, was under pressure to play me.

Martin O'Neill was working as a pundit for the BBC. He had recently left Leicester to take over at Celtic. Regardless, he re-ignited his one man Muzzy Izzet campaign. "Muzzy would cope brilliantly in this competition," he told the media. "He's got the temperament for it, he's very confident in his own ability, he can go past players. He perhaps lacks that phenomenal turn of pace to go – and then stay – away from players but he's got such magical feet he can create things. He's a brave lad as well."

I don't know if Denizil was listening but it worked. I was in, and I made my debut against the Swedes. Well, that's what the record books say. I remember nothing of it save for the fact I was injured in the 58th minute thanks to a diabolical tackle by Celtic centre-half, Johan Mjallby. We ended up finishing second behind Italy in our group. In the quarter-finals we lost 2-0 to Portugal and came home. As an experience, it was alright. My folks flew out and stayed in a nearby hotel. Carly, my partner, came out, as did a few mates. I didn't feel as estranged as I would two years later, on the other side of the world in the biggest footballing competition on the planet.

I played a few times for Turkey in between the Euros of 2000 and the World Cup of 2002. It was good. I enjoyed it. And I was proud. I must have liked it – because the logistics of getting from Leicester to Turkey were an enormous pain in the arse. I first had to get down to Heathrow. Then from Heathrow, a four-hour flight to Ataturk International Airport, Istanbul. Meet up with the squad. Train. Fly wherever we had to go. Even when we had a home game we'd sometimes play in Germany or another major European city – but we'd still meet in Istanbul first. Play the game. Speak to virtually no-one. Come home.

I was always proud to play for Turkey. I knew what it meant to my dad, my family. I was proud to represent my country. But everything that surrounded it – the travel, the whole drawn out pantomime of it all – I could have done without it.

By the time the 2002 World Cup came around, I think my heart was already starting to drift away.

I don't know if I was aware of that at the time, but I can see it now. I was excited about the World Cup. I was looking forward to it. I was proud to be in the squad, but I was tired of all the peripheral stuff that surrounded the football.

On top of this, I just wasn't prepared for how isolated I was going to feel. It was supposed to be my finest moment. It turned into the loneliest experience of my professional career.

SECRET CONTRACT

No regrets. Ask Muzzy Izzet if there's anything he would have done differently and he'll shake his head and tell you no.

"No regrets, son. Life's too short for that."

Push him, though, dig a little deeper – you don't have to dig too deeply, either – and there is one.

It dates back to when he was a kid, 13 years old, six stone wet through, settled at Charlton Athletic, doing well, all the right people saying all the right things – and then leaving for what was supposed to be a bigger club and a bigger chance across London at Chelsea.

It was stupid, he'll say.

Don't leave a small, happy ship – where things are going well, where people know and like you – for a bigger one. You won't have more chance of making it. You'll have less.

He'd been at Charlton for a couple of years. He liked it there. It was a good set-up with good people. And they were skint. Skint is not necessarily a bad thing if you're a young midfielder looking to break into the game.

A club with no money is unlikely to be handing out big cheques to the manager in order to find the next Paul Gascoigne. Instead, a club with no money is more likely to give the kid in the reserves a chance. Not because they want to, necessarily, but because they have to. Skint is good.

Muzzy would have a chance. They told him so. "Keep going and you'll be playing for the first team before too long," they said, and Muzzy would smile and wonder if they were having him on.

And what did he do?

He left and moved across London to Chelsea.

Chelsea made him a secret offer – a suspect, possibly illegal offer – that he couldn't refuse. "Sign for us as a schoolboy," they said, "and we'll guarantee you a two-year YTS. We'll take you on."

Clubs didn't do this.

A good prospect at 14 wasn't always a top prospect at 16.

This is what Chelsea did. There was more.

"Sign for us now," they added, "and we'll not only take you on for two years YTS – we'll give you a first-year contract, too." A contract. He'd be a pro-footballer.

At the age of 14, Mustafa Kemal Izzet was being told he'd made it – he would be a professional footballer.

"If that's the deal, I'll sign," he said.

"That's the deal," said Chelsea.

He signed.

Two years later, they tried to say it wasn't…

Vallance Road, London, E2. Even people who know nothing about East London know about Vallance Road. This was where the Krays lived. It was where I lived, too. Fourth floor, Kingsham House, number 34. A big block of flats right at the bottom end of Vallance Road, London, E2.

There were two of these giant tower blocks; two blocks divided by a small green which was our playground, our Upton Park, our Wembley. I came home from school, ate my dinner and I was straight down on to the green for a game of football.

This is my first memory. The green outside my flat, me, a ball at my feet. My first memory is not of playing football with the other kids, but playing football with my old man. I came home from school, I'd eat and I'd sit by the door, waiting for my dad to come home.

The poor bloke, he'd hardly stepped through the door and I was hanging off him, dragging him down flight after flight of concrete stairs and outside again, on to the green, me and him kicking a ball around. He always did it, too. It didn't matter how hard his day had been, what was on the telly or if it was raining. He'd come down those stairs with our old leather ball and we'd knock it around, until he really did have to go and have his tea.

It wasn't technical. He never pushed me or told me what to do. I was four, for God's sake. How technical do you want it to be? We just knocked it around, lad and dad, outside, on the green, our Wembley, our Upton Park, just by the Vallance Road flats, London, E2.

My dad was a decent player. He played right-back for Tipples, the local pub team. They were a good side and they took great pride – in this rough pub league – of playing proper football;

from the back, passing, moving, ball on the floor. What my dad had, though, as a parent – and it is more valuable than anything else – was patience.

He always had the time. I look back and I think of the people who helped me, good people who encouraged me, who put me on the right track, made me the player I was, and no-one did more than my dad and the knockabouts we had on the green on Vallance Road. It was just fun. But we did it every night. And, gradually – so gradually I didn't realise – I got better.

Other kids would come over sometimes and try to join in, but I was a bit funny about that. I didn't like it. I was possessive about my dad. I didn't want to play with other kids. I wanted to play with my dad. Just me and him.

We did this for months, years even, just me and him, and by the time I was eight, I was playing with the big kids and holding my own. Dad would look on and smile. "You know what," he said, one day, "I think it's time you joined a proper team."

Weaver's Field was just over the way from Vallance Road. A big municipal playing field, it was the home ground of the mighty St Matthew's Under-10s. I was eight when I played for them, playing with kids two years older. It didn't bother me much, although there was one obvious drawback: I was small. Really small. I was small for an eight-year-old – and now I was playing against boys who were two years' older and some of them were a foot taller.

It didn't matter, though. I was aware of this height discrepancy – I'd have been daft not to have been – but it never bothered me. All I wanted to do was play. And I was decent, too. At that age, I could do things that some of the 10-year-olds couldn't do. I had two good feet. My dad always made me pass the ball with both feet, dribble with both feet, shoot with both feet. I knew what I was doing. I could pass. I could dribble. I could read the game. I was aware. I had a good first touch.

I could keep the ball up, too. Both feet, knee, chest, head. By the time I was 10 or 11, I could do that all day long. In fact, I did, literally, do it all day long; day after day after day. I didn't know how many keep-ups I could do. I lost count after 1,000. We didn't have computer games in our house back then. And I wasn't really interested in anything else. It was just football. So that's what I did. I went outside and did keep-ups.

I hear some people today say that doesn't matter, that you don't go through a game doing keep-ups. Frankly, that's bollocks. Of course it matters. It improves your first touch. If you can learn how to keep the ball up like that, it helps you in a game. It helps your control, your movement, your anticipation. I knew if the ball came to me in a match, whether it was on my knee, chest, right foot, left foot, it didn't matter – I knew I could deal with it. It gives you a feel for the ball. It makes you a better player.

I don't remember my first goal for St Matthew's Under-10s. I only remember the write-up in the local paper, the *East London Advertiser*, with 'Goalscorer: M. Izzet' noted under our goals total. I cut that out and took it to school with me. I never got bored of seeing that.

I earned my place in the St Matthew's Under-10s side – and football was helping me in other areas of my life, too. It helped me settle in. It gave me confidence. I was a shy kid. I didn't make friends easily at school.

I was also acutely aware of being slightly different to my mates. To all intents and purposes, I was just a scruffy-arsed East End lad, the same as all the other lads in my class.

But I wasn't. That much was clear first thing in the morning, as soon as Mrs Seymour took the morning register: Mustafa Izzet. It was different. There weren't any other Mustafas in my class, or in my school.

I felt that from an early age. Kids, when they're nine or 10 years old, they don't want to be different. They want to be the same. They want to fit in. I only really felt like I started to fit in when I played football. Football was the great leveller. It opened doors. People noticed you. If you were good at football, you gained the respect of the playground. I went from a small kid called Mustafa, with very few friends who wasn't very good at school, to Muz, the little midfielder who kept scoring for St Matthew's and getting his name in the *East London Advertiser*.

Then, as with most kids at our school and virtually every other school at that time, an extra 'ee' was added at the end. Muz became Muzzee, then Muzzie. And that stuck. I only became Muzzy when the *Leicester Mercury* started calling me Muzzy. I didn't mind. It didn't matter to me.

I went from St Matthew's on Vallance Road to St Thomas More Under-11s at Bexley Heath. For two seasons, I don't think we lost a game. We went to Scotland to play in a tournament, the Ayr Cup, and won it.

From St Thomas More, I went to Senrab in Tower Hamlets. Senrab had a reputation. They were the best youth team in East London. You didn't just wander down and see if you could get a game. You had to be invited to play for Senrab. Someone saw me playing for St Thomas More and they asked me to join.

Senrab had some good players and an impressive pedigree. In the 1970 and '80s, so many Senrab players signed for Chelsea that they became known as 'Chelsea Juniors.' There's a long list of top players who have played for Senrab: Jermaine Defoe, John Terry, Paul Konchesky, Bobby Zamora, Lee Bowyer, Ledley King, Sol Campbell and my brother, Kem.

Kem was a good player. There was six years between us but, as soon as he could walk, he had a ball at his feet. We used to play in the front room at home, with a ball made from rolled up socks, ornaments flying everywhere and my mum going mad. It wasn't easy for him, as my younger brother, but he handled it all brilliantly. He's a good lad, Kem.

I played in the same side as Ade Akinbiyi. He was my mate and a good player. Ade will pop up up again later when he became Leicester City's record signing. It was a heavy burden for him, that price tag. He felt the pressure. In training, he was brilliant, day after day. But the expectation was too much. He couldn't handle the weight of expectation, the constant scrutiny. It was a shame, because he was a decent lad, Ade, and a decent player.

Every time Senrab had a game, we played to a small crowd of scouts. This is what annoys me when people say we don't have quality kids in England. We do. I've seen them. I've played with them. I've played against them. There are good young footballers all over our country.

At 12 or 13, those kids I played with and against every week played with an exuberance and a natural brilliance that was just intrinsic. It was like second nature, they didn't know anything else.

We were encouraged to go out, to enjoy it, to pass the ball, to make space for each other, to play possession football, keep it, to make the opposition work. We did that. We did it effortlessly. It was the way we played: game after game after game.

We played Ridgeway Rovers one Saturday morning. They were a good side, too. They had a midfield player by the name of David Beckham. He was excellent, I recall. I often wonder what happened to him...

The bad habits – they all came later, when all the good work we took for granted was coached out of us. It sounds almost blasé to say that now, a cliché even. But it's only a cliché because it's true. I know. I saw it. I saw it first hand.

I signed a year's schoolboy contract at Charlton at the age of 12 and, twice a week, my dad took me across East London so I could train at their ground in Bexley Heath. I signed for Charlton but, frankly, it could have been anyone. Every team sent a scout to Senrab games. There were dozens of them.

I played for and trained with Charlton for a year. When it came to sign on again, I decided I wanted to see what other clubs were like so I looked around.

When I was 13, I trained at West Ham, QPR, Millwall, Arsenal and Tottenham. I spent three days at Forest – which was unnerving, my first time away from home, living in digs in Nottingham – and I went to Chelsea. I went all over. It was good, a thorough footballing education.

I came back to The Valley, though. It was a good set-up at Charlton. They liked me. I liked them. And I knew they rated me. That's important, I think. You've got to go where you're liked. Plus, I felt I had more chance of making the grade at Charlton, playing in the then Second Division, than I did with a bigger club in the top flight. So I signed for Charlton at 13.

And then what did I do?

I made the biggest mistake of my footballing career: a few months later, as things were going well at Charlton, I left and signed for Chelsea. Why? Because Chelsea made me an offer I couldn't refuse. I don't have many regrets in football. But that's one of them. I shouldn't have gone to Chelsea. I should have stayed at Charlton. A few of my mates – Terry Skiverton, Andy Grant, a couple of others – were at Chelsea. Senrab still had close links at Stamford Bridge.

The Chelsea scout kept telling my dad that I'd be better off with them. "But he's happy at Charlton," my dad said. But they were persistent. They upped the ante. They made me an offer and made me promise not to tell any of the other Chelsea youngsters. I never did.

Chelsea promised me a two-year YTS contract This was unheard of; no club did this. I was 14. YTS contracts were two years away. But they said I was guaranteed a YTS. I was tempted by that. But they hadn't finished. They promised me a first-year professional contract, too. I thought this seemed odd. They might have liked me at 14. But a lot of things can happen in two years – to me and to them.

"This is how much we want you," they said. "We are guaranteeing you a first-year professional contract."

I talked it over with my dad although there wasn't much talking to do. They were guaranteeing me that I would become a professional footballer; that, whatever happened over the next two years, I would make the grade. It was all I ever wanted.

I signed on the dotted line and became a Chelsea player. I would be a professional footballer. And I did as they told me: I never mentioned it to another soul.

My dad asked them to jot it all down in a contract.

"There's no need for that, Mr Izzet," they said. "Everything will be sorted. No need for contracts."

My dad insisted though so, eventually, they drew up a contract. Two years later, I was pleased he did. Chelsea went back on their word. That contract saved my skin.

The flip side was that at school, I cared even less than I had before. I didn't skive. I didn't cause trouble. I wasn't a bad kid. I just wasn't bothered. School didn't matter. Football mattered.

I went to Lawdale Junior School in Bethnal Green. Then we moved to Canning Town, and I went to Ravenscroft Juniors and Cumberland High School. I can't tell you what qualifications I got. I think I got a GCSE in English. Don't hold me to that, though. I'm not sure. I didn't care. As soon as Chelsea said they were going to take me on, it was all about the football.

I left school in 1990 and joined Chelsea. Every one of my mates left at the same time. Virtually all of them became builders or black cab drivers. No-one I knew stopped on. I know in most biographies you'll read page after glowing page of someone's halcyon schooldays and teachers who influenced them, who went the extra yard. Not here, I'm afraid.

I liked Mr Gamble at Lawdale. He kept a plastic football behind his desk and, if he heard you chatting, he'd throw the ball at you. He used to throw it at me and I'd head it back to him. He saw through my bluster, though, and he encouraged me to play football. Mr Passad at Cumberland was all right as well. He managed to get me and three of my mates on an all girls' skiing trip when we were 15. We all loved him for that. But my school years were not the happiest of my life.

As a first year YTS at Chelsea, I received £29.50 a week, £35 in the second year. Chelsea paid some towards my travelling – a young person's Travel Card was £100 a month back then and I was travelling from East to West London everyday – and they paid my lodgings. That went straight into my back pocket because I was living at home with my mum and dad.

We trained twice a week at Chelsea, at the Battersea Park grounds in West London. Big Ted Davis was the coach. Ted was an imposing character, with a booming voice and a domineering personality. I was petrified of him. We all were.

If something happened which he didn't like, Ted would slam his huge shovel-sized hands down on the table – BANG! – and we'd all shudder. No-one wanted to cross Ted. He was strict with us – too strict, really; he didn't have to be like that – but, as a player, he seemed to like me. I witnessed his temper many times. But he never aimed it in my direction.

Chelsea didn't play in the same way as Senrab. At Senrab, we were all encouraged to be ourselves, to play, enjoy it, pass the ball, express ourselves. Chelsea wasn't like that.

I played centre midfield. My game was about control, vision, quick mind, quick feet, passing, joining the attack. Well, that's what it was supposed to be about. From the age of 14 plus, during my schoolboy years with Chelsea and with Chelsea reserves, it was rarely – if ever – like that.

Chelsea didn't play football. Going through the academy and into the South East Counties League, it was less about football and more about attrition. We played in rough leagues. The pitches were generally mud baths; two at either end, another muddy area in the middle. It became less about football and more about hoofing the ball into the opposition's box.

There wasn't a lot of quality in the South East Counties League. It was about strength: big men in defence and up front, knocking the ball long to the big centre-forward.

There was no finesse. It was just hoof. We were all right at that at Chelsea.

After the initial excitement wore off – it didn't take long – I quickly started to feel disillusioned. This isn't what I signed up for, I used to say to my dad. I didn't want this. He listened to me and said all the right things – "Give it a chance, son, it'll get better" – but he knew it, too. I could see it in his eyes.

We'd made a mistake.

We came to Chelsea thinking things would be better; bigger and better than Charlton.

They weren't. They were worse. We'd been sold a dud.

At the end of my final schoolboy season, they started handing out YTS apprenticeships. It was all the lads could talk about in the changing room. Who deserved one? Who didn't? Who did the boss like? Where would you go if you didn't get in? I learned pretty quickly to keep my head down during these conversations and to sink quietly into the background. They'd promised me my professional contract two years earlier. I knew that I was safe.

Except, of course, I wasn't. The promises they made when I signed counted for nothing now. They wanted me out. I was beginning to feel in the weeks leading up to 'D-Day' that something wasn't quite right. Just little things: a comment here, a dig, repeated accusations from the coaches, just loud enough for me to hear, that I was too small. That I was not big enough for the big boys' league.

There were 30 Under-16 lads at Chelsea. They gave apprenticeships to 16 of them, 14 were let go. I was one of the 14. My dad came to pick me up. I walked out of the training ground, biting my lip, trying to keep it all in.

He knew what had happened as soon as he saw me. "They haven't offered me a YTS, Dad," I said.

He looked dumbfounded. But they promised? They wrote it all down. My dad went over to see Ted Davis. "There's been a mistake," he said. "No mistake," said Ted. "He's not in. He's not big enough. He'll never make it."

My dad told him about the Secret Contract, the piece of paper that Dad had insisted on. Ted looked surprised. If he knew about the contract, he wasn't letting on. I was out. I went home – I was too shocked to cry. The following day, my dad took the contract in. It was all there, in black and white. The Secret Contract. "You can't back out of that," he said.

We didn't hear from Chelsea for a while. It all went quiet. They called two days later. It was Dave Collier, the youth-team coach, offering apologies and niceties. All I heard was back-tracking. Chelsea would be pleased to offer Mustafa Izzet a two-year apprenticeship, he said. "But know this," he added, the tone changing. "He won't play." I'd be on the bench.

I didn't want to go. I didn't want to join a club that didn't want me. I didn't want to go and sit on the bench. I wanted to go back to Charlton.

At that stage I'd have gone anywhere. But, it was too late to go back to Charlton or anywhere else. All the apprentices had been chosen, all the spaces allocated. I could try somewhere else – but the chances were, at this late stage, that I wouldn't get in. My dad persuaded me to go back. "Two years is a long time in football," he said. "Things change, faces change. It could all be different again in no time." I hoped he was right. I went back. For the first three-quarters of the first season, Dave Collier was right. I didn't get near the team.

I was drinking protein drinks, lifting weights and eating pasta because they kept saying I was too small. It made no difference though. I was eating and training like Rocky Balboa but I still looked like a jockey. I wasn't just small. I was out of the team and small. It wasn't a great time.

And then, after spending most of that first year sitting on the bench, watching the action but never really getting near to it, the Chelsea youth team travelled to Germany for a big 'friendly' tournament between various European clubs. It was meaningless, really, but it was this tournament that turned my Chelsea career around.

We struggled in Germany. The European teams didn't play like Cambridge United reserves or Southend United's youth team in the South East Counties League. They knocked the ball around for fun. We were murdered in the first two games. Our brutal, one-dimensional long-ball game was quickly found out. So, to his credit, coach Dave Collier changed things around.

Rather than hitting hopeful long balls to our big number nine, Zeke Rowe, we started getting the ball down and playing football through the middle of the pitch. "Muzzy," Dave said one morning, calling me over. "You're in tomorrow. Prepare well." I got a game.

Dave had never rated me. I was too small, he told me, and he told me often. But, now, finally, in a meaningless tournament hundreds of miles from home, he was giving me a chance. And this time, we were playing football; keeping the ball on the floor, trying to pass our way through teams, beating them by guile and skill rather than just humping it forward. For the first time since I'd been at Chelsea, they were playing to my strengths.

We played better. Teams didn't carve through us. Instead, we started carving through them. I loved it. I had a chance, finally, to show them what I could do. I took it. I played well. They picked me again. I played well again. I can't remember how many games we played, how many we won or lost. We didn't win the tournament, I know that.

I didn't play any differently in Germany. I was the same player I was back home. It was just that WE played differently. I did well. For the first time, other people at Chelsea could, I think, see what I could do. I'd proven myself. It was virtually the end of the first year. There were only a handful of games until the end of the season. I played in every one.

My relationship with Dave improved, too. Dave liked tough midfielders. I showed him that, even though I was small, I was solid and I had heart. I wasn't scared. I wasn't easily shoved off the ball. And then, typically, just as me and Dave were getting along fine, he left the club. Former Chelsea and Wales midfielder Peter Nicholas was appointed as the new youth-team boss. Peter was renowned as a tough-tackling, no-nonsense midfielder. I felt my heart sink. I won't be his kind of player, I thought. But he kept picking me. Me and Peter – we got along just fine.

This perfectly happy state of affairs continued for the second year. We didn't play like Barcelona under Peter, but we tried to knock it around. I did all right, too. I played well. By the end of that second year, I knew I'd done enough. They were dropping hints to me all the time, stuff like: *'If you like it this year, Muz, you just wait til next year, eh?'* and a wink and a nudge, stuff like that.

According to the Secret Contract, they'd promised me a year. A year's pro contract. But this time – the compliments, the kind words – things seemed different. This wasn't because of a two-year-old contract. I felt like I'd earned it.

On one of the last days of the season, the end of our second year, they gathered us together at Stamford Bridge. The boss was in one room, down the corridor. We all sat in the changing room. It was excruciating.

"I don't care who comes in first or in what order, but one at a time when you're ready," said Gwyn Williams, the chief scout. We only saw Gwyn on days like this. It just seemed to add to the already unbearable tension. This was how we would find out – who would get a contract and who wouldn't.

I saw the players go in, one by one, and I saw them come out. Some sat in silence, some openly wept. Dreams were being made or shattered, one kid at a time. In and out, taking no more than five minutes for each. It was cut-throat. It was harsh. It was unnecessary, the way they did it. It was one of the worst days of my life. I was eighth or ninth in.

"Well done," said Gwyn. "You're in. You've played well, you've improved. We're offering you a three-year contract." *Three years. Blimey.*

I smiled, shook his hand, walked down the corridor, left out of the door and hid round the back of Stamford Bridge. I sat in the kit room, by myself, for the best part of an hour. I didn't want to be there, in that dressing room, sat with lads that I'd known and played with for two years, with me sitting there having been given a three-year contract and them sitting there wiping their eyes on their tear-stained Chelsea shirts.

Four of us got professional contracts out of that intake of players. Four out of 16. Me, Terry Skiverton, Neil Shipperley and Craig Norman. Shipperley went on to play for Chelsea's first team, then went on to Southampton, Palace, Forest, Wimbledon, Sheffield United and others. Craig Norman spent 10 years at Kettering Town. Terry Skiverton went to Wycombe Wanderers and Yeovil Town, eventually becoming the manager there. Terry was my best mate. We travelled in together, every day, across London, from the East End to the West, laughing and joking and talking about the game. He was a good bloke, Terry, and a good player. We're still in touch today.

We had six weeks off for the summer and then, when we came back we had a new manager. Glenn Hoddle.

Glenn Hoddle, I thought.

That will be brilliant.

GOODBYE CHELSEA

"It's Leicester," said Glenn Hoddle.

"Leicester City. They want you on loan."

And with that Muzzy Izzet walked from the manager's office, down the corridor, out of the club's Harlington training ground and out of Chelsea. His six-year career at Stamford Bridge was over.

The grim truth, and Izzet realised the grim truth before this watershed moment, was that it was over long before this day. It was over before it had ever really started.

He thought he might be upset about this, a young lad schooled in the traditions of this great English club.

But he wasn't. He just wanted to go.

There was a new club on the horizon. A chance, finally, to prove himself. To play football. To make his mark.

So, Leicester City. Leicester City.

He didn't even know where it was.

He knew it was north. North of London, yeah. But how far north?

He began his own game of word association.

Leicester: Gary Lineker. Alan Smith. Filbert Street.

The Midlands.

Was it the Midlands? He wasn't sure. Didn't they make crisps there? He'd only ever left London on school trips and to play football.

It didn't matter, though.

If Leicester wanted him, then he wanted them, too. He would go.

A few days later, a man called Steve Walford picked him up from Cockfosters train station, early on Thursday, March 28, 1996.

Walford was the Leicester City coach. He was decent, too. Friendly. Knowledgeable. They talked all the way from London to Leicester.

They'd been watching him for a while, Walford said. They liked what they saw. They were building a new midfield at Leicester. They had one piece of the jigsaw already – a young Irish lad called Neil Lennon. Izzet was next.

Lennon was the foundation, the building block of this new-look midfield. Izzet would make it tick. He would be the dynamo.

They were going places, too, Walford said. "You can be part of that, son." Izzet nodded. He wanted to be part of it. By the time they arrived at Leicester City's Belvoir Drive training ground, Muzzy Izzet knew where his future lay.

Blue was the colour. Except it wasn't the blue of Chelsea.

It was the blue of Leicester City.

I was a West Ham fan as a kid but I loved Glenn Hoddle. If you liked football, you liked Glenn Hoddle. He was class. Quality. He could do the most outrageous things and make them look simple, like anyone could do it, almost like it was the most natural thing in the world when, of course, it wasn't. He had it all.

But that was Glenn Hoddle the player.

Glenn Hoddle the manager was nothing like that. I didn't like him much at all. In fact, I fucking hated him. At Chelsea, he wasn't a popular figure.

Hoddle came to Stamford Bridge from Swindon Town in the summer of 1993, taking over from Dave Webb after Ian Porterfield had been sacked a few months earlier. His last game at Swindon was the 4-3 victory against Leicester City in the Wembley Play-Off final, which saw them promoted to the Premier League. However, Hoddle wouldn't be there to steer his side through the choppy waters of the top flight. He was coming to Chelsea. Swindon, as it transpired, went straight back down the following season.

I didn't know Ian Porterfield, not properly. I wasn't in the first team so my dealings with him were limited. But he seemed all right, a decent bloke. He took an interest in the youngsters. It's nice, that, as a kid, when the boss knows who you are; when you're playing in the reserves on a rainy Tuesday night and you look around and there he is, collar up, watching the game, telling you that you "did all right there, son" as you trudged off.

Porterfield was a footballer's manager. He wasn't much of a disciplinarian. He didn't crack the whip at Chelsea. His regime, from what I could see as a young lad looking on, was very relaxed. But it wasn't his easy-going management style which cost him his job. It was the results.

Porterfield was sacked in February 1993, the first boss to be sacked in the new Premier League. It wasn't a surprise. The club was in freefall. Ex-Chelsea and Leicester centre-half Dave Webb came in to steady the ship until the end of the season but he was only on a short-term contract.

When news spread that Hoddle was on his way, there was a palpable rush of excitement at Chelsea. 'He'll want us to play football,' we all thought. *Proper football.* We all wanted that, too. No-one wanted that more than me.

I wasn't having a great time at Chelsea. I'd come through the worst of it, but it still wasn't great. Chelsea was a club split three ways: there were the experienced pros at the top of the pile, the first-team regulars. To an outsider looking in, they seemed to run the show under Ian Porterfield.

Then there were some other fringe first teamers and some of the more confident reserve-team players in the second camp.

And then there was everyone else, who wanted to be in one of the other groups but wasn't. I was with everyone else.

It just never seemed to happen for me at Chelsea. I knew what I could do. I would sit there and watch some players and think: *'You know, I can do that, I'm as good as him...'* but I always felt like I'd get to one level, climb one hurdle, get so far – and there'd be another right in front of me. You have to put this into context.

This was the early 1990s. It wasn't a great time for English football. Graham Taylor was the England boss. English teams had only just been allowed back into Europe. On the domestic front, English football wasn't about nimble midfielders. It wasn't about possession football and the clever pass-and-move midfield-dominated game that we've become accustomed to watching today. It wasn't attractive. It was like World War One.

It was muddy pitches. Hoof football. The big up-and-under. Wimbledon: The Crazy Gang. Carlton Palmer playing midfield for England. Route one football, not just in the lower leagues, but in the top flight and in the England team. It was hitting the ball out wide and then banging it into the box for the big

49

number 9. Every English team, it seemed, had a big number 9. Hit and hope. Bang, bosh, bang, bosh, over and over again.

There were some games when it seemed more like rugby than football. I remember matches, especially during my early years at Chelsea, when I'd be in central midfield and I'd hardly get a sniff. The ball would fly over my head, one big clearance, one big hoof, from one end to the other, and then back again.

If it taught me one thing, this game of mud and attrition that I barely recognised from my youth, it taught me to be tough. You had to be tough, to stand up for yourself and never get bullied. I wasn't the biggest player, but I would never, ever roll over and I would never give in. I learned to stand my ground. It taught me that at least, and I was glad it did, because I needed it. I needed that in my game – especially at Leicester.

But it wasn't football back then. Not really.

My size – or lack of it – was a constant issue at Chelsea. You were no good if you were small. That was the message, the accepted wisdom. It didn't matter about the size of my heart. It was how tall I stood in my socks, how broad my shoulders were, how muscular my legs looked. I was a skinny 18-year-old kid with legs like pipe cleaners. I weighed eight stone wet through. I didn't get a look-in.

Chelsea were by no means unique here. I would play some youth or reserve-team games and I would line up against young men the size of grizzly bears. It's why we produced a generation of Carlton Palmers rather than a generation of Gazzas. It wasn't about what you could do with the ball at your feet, how you read the game, how quick your mind worked, how quick your feet were. It was about size and strength. Do you know the worst thing? We're still feeling the legacy of that today.

It made my heart sink – and yet I bought into it. I wanted to be big and strong. I drank milk every night, pumped iron, ate pasta and gulped down daily protein shakes.

I'd do all these things, anything, any new fad or whim that might make me a bit bigger, because I thought the key to success was to be bigger. I had to be bigger. Bigger and stronger, and therefore better. I think about that now and I laugh. I wasn't laughing then. It was humiliating and depressing.

On his first day at the club, Glenn Hoddle gathered all the players together at our Harlington training ground near Heathrow. He gave us *the* speech; the archetypal New Manager's Speech.

"I don't care what has happened before here," he said to us. "It's clean slate time. You'll all get a fair crack of the whip."

We all nodded. I nodded. I'm sure I nodded more vigorously than anyone else. It was July 1993. I was 18, a first-year professional on £225 a week.

I'd enjoyed the craic and the camaraderie of my first two years as a YTS at Chelsea but I hadn't enjoyed the football. Now, here was one of the most cultured midfielders in the history of the English game telling us, telling all of us, but telling me directly I felt, that this was my time.

My excitement was short-lived. Hoddle may have believed what he said on that summer's day in 1993, about clean slates and everyone having a chance but, in reality, I didn't get one.

There were two main reasons for this: one was Hoddle, the other was his assistant, Peter Shreeves, the former Spurs boss. I didn't like him and I didn't rate him. He made it fairly clear he didn't like or rate me either.

Shreeves was fine with the senior players, but from what I saw, he spoke to the juniors like shit. There was already a chasm at Chelsea, between the haves and the have-nots, the chosen few and those on the periphery. Under Hoddle and Shreeves, it grew wider. With Shreeves, you felt that whatever you did, regardless of how well you played or how hard you tried, it was never enough.

I played in reserve games where I played well, where I know I played well, and Shreeves would stand on the touchline, arms crossed, saying nothing. Yet if you were a senior player coming back from injury, playing a tentative last 30 minutes or so, a run out to get a bit of fitness, Shreeves would be all over you. *'Well done, son, great game,'* and ruffling the player's hair and patting his arse. All of that. That's how he was. If you weren't one of those players, then he didn't give a toss. You were nothing.

It's tricky at a big club, trying to please all the players, to keep all the different personalities and egos happy. I know that. Even if you try your hardest, it's a difficult thing to get right. Shreeves didn't even try. It lead to a fractured, uneasy atmosphere.

By the beginning of 1996, I was a third year professional at Chelsea. I was in the final year of a three-year contract; a contract Chelsea had promised me when they signed me from Charlton but had desperately tried to wriggle out of when the time came to talk terms. It was a valuable little lesson in the ruthless skulduggery of top flight English football.

I started as a pro on £225 a week, up to £250 in my second year and £275 in my third. It seemed like a fortune at first, as an 18-year-old, coming from a two-year YTS on pin money.

But by the time I was 21, it didn't seem so great. I had mates who were earning that sort of money on building sites or driving cabs. I wasn't earning enough to move out and get a place of my own. I was still living with my folks, going across London on the Tube, from the East End to the West End, by train every day; an hour-and-a-half there, an hour-and-a-half back.

But it wasn't about that. It wasn't about the money. It's never been about that. It was about the football. I'd had enough of playing for the reserves. It was make-or-break time.

I found the answer during a home Premier League game against West Ham, the club I supported as a kid. I was named on the bench. By then I'd played a lot of reserve games. The word seemed to be that I'd done all right. I hadn't let anyone down, anyway. Finally, a chance. I was thrilled.

It was Saturday, February 17, 1996. Stamford Bridge – 25,252 people were there. I was on the bench with Frank Sinclair. West Ham had Tony Cottee as one of their subs. Cottee was my boyhood hero. I had posters of him on my bedroom wall. It was strange to think that, in a few years' time, I'd be lining up with both of 'em in the blue of Leicester City.

The game started and I was nervous. Then, commotion. Eddie Newton was injured. I liked Eddie, he was a decent bloke and a good player, too. He was a midfielder. I was the only midfielder on the bench. I started to take my tracksuit off. *This was it. This was it. I was about to make my Chelsea debut.*

Not so fast, son.

Hoddle put his arm across my chest.

Sit down.

He had other ideas.

He gesticulated towards Ruud Gullit, pointing in front of Gullit to the midfield. The Dutchman looked bemused. You could see he didn't know what Hoddle wanted.

What he wanted, it quickly transpired, was to push Gullit up from playing as sweeper to fill the gap left by Eddie in midfield. I could see Gullit pointing at me. I could hear him shouting: *'Bring Muzzy on.'*

But Hoddle didn't. He wouldn't. He pushed Gullit into the midfield and he brought on Frank Sinclair, a centre-half. I sat back on the bench. And right there, right then, in front of 25,252 people, against the team I supported as a kid, I knew. I'd known it for a long time, really, but I hadn't admitted it.

It was never going to happen at Chelsea. It was over. We lost 2-1 that day. It was the day I knew my Chelsea career was over. Over before it had started.

The signs had been there, of course. I'd just refused to see them. There were games where younger and less experienced players were appearing ahead of me in the Chelsea pecking order. Hoddle fancied Jody Morris, I remember. And then, at the opposite end of the scale, I remember him playing Graham Rix, the old Arsenal winger, in midfield in one reserve game. Rix was the youth-team coach. I'm sure Rix even got a game in the first team. By then he was 37. I knew what all of this meant. It was time to go.

I came home from training a few days after that West Ham game and sat down with my dad. I'd had enough. "You'll have to have it out with him, son," my dad said. I knew he was right. But I didn't want to. I'm not the kind of guy who enjoys any kind of confrontation, even now. As a wet behind the ears 21-year-old, frozen out of a side I thought I was good enough to play in, it was daunting. I didn't want to knock on Hoddle's door and complain. But there didn't seem to be an alternative.

The following day, after training, I went to see him. By then, there was a mutual feeling of unease, let's say, between me and the Chelsea boss. I didn't rate him. He didn't rate me. I was in the last months of a three-year contract. I needed to know where I stood. It was an uneasy conversation.

"All I want to know is if I have a future here," I said. And Hoddle looked at the floor, refusing to meet my gaze. He ummed and ahhhed and did everything except answer the question. I remember being struck by this surprising feeling that he was more uneasy than I was. I wasn't expecting that.

He couldn't tell me where I stood. He said he'd try to get me out on loan. It wasn't the answer I was looking for. I wanted to know if I had a future, where I stood in his eyes and at Chelsea. It didn't seem an unreasonable request to make. He stuttered and changed the subject. Looking back, I'm not sure if he actually knew where I stood.

So, he hedged his bets. He played for time. What about a loan deal, he said. It'll be good for me, he said. Good for the club. Better for Glenn Hoddle, I couldn't help thinking. He would sort it out as soon as possible, he said.

But nothing happened. No clubs came in.

It doesn't look great, Hoddle told me a week later.

I had an agent. I don't know why I had an agent as a 21-year-old reserve player at Chelsea on £275 a week. I didn't need one. My agent said he was touting me around but that no-one was interested. For the first time in my life, I began to think that football wasn't for me.

I still went every day – from Canning Town in East London, across the city to the Harlington training ground near Heathrow – 90 minutes on the train and the Tube, there and back. But my heart was sinking. My mind was drifting. Doubts were creeping in. I started to think that maybe Hoddle was right. Maybe I wasn't good enough.

I thought of other jobs I could do instead. But what could I do if I wasn't a footballer? I'd never contemplated that. At school, whenever I was asked what I was going to do, I always said the same thing: footballer. It was all I could do.

And now I was beginning to wonder if I'd got it all wrong. I thought about roofing with my old man. I could do that. It wasn't like playing football. But I could do it.

I started to think that maybe this was as good as it was going to get for me: Chelsea reserves, sitting on the bench for the first team against West Ham, the manager preferring an old Arsenal winger in midfield to me.

And then finally, at last, there was some interest.

Eddie Niedzwiecki was the old second-team boss at Chelsea. A Polish-born Welsh international, Eddie was Chelsea's old goalkeeper. He had been forced to retire at the age of 28 after a series of injuries but stayed on and coached the kids and the reserves. He was almost a part of the fixings at Chelsea, Eddie. We all liked him. Shreeves might have been stand-offish and aloof but Eddie never was. Eddie was decent.

There was a club that wanted me on loan, he said. He couldn't tell me who it was. That was up to the gaffer. But expect a call, he said. The gaffer would call me in tomorrow.

The next day, Hoddle asked to speak to me after training.

"There's a club that wants to take you on loan." Great.

"Who is it?" I said.

"I can't tell you who it is."

"Why can't you tell me?" I said.

"I just can't tell you. Not yet," he said.

"I don't understand. It's hardly a state secret, is it?"

There was silence. I tried to figure out his logic. I didn't get it.

"Now is not the time," he said. "This is the last year of your contract, so I can't let you go out on loan until you sign another deal with us."

I didn't want to stay at Chelsea but to move, I had to sign a new contract committing me to Chelsea, a club where I had no future. Welcome to the mad world of football.

"What do you want?" Hoddle said. "How much are you looking for?"

I had no idea. What I really wanted was a go in the first team. I just wanted to play. The money? I didn't know. I didn't know what to ask for. I shrugged.

"Think about it," he said. "We'll talk tomorrow."

He rang me at home the next day. My mum took the call. None of my family liked Glenn Hoddle. I'd come home from training and moan about him, every night, as I ate my dinner. It became a nightly ritual.

My mum had never met him, but she'd heard these moans every day for the best part of three years. She handed the phone over to me. "It's Glenn Hoddle," she said, and she pulled a face as though she might be physically sick.

"So then," he said. "How much do you want?"

I was on £275 a week. I thought I'd go for double that. "£550," I said. "That seems reasonable."

"I'll give you £500," he said.

"Right," I said.

"Right," he said. Deal.

I wasn't likely to ever receive this extra money. We both knew this. I was signing a contract that meant nothing to me or to him – it just meant that whoever wanted to sign me would now have to pay Chelsea more money. That's just how it is. That's how football works.

"Come to Stamford Bridge tomorrow and sign the contract," he said. I signed the next day; a three-year contract which paved the way for me to leave.

Hoddle called me in later that day. He beckoned me over.

"It's Leicester City, by the way," he said. "They want to take you on loan."

Leicester City.

I didn't even know where it was. I'd never been there. I knew nothing about them, the city or how they were doing. I went home and told my dad.

"What do you want do?" he said.

"I just want to play," I said. "I want to go."

And that was that. I told Glenn Hoddle I wanted to go. He didn't say much. I didn't say much. By then we didn't have much to say to each other. It was over. We both knew it. I walked out of his office. And that was that. Goodbye Chelsea.

Steve Walford, the Leicester City coach, called me that night. They wanted me to travel up to meet them the next day. He assumed I could drive. I couldn't. I heard him sigh. "Don't worry," he said. "I'll pick you up. Tomorrow morning, 6am. Cockfosters train station."

There are some London stations that have an odd sense of faded Victorian splendor that even on a damp and miserable winter's morning can still feel grand, romantic and beautiful.

Cockfosters is not like that. Especially at 6am on a cold winter morning. It wasn't pretty. It was Thursday, March 28. 1996. My life was about to change.

Walford picked me up in his car and we talked all the way up to Leicester. He was good. He spoke about Leicester and what they wanted to do and he seemed to fizz with an enthusiasm, which was infectious. I loved it.

I nodded along in what I hoped were all the right places and tried not to appear too nervous or too keen. I doubt if I pulled that off. Secretly, I was thrilled. He said they'd been watching me. Not just once or twice, but a few times. He told me the games they'd seen, the things I'd done that had impressed them. He knew more about me than I did.

They'd seen a few players, he said, but they wanted to be sure so they came back and saw me again and again. They liked my industry, he said. My attacking instincts. The manager, Martin O'Neill, had a plan for his team. Square pegs and square holes. Round pegs and round holes. They knew what they wanted me to do, where I'd fit in.

I was realistic, though. I didn't think he was bringing me to Leicester for me to walk straight into the team. I'd have to earn my place, I knew that. And yet the way he was talking, it sounded so positive. I sat in the passenger seat of Steve's car and in that two-hour trip up the M1 he made me feel like someone. Peter Shreeves didn't come close to that in three years.

We arrived at Belvoir Drive, the Leicester City training ground; a couple of football pitches at the end of a 1950s housing estate on the outskirts of the city. It was just before 9am.

I took my bag from the boot of Walford's car and sat in the

changing room, waiting for everyone else to turn up. They came in one by one.

Garry Parker, Scotty Taylor, Neil Lennon, the midfielders. Steve Walsh, the captain and centre-half. Goalkeeper Kevin Poole. Full-backs Simon Grayson and Mike Whitlow. Fellow Londoner Jamie Lawrence. *"Facking hell, awright mate."*

They shook me by the hand. They patted me on the back and made me feel welcome. And then they started to take the piss out of me and I don't think it stopped, the piss-taking, for the next four years.

"Izzet?" said Garry Parker. "What Izzet? Izzet me you're looking for?" I got that for days.

New signing Steve Claridge was late. I would soon discover that this was a regular occurrence.

Was I intimidated? No, I wasn't. A few days earlier, I'd been training with Ruud Gullit and Mark Hughes. I'm not easily intimidated by things like that.

But I was nervous. I was *'new-kid-at-school'* nervous.

I didn't want to do anything wrong. I didn't want to stick out. I didn't want to make a twat of myself.

I remember that the training pitch was terrible.

I remember the canteen was tiny.

I remember the training kit – a size small, Fox Leisure – *What the fuck is Fox Leisure?* – was poor quality.

John Robertson, the assistant manager, and Martin O'Neill were already there.

Martin came over and greeted me like a long-lost nephew or something. It was the first time I'd met him. I knew he'd watched me a few times. I knew he rated me. But this was the first time we'd met.

60

He shook my hand vigorously and he told me this was my time – my time to prove myself, to take my chance. "But more than that," he said, "enjoy it." And with that he disappeared into his office.

Enjoy it.

I would, I said to myself. I would enjoy it.

I didn't know any of them. I'd seen some of them on the telly. I knew who they were. But they were decent. Friendly. Welcoming. No airs. No graces. Just decent.

I could see them looking at me, this wiry little Cockney kid with the funny name and thinking: 'Who the hell is this? Where does this geezer fit in?'

I changed into my kit and went out to train. It was tougher than I was used to. Competitive. Even training at Leicester was competitive. The tackles were flying in but I didn't mind that. I liked it. I did all right, too. I did enough to hold my own.

That summer, I settled into an inner-city hotel near the edge of Leicester, at the bottom of Humberstone Gate, a big concrete monstrosity with decaying windows and a fading reputation. It may have been a top hotel once. It wasn't, though, by 1996.

I used to walk around, unrecognised, untroubled, a stranger in a strange land getting my bearings. This wasn't the most salubrious pocket of Leicester, I would soon discover, when the city became my new home. It didn't matter.

I was from the arse end of East London. It looked all right to me. I felt good. The nerves were gone. A new start.

Enjoy it, the man said.

I promised myself that I would. I really would.

HELLO LEICESTER CITY

Leicester City played 15 games in the first three months of 1996. They won just three of them. Perched comfortably in the top three for the first half of the season, promotion had looked almost certain under previous manager, Mark McGhee.

And then, as it often does in football, everything changed. McGhee was lured away by what seemed – to him at least – a better proposition at Wolverhampton Wanderers.

Enter Mike Walker, the former Norwich City and Everton boss who, it had been widely claimed, would become the new City manager. Secretly, Walker had already met the fans. "I'm delighted to be here," he told them. "I hope we can get promotion."

Behind the scenes, though, all sorts of things were happening. City chairman, Martin George, was frantically persuading Martin O'Neill to swap his current club, Norwich, for Leicester. At the 11th *hour, O'Neill finally agreed. The move was ratified by the City board of directors during an often fractious and heated meeting. Walker was out. O'Neill was in.*

It was by no means anonymous. This fissure in the Leicester City boardroom would continue to ferment throughout O'Neill's four-and-a-half year tenure at the club. The Irishman arrived to great fanfare. Promotion is the aim, he told the Leicester Mercury in December 1995. It didn't go immediately to plan.

City struggled. O'Neill lost or drew his first seven games. There was a morale-boosting victory at McGhee's Wolverhampton Wanderers, but an ailing City slumped from second in the table to ninth in three months. The fans – who had thought promotion was a certainty – were getting restless. On Saturday, March 30, 1996, Sheffield United came to Filbert Street. Sitting on the bench in the number 14 shirt, just two days after his arrival, was Muzzy Izzet.

It was an old-fashioned ground, Filbert Street. The stands – two decent, two pitiful – were right next to the pitch. Muzzy Izzet could hear the boos from the subs' bench. They grew louder and louder as Sheffield United went one-nil up, then two.

That afternoon – the afternoon Izzet made his debut – three months of frustration came to an ugly head. A chorus of pent-up anger and resentment. Protests outside the ground. Calls for O'Neill to go. That day stayed with O'Neill. It was the lowest moment of his City career – the day his own people booed him. He never let them forget it.

The fightback started immediately – with a midweek away game at Charlton Athletic. After a brief cameo versus the Blades, Izzet was put straight into the first team. The win at The Valley began a dazzling run that would lead to a victorious push for the top six, the play-offs, Wembley, promotion, four years in the Premier League, a top-10 finish in each of those years, three League Cup finals (winning two of them), two spells in Europe and a seat at football's top table.

Muzzy Izzet, meanwhile, 21 years old, taking his seat on the bench at 3pm on Saturday, March 30, 1996, wondered what on earth he was letting himself in for.

It's a bewildering time, joining a new club. You don't know the area. The players. The rituals, who does what and why that might be important and *what it all means*. It feels like landing on another planet.

This was how I felt when I first came to Leicester; a wet behind the ears kid from East London, living away from home for the first real time in my life, pitched up in a strange new city in the East Midlands with a load of lads I didn't know. Welcome to Leicester. Hope you enjoy the view.

I'd had a cursory look at the table. On Saturday morning, March 30, 1996, City were ninth. Not bad. Just outside the play-offs. Poised, you might think, for better things.

But football, like life, is all about context, isn't it? I didn't know what had gone before at Leicester. I'd been too busy concentrating on Chelsea, why Hoddle wouldn't pick me and when I could leave. I didn't know that, a few weeks earlier, under a different manager, City had been comfortably camped out in the top three.

That Saturday, Leicester City faced Sheffield United in the old Endsleigh Football League Division One. I was on the bench. I wasn't to know this but that day, my debut, would go down as the lowest point of Martin O'Neill's four-and-a-half year tenure at City.

I sat in the dugout at Filbert Street, the ground about three-quarters full, the smell of matchday in my nostrils, the same smell at Leicester as it was at West Ham. They were similar grounds in many ways, Filbert Street and Upton Park. Old fashioned. The stands right on the very edge of the pitch. A good atmosphere. Loud, loud fans. Not slow to let you know, either, if they didn't think you were pulling your weight.

The air was thick with the smell of Benson & Hedges, stale beer, adrenalin and expectation. I looked out from the dugout on to the pitch. It was abysmal. There was a giant mud bath in the middle, mini-mud baths at both ends. I've played on better pitches at the local park.

Today, Leicester City play their games at the King Power Stadium. It's a great venue, and the pitch is *magniff*. I had two seasons playing there – when it was known as the Walkers Stadium – and I liked it. I go there as often as I can to see Leicester. I take my lad, Dylan, and the club and the fans always make me welcome. I grew up a West Ham fan and I still am a West Ham fan – but Leicester City are my club. They're part of me.

As much as I like it at the KP Stadium, though, it doesn't mean the same to me as Filbert Street did. Granted, I never had to wade through the puddles of piss in the bogs in the back of the old Kop and I never had to queue, endlessly, for a barely warm pie or a luke-warm cup of tea at half-time. But there was something about Filbert Street that was special. I had some magical times there and I miss it.

On Saturday, March 30, 1996, I didn't know the gaffer was under pressure. I didn't know City had won just three of their 14 games since the beginning of the year, slipping from third in the table to ninth. I wasn't looking at the big picture at that stage. I was too wrapped up in my own game.

The team that day contained a few surprises:

Poole,
Carey, Walsh, Watts,
Grayson, Taylor, Lawrence, Heskey, Whitlow
Claridge, Roberts

Me, Neil Lewis and Mark Blake were on the bench. We played a 3-5-2 formation. It was the way O'Neill liked to play; solid, hard to beat, with three big centre-backs and two marauding wing-backs. But it wasn't the formation which let us down that day against Sheffield United. It was the personnel, or more accurately, the lack of personnel.

There was no Neil Lennon, who had signed a few weeks earlier from Crewe Alexandra – right under the nose of Ron Atkinson. Big Ron was convinced he'd persuaded him to sign for Coventry City. What he hadn't reckoned on was Martin O'Neill and John Robertson nipping round to Lenny's pig-sty of a flat at the 11th hour and persuading him to come to Leicester instead. Cov's loss was our gain.

Lenny settled in immediately, quickly becoming the anchor of the City midfield. Lenny wasn't just a brilliant player, he was a brilliant bloke. He was a leader. And he had a brilliant footballing mind. He read the game so well. He sat in front of that back four and he was on, constantly, at the people around him.

There was no Garry Parker, either.

Martin O'Neill has said in the past that one of the reasons for City's poor run when he took over the side was that the team – essentially, Mark McGhee's team – was too one dimensional, too reliant on Garry Parker: stop Parker playing and, basically, you stopped Leicester.

I don't know if that was true. Scotty Taylor was a decent

player, too, so it seems unlikely that City were ever solely reliant on Parker's guile. I know this, though: I've played with some great midfield players over the years, and Garry Parker was right up there with the best of them. Was he a better player when he was with Villa? Or Forest, even? I don't know. If he was, he must have been some midfielder then because he was a consistently brilliant player for Leicester.

So, on Saturday, March 30, 1996, City were missing the heart and soul of their midfield.

Of course, I didn't know any of this then. I didn't know who was who and who did what. I'd only been there two days and was just pleased to be there at all. I took my seat on the bench and tried to look like I was taking it all in; calm, reflected, knowledgeable, ready for action. I was none of those things. I was fucking petrified.

I remember very little of the next 90 minutes. I recall the atmosphere slowly changing from excitement and expectation to frustration and then anger. I heard one boo. Then another. And then the boos getting louder and uglier.

Sheffield United scored in the 62nd minute. O'Neill responded by bringing on me and Neil Lewis. A double substitution. It would be nice to say this injection of fresh legs and ingenuity did the trick with around half-an-hour left to play. Nice, perhaps, but a lie. It made little difference.

I got a half-decent reception. There was a bit of a cheer. Maybe that was for Neil, I don't know. I took a corner early on and as I put the ball down by the corner flag, some people in that area of the ground stood up and cheered and double-thumbed me. I'll never forget that. I don't think I did anything special that day. I had a few early touches of the ball – and I tried hard not to do anything stupid. Sheffield United scored again, seven minutes from the end to seal the win but, really, we could have played until midnight and not scored. It was just one of those days, one of those games. The final whistle went – and that's when the boos really started.

On the Monday after the game, the headline in the *Leicester Mercury's* match report was blunt. *'No Excuse For This Shambles.'* It was difficult being without both Lennon and Parker, argued O'Neill on the backpage. "With one or both of them I think it would have been a different story," he said. "But with neither of them – well, we didn't do enough and we didn't deserve anything from the game."

'Ugly, just plain ugly,' was the write up from seasoned *Mercury* reporter Paul Jones in his 'View From The Terraces' piece.

'Ugly is the only to describe events on and off the field on Saturday. And you can't blame the fans for their furious reaction. The only surprise was that so many wanted to stay behind after being subjected to such a dreadful 90 minutes. The early bus home seemed like the best option – and many took the chance.'

I scanned the report to see if I had been mentioned. I had. It was mercifully brief.

'When Izzet came on he instantly became City's best midfielder on the day. He looks a bright prospect for the future...'

I was happy enough with that; there was more...

'...although now he has seen this, that future will surely lie back at Stamford Bridge once his loan ends, if he is any judge.'

There's one good thing about hitting the bottom, though. You can't go any lower. We couldn't play any worse than we did that Saturday against Sheffield United. It's not nice, hearing your own fans boo you, seeing banner headlines in the local paper saying: 'No Excuse For This Shambles.'

It wasn't good, looking at the table – three wins in 16 games, falling from second to ninth in three months. It was worrying, too, hearing that the man who had brought you here was having to meet angry fans outside the stadium an hour after the game with supporters calling for his head.

We'd hit the bottom. We could only go one way from here. The only way was up.

Three days later, we had Charlton away. O'Neill put me straight in the team; me, Lenny and Scotty Taylor in midfield, against the team where it all began for me.

It wasn't a great game. In fact, it was dire; a proper backs-against-the-wall Division One affair on a cold Tuesday night. But we stuck it out and won 1-0 thanks to Stevie Claridge.

Four days later we were back again in south London playing Crystal Palace at Selhurst Park. Again, it wasn't pretty. If they weren't pumping long balls into our box, David Hopkin, their ginger-haired midfielder, was hurling long throws into our area. Every time the ball went in, Steve Walsh rose to head it out.

I didn't know much about Steve, this big, strong number five, when I first arrived at City. But he was immense that day. He won everything. He was immense all the way through that run. We won 1-0 again. Two games. Two wins.

By now, I already felt part of it. I wanted to stay. I knew that already. I wasn't just playing to get Leicester promoted; I was playing for me. I was playing for a move. I wanted to come here. The club had put me up at Sketchley Grange, this beautiful big, country hotel in Hinckley, a town in west Leicestershire. It was where Lenny was staying. They put me in a room near him. It was the start of a brilliant friendship, on and off the field, which has lasted to this day.

We got on well, me and Len. Plus, he could drive. He took me to training every day in his little green coloured club car and he'd fill me in, what it was like at Leicester, who was good, how Martin could be scary but he was decent, that he was a good boss, that we'd been struggling but we'd turn it round. I'd take it all in and nod and then Lenny would pull out his Oasis tapes and we'd listen to Liam Gallagher all the way in. I liked living at the Sketchley Grange and driving in with Lenny.

It didn't last long, though. The club moved me to a hotel at the bottom of Humberstone Gate. It was where a fair number of the city's asylum seekers were housed. I'd stay there at night and get a cab into training in the morning. It was a shithole. But, you know what, I didn't mind.

I didn't go out. I didn't really drink. Not then, anyway. The drinking came later. I didn't want to do anything that might jeopardise any potential permanent move. I just wanted to train, to be with the lads, be a part of it, in the thick of it. I just wanted to do everything I possibly could that would help get me out of Chelsea and into Leicester.

It was good at Leicester. Steve Walford took the training. It was decent – varied, interesting, competitive. We all loved Wal. He never, ever judged you. He was always positive, always telling you that you could do it.

It was never strict. He wanted things done right and, by and large, things were done right. He got his own way – but he got it with our compliance. We wanted to do it.

That's always a tough thing to get right in any workplace, whether it's an office, a factory or a football club – especially a football club where there are two dozen young men who all think they know better. But he made it look easy.

Robbo would come out now and again. You got to know his routine, the way he worked, but you never grew tired of it. He was always encouraging, always clapping on the touchlines and putting an arm around your shoulder to tell you how well you'd done. He was relentlessly positive.

As a number two, he was the complete opposite to Peter Shreeves. Robbo was like this with everyone. He worked hard to make *everyone* feel part of it at Leicester. We all loved him for it, too. You'd see him sometimes with a fag on, and it's fair to say that by this stage of his life he was carrying a bit more weight than he was in his playing days, and yet he'd still got it.

We sometimes played five-a-sides at the end of training and he'd come on and play for 10 minutes and he was always the best player on the pitch. Every time. It was like the ball was glued to his feet. No-one could get near him. He had his knee brace on and his old boots, but he could still drop a shoulder and glide past you.

By the end of the week, as Saturday approached, we'd start to see a little less of Robbo and a bit more of Martin O'Neill. He wouldn't say much. He was happy to leave the lion's share of the training to his two trusted lieutenants but he'd pick players out, one by one.

He'd come to you as you walked off the pitch and say: "I was watching you closely on Saturday. I loved the way you were running off the ball and opening up their defence" or, if not that, some other minor aspect of your game, something he'd clearly noticed and something that made you feel special.

It was so simple, just basic psychology. But it worked. It worked every time. I'd walk off the pitch thinking: *'He noticed. He saw what I was trying to do. He's happy with me.'*

And then he'd say something the next week. He'd find another small aspect of your game and again, in a quiet moment, arm around your shoulder, he'd whisper in your ear and I swear, you'd feel 10ft tall. *He's happy with me.*

It got to the point where you wanted to hear that every week and, if you didn't, you wondered why not. Had he not been watching you? Had you not done enough? So, the next game, you'd do more. You wanted to please him.

It doesn't bear a great deal of scrutiny, that, really. In black and white, written down, it looks simplistic, like you're some kind of kid and you want to please your favourite teacher. And yet that's *exactly* how it was. That's how he made you feel.

Our good run continued. After losing 2-1 at home to West Brom, we went to Tranmere and drew 1-1.

We beat Oldham, thanks to two goals by Steve Claridge, then Huddersfield, 2-1 (Walsh and Claridge, again – the two Steves did more than anyone in that run-in to push us back into contention) and we came to the last game – Watford, away.

I'm pretty sure we needed to win or we wouldn't make the play-offs. That's my memory of it. I remember the pressure was massive. It was a Sunday game, early May; the ITV cameras were there and the away end was absolutely packed with Leicester City fans. They were throwing bits of paper and blue and white balloons. They made an incredible noise. I don't think I heard the Watford fans. It was like playing at home.

I scored my first Leicester City goal, my first League goal, that afternoon; right in front of the away end. There was a scramble, someone tried to clear and rather than clearing the ball high and wide, they directed it right on my head – and, somehow, I headed it into the goal: 1-0. I ran straight into the away end. It was delirium.

My team-mates jumped on my shoulders, cheering and shouting, lifting me up off my feet. The noise was deafening. It was pure exhilaration. And even though I could barely get my breath, I remember thinking: *this is it, son.* This is what it is like to be a professional footballer. For all the highs that were to come – Palace, Wembley, League Cup finals, great victories in the top flight, Europe, Turkey – that game, that feeling, that goal… it's still one of the best moments of my life.

The 1-0 win was enough to take us into the play-offs. We all thought, by then, that if we could get to the play-offs, we'd do it. We'd get promotion. We had the momentum and there was this genuine, brilliant feeling of confidence, in and around the side.

I left with my mates to go back to London after that game. They left their car in a local multi-storey car park. All around, it was kicking off. I was in my Leicester tracksuit, walking back to the car. We were in the play-offs, and maybe Wembley. They were relegated. There were fights and stand-offs everywhere. And here I was, the goalscorer, the man who scored the goal which put them down and sent us to the play-offs, walking through it in my Leicester tracksuit.

My mate let me borrow his coat. I walked back to the car in his coat, head down, as fast as I could, my Fox Leisure tracksuit bottoms showing under his coat. We drove back to London, laughing and laughing.

We were drawn to play Stoke City in the play-off semi-finals. Stoke had finished fourth. We'd finished fifth. They had beaten us home and away that season. It was a two-legged affair, but it didn't matter that they'd beaten us twice. That was then. We were a different team now. We fancied our chances.

The first game finished 0-0 at Filbert Street. My abiding memory of that game is of our goalkeeper, Kevin Poole, keeping us in it with a string of brilliant saves. He saved my skin. I lost my marker at a corner and, typically, the ball found the player's head and it looked for all the world like a goal, until Poole's outstretched fingers pushed it wide.

I was frozen to the spot. I knew it was my fault. I knew, too, if it had gone in, Martin would have known it was my fault. There was no escape, I was quickly learning. He saw everything. I breathed a huge sigh of relief and vowed that he wouldn't give me the slip again. The game ended 0-0.

We needed to win or get a score draw at the Victoria Ground but we had a good record away from home. We were still confident. Garry Parker came back to bolster the midfield and he scored with a left-foot volley 30 seconds after the start of the second half. We had chances to score again after that. We played much better in the second leg than we did in the first.

When the final whistle went, we ran towards our supporters and threw our shirts in the crowd. Then our boots and our shin pads, then our shorts. Everything went. We were standing in front of the away end at the Victoria Ground in our pants and socks, laughing and cheering and singing with the fans.

And then there was a pitch invasion; Stoke fans, hundreds of them, thousands even, not in the best of moods either, all pouring onto the pitch. I remember a police cordon, horses charging at the Stoke fans – and me, Lenny and Parks being hastily escorted into a little wooden hut at the corner of the ground as the other players were rushed down the tunnel.

We sat in that little wooden hut – in our underpants and socks, exuberant, laughing, on our way to Wembley, as a couple of hundred Stoke fans ran riot for the best part of half an hour. I dread to think what would have happened if they'd found us.

So, Wembley. I'd been at Leicester for only two months and I was already off to the national stadium. We had suits made. We were all over the papers. I began to notice that, if I went out in Leicester, people would stop and chat and ask for my autograph. They said nice things about the way I was playing. I was getting recognised, and I liked it; but what I liked more was that I was playing regularly and playing well, too, and I felt part of it. It's all I ever wanted.

In the run-up to Wembley, we didn't train harder – we trained less. It was all psychological. O'Neill told us daily that we were brilliant. He used to take me to one side and tell me I made the midfield tick, that it had all started to click the day I arrived.

I'm sure he was saying the same things to Lenny, Scott Taylor, Julian Watts and the rest but, nonetheless, it did the trick. As Wembley loomed, I was brimming with self-belief. I ran onto the pitch at 3pm on Bank Holiday Monday, May 27, 1996, and I felt like a world-beater. I was brimming with confidence. We all were. Walking out there, the pitch, the stands, the crowds, the noise. It was massive, all of it, and it was magical.

It was Leicester's fourth time at Wembley in five years. Palace, managed by Dave Bassett, were the favourites. They started brighter than we did, too. I remember the ball going out of play early on, looking around, seeing all the fans and being momentarily overwhelmed by it all. I had to pull myself together.

Just play. Concentrate on the football, not the surroundings.

They went 1-0 up.

Then I won a penalty.

A beautiful ball from Steve Walsh, me cutting in from the left and their defender, Marc Edworthy, lunging in front of me just inside the box. Could I have stayed on my feet? Maybe. But it was a foul. He was late. There was contact, it was inside the box and I made sure I went down. The ref blew for a spot-kick. Up stepped Garry Parker. I knew he wouldn't miss: 1-1.

It stayed 1-1 until extra time. I was dead on my feet by then. I don't know how I managed to put one foot in front of the other. I was like a car running on empty. At the back of my mind, I was gearing myself up for penalties. I knew I'd have to take one. I couldn't feel my legs. I was dreading it.

And then there was a commotion on the bench. I didn't see him until Kevin Poole started to come off. O'Neill was bringing on Zeljko 'Spider' Kalac, the club's reserve keeper. It was tough on Kevin Poole – a fine goalkeeper and a man who had done more than most to get us to Wembley.

Spider was 6ft 8ins tall. He'd had what you might diplomatically call mixed fortunes at Leicester. He was a nice lad, we all liked him but he'd dropped a couple of clangers in his first two appearances under Mark McGhee and you could see O'Neill didn't fancy him. But you could also see O'Neill's thinking. A game heading towards penalties – who do you want in your goal: Kevin Poole, at 5ft 10ins, or 6ft 8ins of Spider Kalac?

I bought Spider's old house in Markfield a few months later. I remember all the door openings had been made higher. He'd got someone in to do it. "I had to do it, Muz," he said, when we looked around the house. "I kept banging my head on the door frames." When we moved in, we had the tallest doors and the biggest door frames in the whole of Leicestershire. So on came Kalac. I was shocked, so I can only guess what the Palace players were thinking.

Play restarted. A free-kick in our own half, punted hopefully forward, knocked down to Steve Claridge who took an equally hopeful shot. He mishit it. It came off his shin. I know he's tried to say since then that it didn't, but it did. And yet, somehow, as time stood still, Claridge's mishit shot flew past a dumbfounded Nigel Martyn in the Palace goal and into the top right-hand corner. I thought he'd hit the corner flag with it, frankly.

But that was that. The last kick of the game.

We'd won.

We travelled back up the M1 – cheering and waving at all the Leicester fans who were making the same journey up the M1 back to the East Midlands with us.

That night, we had the biggest party at Sketchley Grange. All the players, management, staff, friends and family. It was a brilliant night. It was the most drunk I'd ever been – and the next day we had an open-top bus tour around Leicester, which made us all feel a bit queasy.

We'd made it. The Premier League. Big time.

We'd arrived.

It was the first day of the best four years of my life.

WELCOME TO THE PREMIER LEAGUE

The 1996/97 Premier League campaign – remembered in the history books as the season Manchester United won their fourth Premier League title in five years, the year Eric Cantona retired, when Kevin Keegan walked out of Newcastle United, Arsene Wenger arrived at Arsenal and Forest were relegated to the First Division.

Most observers had predicted Martin O'Neill's team of bargain basement top-flight misfits as being favourites for an immediate return to the second tier. After beating Crystal Palace in the play-offs that May, City had been promoted, along with Sunderland and Derby County, to English football's top table.

O'Neill bought only goalkeeper Kasey Keller from Millwall (£900,000) and Spencer Prior from Norwich City (£600,000) in the close season. You could argue – and you'd probably be right – that the gulf between English football's elite and the rest was not quite so yawning as it is today. But if that 'spending spree' doesn't seem like much in the way of strengthening by today's standards, it didn't seem like much then, either. Only fans with the rosiest of rose-coloured spectacles didn't fancy City as odds-on relegation favourites.

O'Neill made one more signing before the season started. A 21-year-old Chelsea reserve, Mustafa Izzet, signed permanently after an impressive loan period at the fag end of the previous campaign. The fee was £650,000, rising to £800,000 on appearances. After just three months at Filbert Street, the City fans knew that was a steal.

Izzet joined a midfield of Neil Lennon, Garry Parker and Scott Taylor. That year, they would come up against some of the finest players in European football. And yet few teams, few midfielders, got any change out of that four. The plan was simple.

They would not be afraid.

They would not be bullied.

They would always compete.

If they could not beat teams by skill, guile or footballing finesse, then they would beat them through endeavour and effort. They might not be the best team in the land. They would, however, be the fittest and the most competitive.

And that's what they were: that season, and the next, and the one after that, and the one after that. They raised eyebrows and defied predictions that year, and in the three seasons that followed. They enjoyed that – especially the skinny lad in the number 6 shirt...

The real genius of Martin O'Neill, more than anything – his eye for a player, his straight-forward honesty, his skill as a motivator, even – was his simplicity. He never over-complicated things. He was clever. We knew that. He also knew that we weren't.

We had the collective concentration span of a tank of goldfish. Imagine all the disruptive kids from your old school, all herded up and plonked in a changing room. That was Leicester City Football Club. Mercifully, Martin knew this. He kept his team talks short and his tactics simple. And we loved him for it.

When we met up for pre-season training in July 1996, he gathered us together at the Belvoir Drive training ground. The club was still bouncing. We'd been promoted when absolutely everyone had written us off. The atmosphere around the club was brilliant. We were excited.

"We might not be the most skilful team in this league," he said. "But I will tell you one thing – we will be the fittest. I will accept defeat, if it is an honest defeat. I will accept defeat if we lose to a better side and as long as you have given your all. There is no substitute for hard work. I will accept nothing less."

And he didn't. And we knew that. Every single one of us.

These were the ground rules, what Leicester City was built on during O'Neill's time as boss. It was set in stone, like one of the commandments. Before a ball was kicked, Leicester City were favourites to be relegated. We understood that. There was a gap between Division One and the Premier League – not as big as it is today, perhaps, but a big gap, nonetheless.

But we also understood that we had something. We were a team – on the pitch and off it. We liked each other. We all got on. There weren't two, three or more rival camps at the club, and that happens, believe me. I saw it often. We were one. We had a genuine camaraderie. You can't buy that and, if you have it, it's precious. I don't know how many points that was worth to us. I know how it felt, though, when that carefully nurtured camaraderie disappeared five years later. We were relegated.

Still, Martin was cautious at the start of the 1996/97 season. It was his nature to be quietly cautious. "Let's get off to a good start," he said. "Let's aim to get 20 points by Christmas." Reach that target, he said, and we'll build from there.

I'm sure this was not the way Alex Ferguson started the pre-season at Old Trafford but it seemed like an obvious target to us. We were the new boys; the bookies' favourites for the drop, an unknown quantity. We hoped for the best, but we didn't know how we'd cope. Not really.

I watched a lot of Premiership football in 1996. I'd played with and against quite a few of the players. It's one thing watching it on telly, or even in the stands at Chelsea. It's another thing playing it, though; week in, week out.

It was the quality that made the difference. The quality, the standard, was relentless. It was unforgiving. Tiring. And if you weren't prepared – if you weren't concentrating, if you weren't quite fit enough – it found you out. You might slightly miscontrol a pass in Division One or miss a half chance and it didn't matter too much. Another chance would come along.

Do that in the Premier League and you'd be punished. Lose possession in midfield and you'd be on your arse. In Division One, you perhaps needed four or five chances to score. In the Premier League, it was two. You mishit a pass, you'd be punished for it. You miscontrolled the ball, you could guarantee the opposing midfielder wouldn't and he'd be away.

I had to pull my socks up. We all did. I worked on my fitness but, more than that, I worked on my concentration. I couldn't afford to switch off. There was no coasting. Every game was intense. Ninety minutes, bang on it. I'd leave the pitch after most games absolutely shattered, physically and mentally exhausted.

The first game in the Premiership was at Roker Park – the last season of the old ground, against Sunderland, Saturday, August 17, 1996. We were relieved when the fixtures came out that we got Sunderland first up. They had come up with us from Division One. At least it wasn't Man United, Liverpool or Arsenal. We already knew what Sunderland were about.

It was a boiling hot day, a tough game with not much in it. Both teams cancelled each other out and, unsurprisingly, it finished in a dour scoreless draw. At the start of that season, there was little between us and Sunderland. At the end of it, they were relegated while we finished ninth.

How did that happen?

There were all kinds of football reasons: we had a strong defence, a combative midfield, Heskey's pace and unselfishness up front, Stevie Claridge's guile and we created plenty of chances. But, more than that, we had a determination that ran through the team like lettering in a stick of rock. We were hard to beat and we never gave in. There was no substitute for hard work. That's what the boss told us. We took him at his word.

When we played, we knew we could get among teams. Me, Lenny, Parks – we weren't scared to do that. I was the one who usually liked to get forward – although Lenny, Parks and Scotty Taylor could do that, too. But when I went forward, Lenny sat back. If he went forward – he didn't do it often, but he did – then I sat back. It was about the team. We had that discipline.

We never had the luxury of having fast defenders at Leicester. We knew we were vulnerable there. We could be undone by genuine pace. So, as a midfield, we tracked back. We helped out, we were that extra line of defence. It's the way Martin wanted us to play: you put the team first.

I remember playing Liverpool once, a few years later, and everyone was talking about Steven Gerrard and, yeah, you didn't need to be a football expert to see that Gerrard was a class player. He was a great midfielder. Gerrard back then loved to bomb on – but if Liverpool lost possession, he didn't tear back to try to win the ball. I remember standing on the green pitch at Anfield, hands on hips, blowing out of my arse and thinking: *'Why isn't he tracking back like we're tracking back?'*

And it was because he didn't have to.

We might not have had the fastest back line – but we had one of the toughest. I can't imagine there were many forwards who would get our team sheet, look down, see the names Walsh, Elliott, Prior (and later Taggart and even Sinclair) and let out a little sigh of relief. They knew they'd be in for a game. I don't think there was a better back line at dealing with set pieces during that time – and, also, coming up and being an attacking threat at corners.

We were inconsistent in that first season. We'd win back-to-back games against Spurs and Leeds, and then lose to Chelsea and West Ham. We dealt pretty well with the physical aspect of the Premier League. We were fit. We were tough. We always got stuck in. It was just the mental side. The concentration. You couldn't switch off. Each game was relentless.

The step up in quality took some time to get used to, but we hit our 20-point target on December 3 with a 2-0 victory at Middlesbrough. They were a team that loomed large for us that season. Of all the top-quality midfield players I came up against in that first year in the Premiership, one opponent stood head and shoulders above the rest: Osvaldo Giroldo Junior, better known as Juninho.

You knew that Roy Keane was a fiercely competitive, tough tackling, box-to-box midfield player. You knew what David Beckham could do from a dead ball. But no-one could hurt you – *really hurt you* – like Juninho. He could pass, he had vision and boundless energy, but he also took players on – and he was brilliant at it, too. He could get the ball just inside your half, look up and with a jink and a shimmy, a dropped shoulder and a deceptively quick turn of pace, he'd be one-on-one with your goalkeeper and Middlesbrough were one-up.

We were 10th in the league when Boro came to Filbert Street on March 15, 1996. By that stage, we knew we were going to play them in the Coca-Cola League Cup final. It was a good chance to really see what they had and what we were up against.

What they had was Juninho. He was their fulcrum. I don't think there was another Premier League team that season who relied on one man quite as much as Middlesbrough relied on Juninho. Everything Boro created came through him. He carved us apart that afternoon. Boro won 3-1. Juninho scored one, and made one. He beat us singlehandedly. The boss decided that afternoon that, if we were going to beat Middlesbrough in the final, then we had to stop Juninho.

First, though, there was a surprise. We finished training one day and the boss gathered us round. "I'm taking you away," he said. "We're all going to Marbella for a few days."

We met at the airport and we started drinking. One round. Two rounds. We were three in by the time they called for us to board. Everyone else was eating their breakfast. But you look at those players – Steve Walsh, Ian Marshall, Simon Grayson,

Lenny, Claridge, Parker – we were old school. We didn't even know how to spell sports science, never mind know what it was.

There are two types of players: honest ones, and then the rest. We were honest, old-fashioned footballers. Working-class lads, mainly, who had come up the hard way. We were professional footballers – but we'd come up as YTS trainees, cleaning boots and sweeping terraces. We stuck together and helped each other. We took the piss out of each other – at every opportunity – and we liked a drink. I look down that list and it's easier to name the players who didn't drink than the ones who did.

Emile wasn't a big drinker. Kasey Keller, an American, was a bit bemused by the drinking culture. He didn't come out very often. Neither did Pontus Kamark. Spencer Prior wasn't much of a drinker and I think Mike Whitlow had some kind of condition which meant he couldn't drink much. Mike Whitlow was hyper without any ale. He'd still come out, though. Stevie Claridge wasn't a big drinker, but he'd still come out, too.

The rest of us? We were on it (apologies if I've missed anyone out and wrongly libelled them as a semi-alcoholic but I really don't think I have). We all liked a few beers – and when we started drinking, it would go on and on and on.

We drank for four days solid in Marbella. We might have a bit of a light training session in the morning, but nothing serious. We'd get back to the team hotel, shower, change – and the rest of the day was ours. Which meant we'd be in the bar for midday, and we'd be on it all day.

There was a photo session one afternoon for the *Mercury*; we were asked to wear some red noses by the pool, which we did – but Jamie Lawrence decided to slip his old chap out from the side of his shorts and put his red nose on that.

The photographer didn't say anything at the time. I don't think he noticed, but I'm not sure that picture was ever used. He must have got back, processed the film and saw what Jamie did and thought: "Ah, well I can't use that one then…"

We used to have big games of team cricket on the beach. Martin wanted us to meet in the hotel foyer at 10am before going over. The night before, we'd been out until 3am. Despite that we were all there on time in the hotel foyer – reeking of San Miguel and wearing dark glasses. We walked gingerly down to the beach and played the worst game of beach cricket you've ever seen in your life. It was pathetic.

There were well-known Leicester City players – I'm not naming them, I was every bit as bad as they were – passed out on the beach, sunglasses on, unable to field. It seemed to sum up our trip away. We came back with swollen livers but, if possible, better mates; closer than we were before we left. The team spirit was fantastic – and we took it onto the pitch with us.

We all had suits fitted for the final. We did interviews. One newspaper had me and Lenny dressed in suits, standing outside a door, like Ron and Reggie Kray. I was uncomfortable with that, having been brought up where the Krays had lived – but we went with it.

Middlesbrough were the bookies' favourites. They had Juninho, Ravanelli and Emerson. Big names. Big stars. No-one really fancied Leicester but that suited us just fine. We went into that final and we didn't feel the pressure. However, I'm not sure, from a fitness point of view, if it helped us when the ref blew for extra time in the final with the score still goalless. Four days of solid drinking wasn't the best preparation for a Wembley final.

We felt a bit leggy that afternoon, no-one more so than Pontus

Kamark, a player who oozed class and had stuck to Juninho like a limpet – on the boss's orders – all afternoon. Pontus didn't let Juninho play. He never let him out of his sight. Pontus had pace, he was nimble but, more than that, he was a good player and he read the game well. He had a brilliant sense of anticipation. It was his job to keep Juninho quiet, and he did it magnificently.

There were some critics who complained after the game, who said it 'wasn't in the spirit of the game' but, frankly, that was just rubbish. Maybe they'd have preferred it if we'd allowed Juninho to carve his way through us, just like he had a few weeks earlier at Filbert Street? Maybe that would have been more in the 'spirit of the game'. But then, maybe, the history books would say today that Middlesbrough won the 1997 League Cup final, not Leicester City. I think the ends justified the means.

Neither of the two final games that year – the first one at Wembley and the replay, 10 days later at Hillsborough – were classics. They were cagey, tentative encounters; both teams being far too aware of what was at stake, neither wanting to make an error that might prove costly. We won the replay not because we had a better team. We didn't – they did. But we won because we had a better team spirit. We wanted it more.

I played terribly at Wembley and was substituted in extra time. I just couldn't get into the game. I was pushed out on the right and the game just seemed to pass me by. Thankfully, Lenny and Parks were brilliant. They carried me that day. They never said anything but they didn't have to. I knew – and I suspect they did, too. Ravanelli scored for them and Heskey equalised as the extra 30 minutes was running out.

Ten days later, we met again. I was determined to be more involved in the replay, to get into the game. Thankfully, I did.

I had a much better game. It was a great atmosphere at Hillsborough, probably better than at Wembley, and when Stevie Claridge volleyed in the extra-time goal from Walshy's header, I knew we wouldn't lose.

Walking up to collect the cup – through a sea of jubilant fans – was a brilliant feeling. My first final, my first winners' medal, as a professional. Would we have won if we hadn't been to Marbella and drank like a stag party weeks earlier? I don't know. Maybe we'd have been a bit sharper in the first game at Wembley and we might not have needed the replay. But I doubt it. I think the holiday helped.

We enjoyed three good victories in succession in early March – then we didn't win for the next nine games. This seemed to happen to us every campaign; our seasons fizzled out around February, March time. There was an obvious reason why. We were all knackered. We played such an intense, high energy game that we couldn't keep it up all season.

I was injured for our final two matches of the season. We beat Sheffield Wednesday at home and then Blackburn Rovers 4-2 at Ewood Park, finishing ninth in the league.

The boss called us in before we left for the summer break. "Well done," he said. "You've surpassed the club's expectations this season. I'm proud of you all."

And then he told us about the bonuses: £100,000 in total, for staying up, winning the League Cup and getting into Europe. Brilliant. We'd arrived.

The first year in the Premiership. Finished ninth. Won the Coca-Cola League Cup. Qualified for the UEFA Cup. A total of £100,000 in bonuses in the bank. Lovely.

In the close season, Martin had bought me, Kasey Keller, and

Spencer Prior, adding Ian Marshall, Matt Elliott, Rob Ulla-thorne and Steve Guppy later in the season.

For 1997/98, he added Robbie Savage, Theo Zagarakis and Graham Fenton to the squad. There was a pattern here. Martin had an eye for bringing in honest players, lads who would be no real trouble off the pitch, who would fit in, work hard and play for each other.

You can analyse tactics and formations and Opta indexes, statistics and possession counters and who made the most passes; but you can't measure team spirit. Camaraderie. We had it in spades at Leicester.

And it was all down to O'Neill, and his two assistants.

DRINKING

Baffone's. A modest Italian restaurant in Leicester, a nice enough place which suffered from the misfortune of being situated in what learned experts of this old Roman city have come to know, technically, as 'the arse end of town.'

As the civic leaders who ran Leicester spent millions of pounds beautifying the city, they decided, year after year, to ignore this corner, as if it was being punished for a former slight or misdemeanour. So the pavements grew older and dirtier, the graffiti got more detailed and potty-mouthed and it was where the bad boys started to hang. A nice enough restaurant – but not the smartest neighbourhood.

So who exactly would drink in a place like this?

The players of Leicester City Football Club – most of them, anyway, every Saturday night.

They'd perhaps start somewhere a bit more salubrious; a nice pub or bar in the city but come 11pm, when the pubs were kicking out and all the cool guys and pretty young things were heading to the clubs, the players of Leicester City Football Club would make their way to the arse end of town, to a little restaurant called Baffone's.

And then it would start.

There might be some food; some pasta, maybe, some grilled chicken and bread. But it was never about the food at Baffone's, as nice as it may have been. It was about the incognito drinking.

The curtains would close, the diners would make their way out and the drinking, the serious drinking, would begin.

It's no secret that there was something of a drinking culture at Leicester City Football Club. Lots of clubs had one. At Leicester, however, they drank like they played – with an all-consuming enthusiasm, an all-for-one, one-for-all passion that made them mates, not just colleagues. If it was a midweek session – and there usually was one – they'd wake up, go to training and sweat it all out.

The changing room would hum the next morning with the smell of last night's ale and last night's stories – who did what to who, and who embarrassed themselves the most; and, oh dear, did you hear Walshy murdering 'Your Song' again?

No-one loved it more than City's number 6, the little Turk who didn't have his first drink until he was 17…

I was a late starter when it came to boozing. I had an occasional sip of Carlsberg at family parties – it always seemed to be Carlsberg, too, for some reason; I have this vivid memory of tables covered in mountains of green cans, but I didn't really like it.

I was small as a 16 and 17-year-old. I had mates who regularly went to bars and clubs. Not me. I was this skinny kid, eight stone wet through, with big teeth that stuck out like broken piano keys. I still wore a brace. I don't think I'd started shaving. They went to pubs and I'd be left outside, like an East End urchin, looking in through the window wishing I was bigger.

Eventually, they smuggled me into the Army & Navy in Canning Town. They must have known I was underage. Back then, it didn't seem a big deal. I suppose they thought: 'Well, he's with some older lads. We know them. He'll be all right.'

On my first drunken night, at the age of 17, I drank five pints of lager. At the end of the evening, they had to carry me home. I wasn't sick – I wasn't sick that often. But I didn't like it. I didn't really like the taste. I am nothing if not determined, however. I persevered. I practised. And it's like anything, boozing. The more you practise, the better you get. I got pretty good at it.

The Army & Navy is a big old-fashioned drinkers' pub in the East End. That was my local. It's nothing special, the Army & Navy. It's a West Ham pub. It's carpeted throughout in claret and blue, the West Ham wool mix. I liked that then and I still do now. I don't like fancy pubs. I like proper pubs. The Army & Navy is a proper pub.

I'd finish training at Chelsea on Friday afternoon, get the train back to Canning Town and catch the bus, which dropped me off right outside the Army & Navy.

The bus would go right past my mate Johnno's fish store, at the end of Barking Road. Sometimes, if he was still there, I'd get off the bus early and help him pack up. And then we'd push his stall all the way to the pub. He'd leave it outside, and go in.

Did he smell of fish? Yeah, he stank of it – but he'd put all the fish he hadn't sold that day – jellied eels, cockles, mussels, whelks – in little tubs on the bar. And everyone could help themselves.

It was that kind of pub. No-one minded the smell of fish with Johnno because he was that kind of bloke and you knew, if you could smell fish, there'd be a small tub of cockles you could tuck into on the bar. East End tapas. *Beeauutiful.*

I rarely had a game on Saturday when I played for Chelsea's youth team and the reserves. We usually played midweek, so on Friday night I had a few. I'd drink Carlsberg, Foster's or Castlemaine XXXX. I'd drink with my mates Stu Hibberd, Danny Youles, Matty Graves and Johhno. I don't remember who started it but we formed a Guinness Club, where we'd meet in the pub and the rule was you could only drink Guinness.

It was ridiculous but we did it, and we stuck to it. I hated Guinness to begin with but, again, I ploughed on. I remember the first night I had six or seven pints. It felt like I'd been out for a meal.

They liked a drink at Chelsea. I'd hear Andy Townsend or Dennis Wise talk about going out at the end of training. The first team lads went out. I never went with them. I wasn't part of that gang. No-one ever invited me. I didn't go to fancy night clubs or plush places out West. I was never interested in that. I didn't want to go to the 'right' clubs in the 'right' clothes, dancing to the 'right' music. I'd rather have seven pints of the black stuff with my mates in the Guinness Club at the Army.

I didn't get hangovers then. I could drink all night and I'd wake up the next day, feel a bit rusty – but I'd just get up and run it off. That always worked. I was fit. The drinking left no mark on me. The hangovers came later. They last two days now.

So that was me. I thought I could drink. But, really, I couldn't. This was just an apprenticeship.

I joined Leicester at the end of March 1996. At Leicester,

under the tutelage of some of the finest beer drinkers and hell-raisers British football has ever produced, I learned to drink. I settled in quickly. We started winning games, I was playing and I felt part of it. I knew the lads liked a drink. They used to talk about it. I didn't go out with them at first.

I was a bit shy. I didn't know them. I didn't feel like I could invite myself. Plus, I was worried. I didn't want to screw it up. I liked it at Leicester. They kept telling me they liked me, too. I wanted to move. I didn't want to jeopardise that by drinking, by letting them think I was some kind of boozer.

It turned out I was worrying unnecessarily.

It wasn't until the season was nearly over, Huddersfield at home (a 2-1 win which put us in the top six), that I went out. We all went out. Lenny, Scott Taylor, Steve Walsh, Julian Watts, Simon Grayson, all the Leicester-based lads went out, apart from Big Emile. He didn't come out much.

Drink affected us all in different ways. It helped me relax. I felt less shy. I was more talkative. I felt intimidated at Leicester, at first. I was the new boy. A kid, really. I'd done nothing in the game – but I was playing in midfield with Garry Parker, for God's sake. Drinking took my inhibitions away. The booze provided a level playing field. They said I was funny when I'd had a few, but they say all sorts of rubbish so I won't blame you if you disregard that one.

Lenny was the one with the hollow boots. Lenny could just drink and drink and drink, until someone carried him home. And then you'd see him the next day in training and he'd be as fresh as a daisy. Scotty was the loud one. The prankster, always playing tricks. Sometimes, it was funny. Sometimes, it wasn't.

I didn't hang out much with Walshy, at first. He was the club captain, 10 years older than me. I was always out and he was always out. He was a good bloke, I could see that, but we weren't close at first. We only started to get close a bit later on.

Graham Fenton was a good lad to go out with; a mad Geordie who loved a pint. Matty Elliott was a good laugh. Taggs was great. Guppy liked a drink. Frank Sinclair, too. Frank went out a lot in London. He was a London boy. He knew all the bars and places to go. Frank would go out in London in midweek until 4am-5am, then get a cab, drive up the M1 to Leicester, have two hours' kip in the back and then roll out for training –and still be the best player on the pitch. Unbelievable.

Sam McMahon was a good lad. He came out with us. Larry, Simon Grayson, was always out. As I said earlier, it would be easier to tell you who didn't come out than list the ones that did.

We liked each other off the pitch and we took that with us onto the pitch. Genuine camaraderie. We played hard, we drank hard, we trained hard. We'd do a hard session in the morning, have lunch – and then we'd go to the club gym in the afternoon and have a session in there. And being the blokes that we were, it was always competitive. No slacking. A full day – 10am 'til 4.30pm/5pm – training. I thought all senior clubs had that. And then I moved and realised that they didn't. We took it – I certainly took it – for granted in those days.

I started to get recognised in Leicester. But it didn't really start until the next season. I got a permanent move that summer. There were a few pictures and stories in the *Leicester Mercury* but then, we kicked off the 1996/97 season in the Premiership. Suddenly, we weren't just in the *Mercury* – we were in *The Sun,* the *Daily Mirror* and all the Sunday papers, too.

I shied away from the interviews and the publicity, but it made no difference. People started to recognise me. When we were out, people wanted to buy me drinks. I've lost count of the number of times I've been bought a pint by someone I didn't know in a bar in Leicester. It's only beaten by the number of times I've turned a drink down.

It was nice, though. We didn't go out if we'd lost. We didn't feel like we deserved it. But if we'd won and we were out, people would come up and shake your hand, have a chat, offer to buy you a pint, and there was rarely any hassle. We used to go to Molly O'Grady's a lot. It was an Irish pub and Lenny liked it in there. They'd quite often have a band on and we liked that, too.

We'd go to Simpkins. We'd drink in all the pubs down Churchgate, even though a lot of people wouldn't. Churchgate was the other rough part of town. That didn't bother us. We were all working class lads who had grown up in pubs like that. And then, come 11pm/midnight, as everyone else started heading off to a fancy club, we'd all head off to Baffone's.

It's hard to recall one specific night. They all seem to merge into one. Getting in, being greeted like returning members of a long-lost family, closing the curtains and locking the door, pint after pint lined up on the bar, the Karaoke coming out – usually at Walshy's insistence – and one after another, getting up to make fools of ourselves singing.

I can't sing. I'm tone deaf. Neither could Lenny. But every time the Karaoke came out we'd get up and do *Wonderwall* or *Don't Look Back in Anger*. I'd sing with Macca, Paul McAndrew, our kit man. Occasionally, I'd do *Sweet Caroline* by Neil Diamond. Was it any good? I'd like to pretend it was but I'm sure it wasn't.

I could console myself with the fact that as bad as I was, as bad as we all were, we weren't as bad as Walshy. He really was

96

woeful. Wal was one of those blokes who thought he could sing, who fancied himself as a bit of a crooner, but he genuinely couldn't hold a note. He'd do *Your Song* by Elton John and he'd really go for it, too – closing his eyes, pulling all the faces – and he'd murder it. We'd all be shouting and booing and yet he seriously thought he was brilliant. We couldn't get him off.

Occasionally, other people would try to get in. I think word got round that Baffone's was where some of the City players went drinking on a Saturday night. But the door was locked. Pepe, the owner, wouldn't let them in. With the curtains drawn and the doors locked, the beer flowed. Pepe kept it open for as long as we were still standing and drinking. He didn't seem to mind. We'd give him a signed shirt – he had them all up on the wall – we'd get him tickets to the match and see him right, and he was happy. He was good to us. We appreciated it.

It was often 5am or 6am when the party came to a halt. Sometimes, a few of the lads would stay over. I remember seeing a player who, a few hours earlier, had brought the house down at Filbert Street, asleep on a row of chairs, absolutely out of it. I never stayed over. I don't think I ever stayed until 5am. I was usually ready for my bed by 1am or 2am. I'd wait until they were all distracted and I'd sidedoor it.

I've always done that, bolted before the end. I learned the hard way that it was for the best. I used to go round and say cheerio to everyone and invariably I'd be talked round to staying. 'Come on mate, you can't go, I've just got you one in', all that kind of stuff so I'd stay and then 15 minutes later I'd be nodding off in a corner, wishing I was home and in bed. So I stopped doing the grand goodbye thing and started just nipping out without telling anyone. "I'm off to the toilet" and then – whooosh – off and into a taxi and home. I still do it now. Now, all my mates who used to tell me off for doing this when I was in my 20s are doing it now they're in their 30s and 40s.

Back then I'd ring my mate, Gaz, a cabbie in Leicester. No matter where he was, he'd come and take me home. Most of the players used Gaz. We knew we could trust him. I remember once going back to East London, having a night out there and ringing Gaz to fetch me. And he did, too. I paid him – it must have been £100, £150 – but he got me and brought me home.

We trained Monday, Tuesday, Thursday and Friday at City. Never Wednesday. So we had a Tuesday Club, our little drinking gang. We'd go to Willie Thorne's to play snooker. Fat Cats in Leicester. Old working men's clubs. Anywhere where we could have a quiet drink. I remember we went out one Tuesday after training and we took Macca, the kit man, with us. We went straight from training. Macca was in his kit. He didn't have any clothes. So we marched him to M&S, bought him some clothes, binned his training kit and got on it.

We went to the Cheltenham Festival every year. We hired a bus and we'd drink on the way down, and drink all day. I don't think I even saw a horse for the first four or five years. It wasn't about the horses. It was about the drinking. A few years later, under Micky Adams, we went to Cheltenham and on the way back we got Jordan Stewart's clothes – he was very particular about his clobber – and burned them all. He went home naked.

We went to Portmarnock in Dublin a few times, usually during an international break. Portmarnock is renowned for its excellent golf courses. We stayed in a lovely hotel near the golf course, with a lovely little bar. We met in there one morning, which was a silly idea. It was 9am. The plan was we'd have one pint and then we'd go golfing. But it was a good bar. We liked it there, so we stayed all day. We sat, in our golfing gear, our golfing bags by the bar and drank all morning, all afternoon and all night.

We didn't play a round of golf.

During one night out in Portmarnock, we came back late. The curfew was 1am but, somehow, we missed it. We were coming back in a taxi – there was me, Walshy, Lenny and Garry Parker – and as we pulled up to the team hotel we spotted John Robertson and Steve Walford waiting in the front room. "Don't stop here," Walshy told the cabbie. "Take us round the back."

So we went round the back and we tried every door and every window of the hotel. They were all locked. One of the porters found us. I think he thought we were trying to break in.

"We need to get to our rooms," I told him, "but we can't go in past the reception. The boss is there. He'll tear a strip off us."

"Right," he said. "Follow me – but you'll need to get on your hands and knees when we go through the reception."

So we came in through the back door, through the kitchen and down on all fours to crawl under the bar in the hotel reception, round to the stairs, up to our rooms. And I can still see it now, a drunken train of us – this young Irish lad, then Walshy, me, Lenny and Garry Parker bringing up the rear – crawling through the reception area of this hotel at 2am.

Just as we neared the lobby, where Wal and Robbo were sitting, the young Irish lad turned round and put his finger to his lips. "Shhhhhh," he said. Walshy – the club captain, this 6ft 4ins bloke, this supreme leader of men, on his hands and knees in an Irish hotel – turned to me and did the same thing. "Shhhhhhhh," he said, his finger to his lips, his arse virtually in my face.

I was pissing myself laughing, but I turned round to Lenny and did the same. "Shhhhhh."And then Lenny turned to Parks and he shhhush-ed him, too. It was ludicrous. I'm amazed that Robbo and Wal didn't hear us; four pissed blokes, on their hands and knees, crawling through an Irish hotel in the early hours of the morning, all shushing each other.

But we made it. They didn't see us.

I couldn't leave it there. I got changed, put an old t-shirt and shorts on, ruffled my hair up a bit and came downstairs with an empty glass. There were Robbo and Wal, sitting by the window, looking stern-faced and tired.

"Facking hell," I said, "what are you two still doing up?"

Robbo jumped to his feet. "What are you doing back? I know you've been out." he said. "I know it. How did you get in without us seeing you? How have you done that?"

I feigned surprise.

"I don't know what you mean," I said, stretching into a fake yawn. "I've been in bed. I'm just getting up for a drink of milk."

He looked at me and knew I was lying, that I was having him on. He just didn't know how. I kept a straight face, poured myself a glass of milk, drank it, smiled and went back to bed.

"I will get to the bottom of this," he shouted after me, "I will find out about this."

He never did.

We played Chelsea at Stamford Bridge in the fifth round of the FA Cup, January 30, 2000. I was injured. Lenny was injured, too. It was a Sunday game, live on the box. We went out the night before, in London, me and Len and some of my mates. It was a late one. Lenny was never sick but he was that night.

The next day we turned up at Stamford Bridge to watch the

game. Lenny was wearing the same clothes he'd worn the night before. I think it's fair to say he was never any kind of sartorial trendsetter or leader in fashion, Lenny. I looked down at his trousers. They were creased up. At the bottom, in his turn-ups, was a thin layer of sick, from the night before.

"Facking hell, Len," I said, "you've got sick in your turn-ups." He looked round, waited until no-one was looking and turned his turn-ups out and brushed the dried puke away.

Did Martin O'Neill know about the drinking? He knew. He couldn't have not known. He might not have known it was as bad as it was, but he knew. We all talked and laughed and joked about what we did or what we could remember from the night before, in the way young lads do after a good night out.

He perhaps didn't know all of it but he knew we liked a drink. I suspect he knew that some of us, perhaps, drank a little bit too much than was good for us. But he never said anything.

Even when we went on a pre-season tour – even when we went to La Manga, and that's coming next – we'd be at the airport for 8am and we'd start. Someone would get a round in, then another, then we'd have some on the plane. It was like a stag weekend. Martin would have seen that.

He must have smelled the stale beer at the training ground. It was the signature scent of Belvoir Drive. But he didn't stop us. He watched us train. He knew how we played. He could see how we were, as a bunch of lads. He must have figured: look how this brings them together. And it did, it really did.

We wouldn't get away with it now.

But we did then.

And it made us who we were.

YOU'RE BETTER THAN BECKHAM, SON

What we could do here is go through every game, kick by kick, goal by goal, of every match Leicester City played from 1997 to 2000. But no-one wants that, do they?

If you want that, go to your local library and flick through the Leicester Mercury archive from 1997 to 2000. It's all there.

So, instead, let's pick out the memorable games; the highlights, matches that meant the most to Leicester City's number 6, the ones that stick in his mind.

Let's try to scratch the surface of those games. Not just what happened, but how and why it happened. All the background stuff you can't get, perhaps, from reading the match reports. This is Muzzy's top 10, his favourite games under Martin O'Neill. His choices are surprising.

1. Manchester United 2-2 Leicester City, Old Trafford, Saturday, August 15, 1998

A nice easy return to Premier League football. Arsenal had completed the Double months earlier and you didn't need to be a connoisseur of English football to know that United boss Alex Ferguson would not want to let that happen again.

It was the first game after the '98 World Cup. There was huge media interest in David Beckham, following his sending off in England's last 16 exit to Argentina. It seemed like all the world's cameras and press men were there. But Martin was ready.

It began on the coach, as we left and headed up the M6. We'd hardly left Leicestershire before Martin started early with the psychology. In fact, it started before that. When we trained on Thursday, he came out and put an arm round us.

"They're not what they were," he told us, one by one, as we came off the training pitch. Cantona had retired. "Big boots to fill and they haven't filled 'em," he said. On it went, throughout Thursday, Friday, on the coach to Manchester, reaching a crescendo in the away dressing room at 2pm.

That's when he read the team out, as he did an hour before kick-off every game. We generally always knew what it was going to be. We had a fairly settled side and if there were to be any changes, usually we'd have trained accordingly in the week. So the team was read out and we started to prepare.

Every dressing room has different characters who prepare for a game in different ways. At City, there were the quiet players – Emile, Tony Cottee, Guppy – who would sit, alone in their thoughts. Then there were Garry Parker, Lenny, Walshy, Taggs, players who would gee everyone up, shaking a fist in your face.

The boss would flutter around, skipping from one player to

the next. I remember that game because the gaffer was brilliant. He got into your mind. I don't know how, but he did. And by the time he was finished, you felt like a world beater.

"You," he said, pointing a finger at Matt Elliott. "I would rather have you in my team than Ronnie Johnsen. You're a better centre-half than him."

He looked at Savage. "They made a mistake letting you go from this club, son," he said to him. "I know that. You know that. Everyone in this changing room knows that. Go and show Alex Ferguson. Show him how wrong he was."

Savage put on his shirt and puffed out his chest. Martin scanned the dressing room. His eyes rested on me. "Muzzy," he said. "I would rather have you in my team than David Beckham. You give me more than he does. You wouldn't have got yourself sent off like he did in the World Cup. His mind will be all over the place. Show him who is the better midfield player."

I don't know how I kept a straight face. I think if he had the choice, he'd plump for Beckham above me. But he said it again. He wasn't pissing about. "I'd rather have you than him. Every day of the week. Go out and show him that today."

And although I knew it was a line and he was playing me like an old Irish fiddle, I felt my heart pound and my pulse quicken. I was buzzing. *He fucking rates me more than Beckham. He rates me more than Beckham.*

Martin had signed Frank Sinclair in the close season for £2m from Chelsea. "You will be majestic today, Frank," he said. "There is nothing for you to worry about here. You are one of the finest centre-halves in the Premier League. That's why I've signed you. Go out there and play your game."

Big Frank had been around football a long time. He'd played

under many managers. I swear, as he tied his boots and pulled up his socks that afternoon, he looked an inch taller.

Martin went round and spoke to every player. He nourished them with love and confidence. He put magic in their hearts. We ran out, in front of 55,052 people at a sold-out Old Trafford, and gave the finest team in English football a game.

Tony Cottee started up front with Emile Heskey. We usually played a 3-5-2 under O'Neill but we played a 4-5-1 that day, with Emile in midfield but pushing up to make it a 4-4-2 when we had the ball. Tony had scored the winner at Old Trafford the season before, when we won 1-0. No-one was more pleased than me. I was a Hammers fan as a kid. I had his posters on my wall. He was delirious about that goal – and so was I.

United were a difficult team to play against, not just because of their quality, but for their work ethic. They ran, they tracked back, they covered. People said we were good at that but United were, too. It was what made them such a difficult side to play.

I set up the first goal, a run down the left, nearly falling over, keeping on my feet, getting past Gary Neville to the byline and somehow poking a ball through to Emile who shinned it in.

In the second half, I threaded a ball through to Sav, playing as right wing-back, and he floated in a great cross for an unmarked Tony Cottee to head home and make it 2-0. Two goals in two games at Old Trafford for TC.

But United didn't give in. They came back, wave after wave of United attack. A Beckham shot, which ricocheted off an unsuspecting Teddy Sheringham – 2-1.

The 90 minutes passed. There were five minutes of injury time. We were clinging on. In the eighth minute of that period – I know, I know – Beckham took a free-kick, 25 yards out.

Kasey Keller had gone off injured, Pegguy Arphexad was on.

He was a nice lad, Pegguy, so laid back. Considering he didn't play often, he had an impressive tally of silverware. He was also what you might call 'a big lad'. Unbelievably big. When he went for a pee, he didn't shake it. He kicked it. The joke in the dressing room was that he used to feed it mice.

Anyway, sure enough, the inevitable happened. Beckham curved his right boot around the ball and it dropped low to Arphexad's bottom right-hand corner to make it 2-2.

It felt like a defeat: 2-0 at Old Trafford and back to 2-2 with the last kick of the game. Martin was gutted in the changing room afterwards. We all were. We should have won.

We went out that night and people bought us drinks and patted us on the back. That was the thing about Leicester City fans. They wanted us to win, of course they did, but if we worked hard, if we put up a fight, did our best, then they recognised that. Well done, they said. We were proud of you.

United went on to win the treble that season – Premier League, FA Cup and Champions League. I wouldn't think they had too many games that were more fiercely-contested than that one.

2. Derby County 0-4 Leicester City, Pride Park, Sunday, April 26, 1998

I didn't see it at first, I only heard it. About 4,000 delirious Leicester City fans loudly singing *cheerio, cheerio, cheerio* as a stream of dejected Derby County supporters headed for the exit. The game was 15 minutes old. We were 4-0 up.

Sometimes – and it doesn't happen often – you play in a game where everything goes right, where everything you do comes off: every pass reaches its man, every attack results in a goal. It's a fantastic feeling – and it happened for us on that afternoon.

It was Derby's first season at Pride Park. They were doing well, too, under Jim Smith. I think we were neck and neck in eighth and ninth place. It was a sunny afternoon, a Sunday game, live on Sky. We didn't always do ourselves justice when the cameras turned up. We did that day. Four attacks. Four virtually identical crosses. Four headed goals. Game over after 15 minutes.

I scored the second. The game was only two minutes old. Heskey had already scored the first header. For the second, he peeled off down the right. Their left-back – I think it was Chris Powell – couldn't get near him. I made a run from midfield. Emile looked up and put a perfectly weighted ball in. It was just in front of me – but I launched myself at it and, bang, 2-0. Emile scored another and then Ian Marshall got in on the act. Four-nil in a quarter-of-an-hour – and the exodus started.

Just before half-time, Emile had a great opportunity, which he squandered. I don't remember it so much as the aftermath. We came into the changing room at the break and were delighted. We were laughing and patting each other on the back. It felt brilliant to be 4-0 up, in a derby, on the telly, the game over. We sat down and O'Neill was furious. He tore a strip off Emile.

"What the fuck was that?" he said. "That was the easiest chance of the lot – and you missed it. We should be 5-0 up."

There were a few stifled laughs but we sat, in stunned silence, and watched as our irate manager ranted on. "If you'd put that one away, then we were safe," he said. "Now we've got to go out and perform because they know they can still pull this back."

In 10 minutes, our cheery mood evaporated.

It was only later that I realised what he'd done. It was a bit of reverse psychology. He didn't want us to rest on our laurels.

He knew we needed shaking up a bit after we cruised our way through the first 45 minutes. So poor Emile – and Derby just couldn't deal with him on the day – felt the brunt of his temper.

3. Leicester City 2-1 Tottenham Hotspur, Filbert Street, Monday, October 19, 1998

I scored one of the best goals of my career in this match – but I don't remember the game for that. I remember it as the day when Martin O'Neill stayed at City.

Martin had been at Leicester for two-and-a-half seasons. After a shaky start, he'd done well. The fans loved him, even if that fondness wasn't always shared by the suits in the boardroom.

In the autumn of 1998, Leeds United lost their manager, George Graham, who had resigned to take over at Tottenham. Peter Ridsdale, the Leeds chairman, had let it be known that O'Neill was his first-choice target.

The papers were full of it, daily. Leeds wanted to speak to O'Neill. City wouldn't let them. This impasse seemed to limp on for weeks. It was unsettling. No-one wanted Martin to go. We loved him. He was the greatest manager Leicester ever had.

I'd be out in town and City fans would collar me and say: 'What do you know? Is he going?' and I'd shrug my shoulders. I didn't know. I had no idea. We spoke about it now and then, the lads, but the boss never did. We just got on with the job.

I didn't think he'd go. I could see he liked it at Leicester. That much was obvious. So why would he leave? But then we heard these rumours that he was house-hunting in Yorkshire, not just Martin but Robbo, too. It all came to a head that night.

Night games at Filbert Street were great. There was always a special atmosphere inside the ground, but especially so that night. The local paper, the *Leicester Mercury*, had printed 10,000 posters with the words 'DON'T GO MARTIN' on them.

We ran out and those posters were everywhere. The stands were a sea of blue and white placards. The crowd were singing his name. It was emotional.

Our opponents were Spurs, managed by former Leeds boss, George Graham. We always seemed to do well against them and it was always a good game. This time, we started sluggishly. Les Ferdinand scored for them and, despite a first-half equaliser from Big Emile, we were struggling to get a real foothold.

At half-time, we came in and Martin was pacing around the changing room, scratching his head and looking anguished.

"I don't know what's wrong with you," he said, and he paused. "If this is anything to do with me, and the speculation, let me tell you now – I'm staying. I'm not going anywhere. Put that out of your mind. Don't think about that – concentrate on the match. There's a game of football to win here."

And, collectively, we breathed a huge sigh of relief. I don't know if he'd made his mind up the day before, two days before, a week before or when he saw this huge outpouring of genuine affection from the City faithful. Whatever, he was staying. We went out and we played much better in the second half.

The goal came in the 85th minute. Every time we had a corner or free-kick outside the box, the big boys would go up – Walsh, Elliott, Sinclair or Tags, Emile – and I'd loiter around the edge of the box. If anything spilled to me, I'd have a go.

Guppy's free-kick came over. He was aiming for Big Frank coming in at the far post but Les got his boot to it and volleyed the ball out. It came to me 25, 30 yards out. It was sitting up to be larruped so I had a dig, right foot, on the volley, and it flew past keeper Ian Walker and straight into the top-right corner.

I knew as soon as it came off my boot it was in. And I was off; arms in the air, running, running anywhere, everywhere, delirious. I ran towards the bench. People said to me afterwards: *'You ran to Martin, didn't you? Was that you saying – don't go boss?'* and it wasn't, truth be told. I wish it was, that would be a nicer story. But it wasn't. I was just running.

Afterwards, he took our shirts off. He gave us a massage. He sponged the mud from our legs. When we won games like that, he was like a kid at Christmas. He couldn't do enough for you. It was one of the most memorable nights of my playing career.

4. West Ham United 3-2 Leicester City, Upton Park, Saturday, November 14, 1998

This was our first defeat in seven and I was substituted as well, early in the second half. I never liked being dragged. And yet, this remains one of my favourite games.

I look back at my career sometimes and it's hard to remember it all. Games merge into each other. I never kept a diary. I didn't have a scrapbook. I just played. I loved it and I hoped it would last forever but, truthfully, I took it a bit for granted. I didn't always realise or appreciate just how magical – especially those times with City under Martin O'Neill – it was.

You'll struggle to find another player or City fan who has good things to say about this game. But not me. I scored that afternoon; the first goal of the game, right up against the Southbank, where I used to stand as a kid, with my dad and his brothers, then my mates, week in, week out, cheering on the Hammers.

I remember the ball coming through to me, taking it forward, the defence opening up and, suddenly, I'm one-on-one with

Shaka Hislop. I never used to freeze at moments like that. I never used to overthink it or feel anxious. This is what you train for. You need to switch off and let your subconscious take over. Trust in your ability. It'll be fine – and usually it is. Not that moment. I was struck by the enormity of the situation.

That only happened to me twice, I think, in my career – once at the Saitama Stadium in Japan, in the 2002 World Cup semi-final, coming on for Turkey against Brazil; and November 14, 1998, one-on-one with Shaka Hislop at Upton Park.

For a moment, I stopped. I paused. I looked up at the South-bank and thought about all those Saturdays watching West Ham. My dad, my uncles, my mates. They were all there that afternoon, all West Ham fans. It was a poignant moment. This was the club I supported as a lad. I was going to score against them. I managed to regain my composure in time. I slotted the ball past Hislop, turned away and raised my arm in celebration.

I stayed over in London that night. I went to my old local, the Army & Navy, in Canning Town. I seem to remember I bought a lot of drinks that night.

We played West Ham on the last day of the season the year before. There was an outside chance that day, if we won and other teams faltered, that we might qualify for Europe.

We didn't. We lost 4-3 in a topsy-turvy game and that was that. We didn't qualify for Europe. We finished 10th on 53 points.

The team stayed over. It was Martin's plan – have a few drinks, all of us together at the culmination of a long season. Someone, I don't know how he knew, heard the directors were not happy about this idea. They were worried about the cost. Word got back to Martin. He was furious. "Ring your wives," he said. "Ring your friends. Get them here. We're having a party."

So we did, with the party going on until the early hours. Everything went on the tab. Martin presented that to the board. "Another good season," I imagine he said. "Here's the bill."

5. Atletico Madrid, UEFA Cup,
(away: September 16, 1997; home: September 30, 1997)

We put so much into these games that it affected our league form – we won two of the next 14 after the home leg. I walked off at Filbert Street – it was one of my best Leicester games – and I was exhausted. I'd given everything. It knocked the stuffing out of us and took us a long time to recover.

I remember the heat at the Vincente Calderon. Walking onto the pitch from a tunnel that came up from under the ground, this sea of red and white, and about 3,000 Leicester City fans among the 35,000 crowd, who were making a hell of a racket. Our walk felt almost gladiatorial, like a scene from *Spartacus*.

We didn't know but our fans had suffered a torturous journey. They had been told "the only way to attend" was to pay £279 for an official package, which didn't even include a stopover.

Fans were then herded, like cattle, to a compound out of town – unable even to exchange money to buy food. Afterwards, the club tried to placate disgruntled fans with the offer of a £35 voucher at the club shop. It all seemed a bit tawdry.

As players, we wanted to do well. It was the first time in nearly 40 years the club had been in Europe and early on Ian Marshall put us 1-0 up. He was injured after 30 minutes and carried off. I don't know what was wrong with him, just that one of the stretcher bearers was absolutely pissing himself laughing at him. He had that effect on everyone, Marshy.

We had a great chance to make it 2-0, which we squandered,

and were then up against it. It was all Atletico. They were a decent side – Juninho, (again), Christian Vieri – a £12m signing from Juventus, Kiko. One of the papers worked out they had £52m worth of players, we had £7.5m. They ran out 2-1 winners, scoring twice in three minutes. But the gulf wasn't that wide. We'd done enough to deserve a draw but we gave a good account of ourselves – and at least we had got an away goal.

We went out that night in Madrid, to the same nightclub the Atletico players were in. I remember talking to a couple of their lads. They seemed all right but I didn't want to know, really. We'd just lost. We didn't want to be pals with them, or re-live the game. We wanted to get them back to Filbert Street. We thought we had a chance. So the scene was set. Another big night game. We were so up for it. We were pretty confident.

We dominated the first half, without much luck. Garry Parker was sent off for taking a free-kick too quickly – the oddest dismissal I saw in my career. It was hard enough with a full team; with one man missing, they got the upper hand.

There was some dodgy refereeing. Three times I was fouled in the area. I was never a diver. I thought all three were penalties. After the game, Martin O'Neill told the media the same. He said, on camera, that he started to suspect the game was one we "couldn't win" and he criticised the ref, Remi Harrel. Interestingly, Martin was never fined for his comments. The following season, Harrel was removed from the UEFA approved ref list.

6. Wimbledon 1-1 Leicester City, Coca-Cola League Cup semi-final, second leg, Selhurst Park, March 11 1997

Selhurst Park is an awful ground. If you live anywhere north of the river, it's a hideous journey – and it's even worse when you're facing Wimbledon on a cold, damp, wintery March night. We knew what to expect and they laid it on thick. Wimbledon always used to have music in their dressing room. That night, their CD player wasn't in their dressing room. It was in the corridor, outside both dressing rooms. They waited until we were all in – and they turned it to 11. It was loud – it was supposed to be. It was supposed to annoy us, to distract. I don't think it did. We weren't a team that were easily intimidated.

When we arrived our kitman, Macca, saw one of the Wimbledon coaches carry a case of champagne into their dressing room. He told Martin and he rubbed his hands with glee. Martin loved that. If he mentioned that once before – "They think they've won, they think they're better than you. They've got champagne in their dressing room, for Chrissakes" – he must have mentioned it 10, 20 times. It played right into his hands. The first leg at Filbert Street had been a bruising but goalless affair. They clearly thought they were going to do it.

You walk from the dressing rooms and down a long, narrow, brick-lined corridor at Selhurst Park. They all came out without their shirts, grimacing. Mick Harford. Robbie Earle. Marcus Gayle. Vinny Jones, who was wearing his ear-ring, I remember, which kind of spoilt the effect. They were shouting and swearing, putting their fists in each others faces. "Come on," they kept saying, leading with their chins, their eyes bulging. It was naive, really. You don't do that to a team that has Steve Walsh and Neil Lennon in it. That doesn't scare them.

It was a terrible game of football. It wasn't football. It was war. It was a game of attrition. Long balls. Big men going up for headers, all arms and elbows. Gayle scored in the first half for them, but I don't think any of us felt unduly worried. We knew we were a better team. We just had to bide our time.

Larry Grayson scored our equaliser, a long free-kick from Garry Parker, Larry running in from the far post and knocking a looping header past Neil Sullivan. It was Larry's fourth goal for the club. He went on and on about it.

I remember coming over to the touchline to take a throw-in and seeing Mick Harford warming up. I was at Chelsea with Mick, although I didn't have anything to do with him. He was in the first team, I was in the reserves. They were like oil and water at Chelsea. They didn't mix. But he remembered me.

"Muzzy," he said, when I collected the ball by the touchline as he warmed up.

"All right mate," I said.

"I'm coming on in a minute," he said. "And when I do, I'm going to break your fucking nose." Gulp.

Walshy overheard. "Don't worry about him. I'll have him."

He'd spent the previous hour smashing Vinny Jones. Walshy enjoyed that. Harford would be more a challenge for him, but he loved that. He genuinely had no fear.

Mick came on in the 76th minute. Wimbledon knocked every ball long, in the air, to Mick. I remember the first ball – up went Mick, up went Steve. *Bang*. It was like a car crash. The noise reverberated around Selhurst Park. There were legs and arms flying everywhere. Miraculously, God knows how, Mick Harford was the only player booked that night.

I see Mick occasionally to this day. "Remember when you said you were going to break my nose, Mick." And he shakes his head and says he doesn't remember. Sure he doesn't.

Knocking out Wimbledon at Selhurst Park was every bit as satisfying as winning the cup at Hillsborough a month later.

7. Leicester City 5-2 Sunderland, Filbert Street, Saturday, March 5, 2000

There's a theory in football that sides are only ever as good as their strikers. I shouldn't buy into that, perhaps, as a midfielder.

But I do. You think of any top-class side in world football, and I can guarantee that they'll have at least one, two or maybe three – Manchester United were at their best when they had Rooney, Ronaldo and Tevez up front – brilliant forwards.

We had some great strikers at Leicester. I loved playing with Tony Cottee and Paul Dickov. Ian Marshall was a brilliant finisher. Stevie Claridge was deadly in the six-yard box and equally good with his back to goal. When we had Les Ferdinand he was 37, at the end of his career, but still brilliant. But Martin O'Neill's Leicester side never looked as dangerous as they did on this Sunday afternoon, as we tore Sunderland apart thanks to our two strikers: Emile Heskey and Stan Collymore.

When the boss signed Collymore I wasn't worried about the baggage that might come with him, that he hadn't played properly for a year, because I knew he'd get the best out of him. If anyone could do that, Martin could. We played Watford at Vicarage Road a few days after Stan signed. He'd trained with us once, possibly twice before that. But he slotted straight in.

I remember someone – I'm sure it was Marshy – left a box of Prozac tablets on his peg on his second day at Belvoir Drive. Stan just picked them up, put them in his pocket and shook his head and smiled. I knew then he'd be fine.

Martin picked him for the Watford game. "Just give us 45 minutes," he told him in the changing room. Stan played the whole game, hitting the bar and slotting in pretty well.

After the furore of La Manga, Stan had a point to prove.

This was his home debut. He was fitter and stronger by the time Sunderland came to Filbert Street. Stan and Emile tore the Black Cats apart. Stan had so much to his game. He was a great finisher, but he could drop deep and pick the ball up, he was strong, he could dribble, he had great vision and a brilliant footballing brain. Like all great players, it all seemed so easy.

In all my time at Leicester City, we had to battle for everything – except that day. That day, we seemed to float through the game. We controlled it. Sunderland weren't bad, but it made such a difference having Heskey and Collymore up front.

I remember walking from the pitch and feeling ecstatic. It was the best game I'd ever played in. We were brilliant that day: 5-2, a hat-trick for Stan, one for Emile, the beginning of a brilliant partnership. This was it. We were going places.

And then Emile was sold to Liverpool for £11m, Stan broke his ankle and all that promise, all that potential, was gone. Still, it was good while it lasted.

8. Liverpool 0-2 Leicester City, Anfield, Wednesday, May 3, 2000

We never lost at Anfield under Martin O'Neill. Liverpool beat us at Filbert Street a couple of times but from 1996 to 2000, they never managed to beat us on their home turf.

We always loved playing away at Liverpool, not just because Anfield is such a special ground, loaded with history and importance and the atmosphere was always good. It was because we always did so well there.

Martin left at the end of the 1999/2000 season. The lure of Celtic – after turning down Leeds, Everton, others too, possibly – was too strong. It was also the season we played our best football. We were never just a one-dimensional long-ball team – we had far too much quality in the side for that – but the more established we became in the Premier League, the better we became, too. The less we had to fear, the more teams started to fear us. Maybe not fear us, as such, but there were certainly a few teams who didn't fancy playing us.

If Sunderland was the best we played with Stan and Emile up front, this game wasn't far behind – except both Stan and Emile were missing. Collymore had broken his ankle a month earlier at Derby and Emile was now lining up for Liverpool against us.

We weren't just missing our front two. There was no Walshy. No Tim Flowers. We had the smallest forward line in Premier League football in Tony Cottee and Darren Eadie. And yet we outclassed Liverpool, at home, in front of over 40,000 Scousers. *'Liverpool Outfoxed'* was the headline in *The Guardian* the following day. 'Leicester,' the report said, 'were simply magnificent.'

We were. There was a 10-minute period in the second half where we knocked it around and I'm sure Liverpool didn't get a touch. They weren't great that night. They didn't play well. But we didn't let them play well.

Tony Cottee scored after two minutes of the first half, Phil Gilchrist after two minutes of the second. It was a frustrating period for them. They were outside the top three and desperately trying to qualify for Europe, but their fans clapped us off.

"At some stage someone is going to realise that we can play a bit," said Martin O'Neill in the following day's *Leicester Mercury*. "For some periods we were sensational. My players fancied the challenge but then again, they generally do."

The first time we played at Anfield – Boxing Day, 1996 – and, unusually, the boss had gone round the away dressing room sticking A3-sized posters on the wall, with their formation, who was playing where, their movement, what they might try to do.

He NEVER did this. We never did this. We never worried too much about our opponents. We didn't have sessions where we would run though how we would counter Saturday's opposition. We concentrated on what we would do, not what they might do. Martin picked up one of the posters.

He ran down the list of names: Berger, McManaman, Barnes, Collymore. He didn't say any more. He scrunched the paper into a small ball and kicked it across the dressing room. "Pah," he said. "Fuck all of that. Just go out there and beat them."

The first game with Peter Taylor, Aston Villa at home, the opening game of the 2000/01 season, the walls of our changing room were covered in posters. Set pieces, who's picking up who, their formation. I swear, we ran out that day and there was so much information in our heads, we didn't know what we were doing. Football is a simple game made complicated by morons. The best managers keep it simple. O'Neill did that.

I remember a game against Sheffield Wednesday at home, early in the 1997/98 season and their Italian forward, little Benito Carbone, was running us ragged. We came in at half-time and Lenny was furious.

"Gaffer, Carbone is doing this," and *"Carbone is doing that."*

Martin listened for about five seconds and told Lenny to shut up. Lenny wouldn't shut up. "But gaffer, he's running off us and dropping deep and we're not getting his runs, boss."

"Lenny," he said. "for God's sake, shut up."

"But Carbone… he's…"

"For fuck's sake, Lenny, just go out there and score a goal. That'll solve the Carbone problem."

9. Southampton 1-2 Leicester City, The Dell, Saturday, April 29, 2000

My third game from the second half of the 1999/2000 season. After four years in the top flight, we were a better, more confident side playing more pleasing football. This wasn't one of those games, though. This was no Leicester v Sunderland. We didn't play them off the park like we would do to Liverpool a week later, either.

But this was special for me. I remember it clearly. Glenn Hoddle was the Southampton manager. By now, four years after leaving Chelsea and having a successful career at Leicester, I'd almost forgotten how much I still didn't like that self-obsessed bastard. But in the days leading up to the game, it came back. I wanted to win this game as much as any League Cup final.

The Dell was an awful place to go. A long drive. We never seemed to do very well there. I'm sure Francis Benali scored against us one year. I think it was the only time he ever scored.

It was a gloriously sunny day on the south coast. The football didn't match the weather. The football was piss-poor. Hassan Kachloul scored in the first five minutes for them as we started slowly. It looked like another one of *those* games.

But Tony Cottee – who had taken a bit of a back seat with the arrival of Stan Collymore – equalised midway through the first half and suddenly their heads dropped. They didn't have any fight, any team spirit. From then on, Southampton struggled.

I scored the worst goal of my career in the 60th minute. Their goalkeeper, Neil Moss, who kept them in the game in the second half, came out to clear a loose back pass. I closed him down and he smacked the ball against my arse and it rebounded into the net. It was my first goal for three months.

"He deserved that goal," Martin O'Neill said in the *Mercury* the next day, "for the tenacity and hard work he always puts in." I ran straight over to the dugout, running past our subs and coaches and started celebrating right in front of Hoddle.

I stood there, my arms outstretched, laughing and laughing, looking right at Hoddle. I didn't say anything. I didn't have to.

That one's for you, son.

Have that.

Have that, you fucker.

We finished 11 points and seven places above Southampton that year. I know because I checked. I was pleased about that.

10. *Aston Villa 1-3 Leicester City, Villa Park, Saturday, November 16, 1996*

My first goal in the Premier League and the moment when a few people realised, maybe even a few of our squad, too, that we weren't there just to make up the numbers.

I remember sitting on the coach after the game, Radio 5 Live reporting from our game, and their reporter damning us with faint praise, going on about our set pieces and paying only the faintest lip-service to the quality we had and the way we played Villa off the park that day.

"Oh, and how they must rehearse those set pieces," he said. And we all groaned and swore at the radio, telling the old twat where to stick his analysis. A team of Leicester City players had beaten the much-fancied Aston Villa 3-1 in their own backyard – and it could have been five or six.

A crate of beer appeared.

The cards came out.

We drank our way home.

LA MANGA – PART 1

February, 2000. At the end of the month, Leicester City are due to play their third League Cup final – now masquerading as the Worthington Cup – in four years.

Just like his mentor, Brian Clough, a generation earlier, City boss Martin O'Neill liked to take his squad on holiday before the big game. Relax. Get away. Let your hair down, boys. Feel the sun on your back. You've earned it, lads.

Unsurprisingly, this always went down very well with the players. He'd done it a few times before. It seemed to work, too. The players trained, they played golf, they had a few drinks – maybe a few more, what did it matter – and they came back tanned and relaxed.

This time, with a high-profile Wembley final just a fortnight away, O'Neil booked his side into the five-star La Manga resort in Murcia. Lovely. What could possibly go wrong?

We got to the airport early on Wednesday morning, February 16, 2000. It would have been around 7.30am/8am, maybe even earlier. I'd have been up for a good three hours by then. We used to go on these early flights because it was cheaper for the club to get the tickets. Ridiculous, really, that they'd fly us out to the lap of Mediterranean luxury, the five-star La Manga resort in Murcia, but we'd have to be up at the crack of dawn to save the club a few quid on flights.

We checked in, put our bags through the hold and did what we always did when we had a few days away – we headed straight to the bar and started drinking. It was too early for breakfast, by rights, never mind a pint. But, you know, we'd been up for four hours. It felt like lunchtime. And we never needed an excuse to start drinking, so we tucked in. It's what we always did.

We'd been away a few times in pre-seasons – Spain, Ireland, Tenerife, America – and we'd start drinking, always, at the airport bar. It was a Leicester City tradition. Martin wasn't flying with us. He was coming out later. That was the plan.

Was that the reason this La Manga trip ended in drunken disgrace? Possibly, but not entirely. Martin was there on other occasions when someone would get a round in at the departure lounge bar. Then another. And then another. He always knew what was going on. He'd shake his head and tut perhaps and say it was *'too early to be bloody drinking like that, you know'* but, crucially, he never stopped us. He knew we liked a drink. This time, without Martin, maybe we all felt the reins were, if not off, then a bit slacker, perhaps.

Robbo and Wal were in charge. We all loved Robbo and Wal but both of them didn't mind a drink – and both of them were also terrified of flying. So they had a couple of drinks, a couple of Bloody Marys, I think, to settle their nerves, before the flight. And we sat in the departure lounge bar, knocking them back.

One round. Another one. One for the road.

Before we boarded the plane, I reckon we were – all of us – well on our way. And it didn't stop. We drank on the plane.

We got to La Manga, checked in and went straight out. I didn't unpack. I've been there twice during my time at Leicester City. Both times, I was never there long enough to unpack my bags.

The idea for La Manga was simple: the League Cup final, versus Tranmere was three weeks away. We'd had a tough run and nothing much had gone our way. We hadn't won a league game in December and January. Played eight, lost five, drawn three. We weren't playing badly – where we had lost, we'd lost, mainly, by an odd goal to good sides – but we'd slipped from fifth to 10th. No-one was panicking. We knew the wheels hadn't come off, but it wasn't great. We looked a bit jaded.

The boss's idea was to take us away, like he had all those times before, like Clough did with him when they were winning things at Forest. Get away. Take our minds off things. Martin knew it worked. Clough had this motto. "You can have the best players in the league – but if they're not relaxed, they won't perform. It's the boss's job to make sure the players are relaxed."

Martin was like that. He took us away every season, because he wanted us to be relaxed. We were always delighted when he did this, too, because we knew what it meant. Light training, plenty of sun, relaxation, yep – and lots of drinking.

La Manga looks impressive: 1,400 acres of the finest sports facilities in Europe, three of the best golf courses in Spain, 28 tennis courts, three top-level football pitches, training pitches, squash, open-air pools and a five-star hotel and spa, all nestled between the Murcian Hills and the Mediterranean. The best teams in Europe come to the resort. The weather is great. The facilities are first class. They treat you like visiting princes. I'm sure there is much to recommend it, although I found it a bit sterile, a bit soulless, really. That's as far as any review goes, though. I didn't see enough of the place to offer any informed critique.

We arrived around lunchtime. We were already hammered. We checked in at the grand, marble-floored reception – trying to keep quiet but laughing and larking around – and then headed straight to the bar. The drinks were flowing. One round. Another round. Then another, the volume increasing.

Norwegian club Rosenborg were at La Manga at the same time as us. I remember them looking down their noses at us a bit. We scoffed at them at the time, ridiculed them. The shandy boys, lime and soda drinkers, with their designer jumpers draped over their shoulders. Maybe, though, they had a point. We grew drunker. Louder. The chat, the jokes, the piss-taking and the laughter was constant. Then an argument started.

It began, as it often did, with Ian Marshall. You won't meet a funnier bloke than Marshy but he's so dry it's sometimes hard to know when he's being serious and when he's having you on. And once he starts, once he gets that bit between his teeth, he doesn't let it go. He's on at you all day. He's like a dog with a bone; gnawing away constantly.

He started a debate with anyone who was prepared to listen. The premise of it was this: if he scored a hat-trick, but then the team went on to lose 4-3, then that wasn't his fault.

"In the changing room, if the boss starts after that, after I've scored a hat-trick, he should open the door and say: *This is not for you, son – you've done your job, go home, put your feet up, take Monday off*' because you know what – it wouldn't be my fault we lost. I've done my job. It's you fuckers who have let the side down. I'll see you on Tuesday."

And Marshy being Marshy, he went on and on about it. He had it out with everyone. Tony Cottee was on his side, nodding along. Mostly, we just weren't biting.

Only Robbo. Robbo wasn't having it.

Robbo said he was a member of the team. If the team lost, they were all at fault. And on it went.

At some stage during this drunken session, Gary Lineker appeared. He was with his brother, Wayne. I vaguely remember us all cheering and launching into a boisterous chant of "Oooh Gary, Gary" which was loud and insistent. He came over. We all shook his hand. He knew, immediately, we were hammered.

"Here, Gary," said Marshy, seizing his chance. "If you played in a team and you scored a hat-trick but the team lost 4-3, when the boss starts with the bollockings, you shouldn't be part of that, should you, mate?"

Gary agreed. They'd spent one season together when Gary was at Everton and Marshy was little more than a kid. And with that, Mr Lineker made his excuses and left. He wasn't daft.

A game of golf had been arranged that afternoon. It never happened. We sat and carried on drinking, moving from the hotel to a nearby Irish bar. We were loud and drunk, but it didn't matter. There was no-one around. It was off-season. We had the bar virtually to ourselves. We got stuck in to more beers.

We came back to The Piano Lounge Bar in the La Manga resort and carried on drinking. It was late by now and we had a curfew, a midnight curfew. Robbo, who was also quite refreshed by this stage, tried to tell us it was time to call it a night. We didn't agree. Ian Marshall asked for an extension.

"I can't agree to that," said Robbo. "You'd have to ask the gaffer – and he's not here."

"Give me your phone then," said Marshy. "I'll call him." We all egged him on. *"You daren't call the gaffer, Marshy,"* all of that, which, of course, just made him want to do it all the more.

It was midnight, 1am. Late. Back home, Martin would have been in bed, I'm sure. Marshy took the phone and called Martin.

"Hello boss, it's Ian Marshall here," he said, in his best, formal, 'I'm-not-drunk-at-all' voice.

"We're all just having a nice, quiet little drink here and I wondered, well, we all wondered, as it's a nice night and we don't have too much planned for tomorrow and we're all being very well behaved, if we could perhaps stay out a little later. Hope that's okay, gaffer, cheers, Ian."

We were all pissing ourselves.

Robbo went to bed and we ordered another round.

I remember, at one stage, Stan Collymore passed round a bottle of Jack Daniels. We were drinking beer and taking swigs out of Stan's bottle, as if we needed to be drinking JD after a day on the booze. The volume increased again. Steve Walsh climbed on to a table and started dancing and singing. Somehow, I don't know how, Walshy's trousers ended up around his ankles.

Stanley Victor Collymore had joined Leicester City a week earlier on a free transfer from Aston Villa. A former England international and a star at Forest and Liverpool, Stan had struggled at Villa, his hometown club. We'd read the stories about him and Ulrika Jonsson, his depression, his rows with Villa boss John Gregory. I knew he was a top player. I'd played against

127

him. I didn't really know what to expect when he arrived. But Stan settled in immediately. Stan was like us – a working class lad, an old-fashioned pro who had come up the hard way. He'd cleaned boots and swept floors. He'd had success with Forest and Liverpool, and he'd had to deal with the media spotlight – for things he had done wrong and some he hadn't – but, essentially, he was the same as us. He wasn't a prima donna.

He came in, he had the right attitude, he wanted to do well, to work hard, to be part of a team. I knew he'd suffered with depression but it wasn't the kind of subject you talked about in the changing room. Stan never brought it up and I never asked.

Stan didn't come to Leicester for the money or the fact that we were a decent side on the verge of becoming a very good side – a couple more shrewd signings and we'd have been a top-six team, I think. Stan came because of Martin. Martin would have said to him: "Come and play for me and I'll look after you. I'll make everything ok."

And Stan, like everyone at the club, would have trusted him, would have wanted to play for him, to please him. That's how it was at Leicester. There was never any problem with Stan.

As the bottle of Jack Daniels was passed round, I sat back in the plush surroundings of the bar and I knew, in that instant, that I'd gone. I was finished. I had to go to bed. I stood up and made out I was going to the toilet.

"Muzzy is bailing," someone shouted. My reputation for just nipping out and leaving, without a word, was now well known.

"Nah, I'm just off for a slash," I said, and I made my way towards the toilet, rummaged around in my shorts for my key and swerved off, back to the room. It was 1.30am. I was fucked. I lay on the bed, in the clothes I'd worn all day, and fell asleep.

128

Young Muzzy: (Left to right) Me, maybe age 3 or 4, in fetching knitwear and at the age of 10, turning out in the kit of St Matthew's, my first 'proper' team

Senrab graduates: Andy Grant, Terry Skiverton and me, after signing for Chelsea at the age of 14. As Terry – accurately – reflected: "You should see Muzzy – he looks about six!"

Chelsea boy: Looking serious (front, second left) ahead of a friendly game with the line-up including Terry (back, third left), circa 1994

Debut: Making my bow against Sheffield United, March 30, 1996 – fortunately the fans weren't booing me; (inset) an early training session and education in sporting fashion

Blue is the colour: (Below) Flying the flag at Wembley, after the play-off final victory over Crystal Palace less than two months after my debut; (below right) at my press conference with Martin O'Neill after completing my permanent move

Head for heights: Celebrating with Garry Parker after our League Cup quarter-final victory at Ipswich Town, January 1997

Samba magic: Showing Emerson a clean pair of heels – one of my few bright spots from the League Cup final against Middlesbrough, April 1997

Cup winners: My proudest moment to date – celebrated next to Filbert the Fox – following our replay win at Hillsborough, the club's first major trophy for 33 years

Driving on: Me with Steve Walsh, Graham Fenton and Robbie Savage ahead of a players versus fans golf day

Attacking threat: David Seaman and Steve Bould can't stop me with their eyes closed, Boxing Day 1997 – while (below) my early goal in the stunning 4-0 win at Derby in April 1998

Mixed emotions: Feeling the strain despite tasting victory in our first game of 1997/98, a 1-0 win over Aston Villa

Jump to it: Avoiding the challenge of Lee Carsley during the following season's Derby v Leicester fixture, and (right) with my Player of the Month award for September 1998

Fancy dress: With Ian Marshall during a Leicester Christmas do at a nightclub in Nottingham

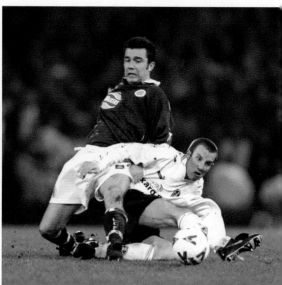

Future team-mate? Challenging Leeds United's Lee Bowyer in March 1999 – less than two years later I was nearly on my way to Elland Road

Suited and booted: (Above, back row, left) In Sunday best with the Leicester squad ahead of the 1999 Worthington Cup final, and (below) riding the challenge of Sol Campbell at Wembley

Lift off: Lenny helps me celebrate my goal against Newcastle United in May 1999

Hello ladies: (Above) With Andy Impey, Big Emile and Marshy during a pre-season training swim at St Margaret's Baths; (left) on a club break with Matt Elliott, Scott Taylor and Jamie Lawrence; (inset) the infamous Baffone's in Leicester, scene of so many musical crimes...

New season, new goals: (Left) Keeping a close eye on Thierry Henry on the opening day of 1999/2000; (above) delight after my late penalty against Chelsea had put us 2-1 up in the 90th minute – only for Frank Sinclair's own goal to scupper our win bonus; (below) the home fans seem pleased following my opener against Aston Villa in a 3-1 victory in September 1999

Blue...and red: In familiar colours with racehorse Izzet Muzzy, named after me by National Lottery winner Sean Taylor; (right) celebrating Worthington Cup semi-final success over Aston Villa in 2000 with the Turkish flag of my father – a decision which would launch an international football career

Final glory: A big hug for skipper Matt Elliott, two-goal hero in our 2000 Worthington Cup final triumph over Tranmere Rovers

Cheeky: (Above) A celebratory pat for Stan Collymore, after his goal against Leeds; a week later, a broken leg at Derby all but ended his brief spell at City; (right) delighted after one of the most satisfying goals of my career, off my arse at Glenn Hoddle's Southampton in April 2000

Welcome to the big time: (Left) Feeling the after-effects of Johan Mjallby's challenge on my full debut for Turkey, a goalless draw against Sweden in Eindhoven during Euro 2000

You want to pay me how much? (Below) A press conference with new boss Peter Taylor after announcing my new contract ahead of the 2000/01 season

Tougher times: (Left) Shooting for goal during the UEFA Cup first round defeat to Red Star Belgrade; (right) new boss Dave Bassett and Dennis Wise in discussion, with assistant Micky Adams also in shot in the first post-Taylor game, 13 months later at Chelsea, October 2001

The end?
A Filbert Street farewell in May 2002 – but it was not quite the end for me at City

World Cup memories: My one appearance in the greatest football competition of them all, in the 2002 semi-final against Brazil; (left) come in number 13...; (above) holding off Gilberto Silva and (below) with Rivaldo

The phone rang just before 9am. It was my wake-up call. "Meet in reception," a voice I didn't recognise said sternly. My head was banging and my mouth was dry. I felt like death. I took off the clothes I'd slept in and got in the shower.

Unsurprisingly, I felt like shit. I had a huge hangover, but I could deal with them then. I'd run and sweat it off. These days, nothing – absolutely nothing – seems to work. They're in for the day, possibly the day after.

The idea was we'd have breakfast and then a light training session at 10am. And then, in the afternoon, we could do what we wanted. I don't think we were planning a big session – but we'd have been drinking. The beers would have been out later.

It wasn't to be.

Steve Walford was standing in reception, talking to an angry member of the La Manga staff. It all looked a little fractious.

"What are we doing, Wal?" I said.

Wal looked despondent. "Go and pack your bags," he said. "We're going home."

He motioned with his head behind me, to the Piano Lounge Bar where we'd been. I looked round the corner.

Jesus.

Everything, absolutely everything – seats, tables, floors, ceilings, the bar, all the fittings – was covered in grey fire extinguisher foam. It looked like a bomb had hit it, and the fall-out, the ash, the cinders, was everywhere. Even through the fog of my hangover, I could see it looked bad, really bad.

One-by-one, the rest of the lads came down. I found out what had happened from their fragmented drunken stories. Stan had set off a fire extinguisher.

"Just one fire extinguisher," I said. "And it did all that?"

Yep. Just one.

I laughed at first. It seemed like a joke. But no-one else was. They stood in the reception of the Hyatt Hotel, La Manga, the players of Leicester City, with long faces and hangovers. And then it hit me: *'Martin. Oh no. Martin will go mad.'*

My theory is if Tony Cottee had let that fire extinguisher off, if it had been me or Walshy, Matt Elliott, Neil Lennon or anyone in that team APART from Stan Collymore, it would have been news, perhaps, in the *Mercury*, and an inside snippet in the tabloids, maybe, but not the news it became. But because it was Stan, and because he had a reputation and a profile that transcended Leicester City, it went everywhere.

We left the resort for the airport that morning. The paparazzi photographers were already lying in wait, trying to bag pictures of Stan Collymore and the Leicester team leaving in shame.

We landed at Gatwick. We didn't go through passport control. They actually came on to the coach and checked our details, and then we drove off, through a back entrance.

I was sitting next to Gerry Taggart on the coach. One of the photographers worked out what was happening. He snatched a few shots as the coach went past. I leaned round Gerry and gave the bastard a V-sign. *Here, have that.* I thought nothing of it until I picked up a copy of *The Sun* the next day – and there's Gerry, by the front window, and my hand, although it looked like it was Gerry, flicking the Vs.

The coach went straight to Sketchley Grange Hotel, near Hinckley, the scene of many famous Leicester City celebrations. This wasn't one of them. Inside one of the conference rooms, the curtains were closed and three rows of chairs awaited us. We took our seats and waited for Martin, and the bollocking we knew was coming. Martin was late. Deliberately late. He made us wait. We were nervous, like naughty school kids outside the headmaster's office.

When he arrived, Martin had a copy of that day's *Leicester Mercury* under his arm. There was one word on the front page: DISGRACE. I saw Martin O'Neill lose his temper many times at City. I don't think I ever saw him so angry, and yet so focused, than he was that day.

"You have let yourselves down, you have let me down, you have let this club down – and you have let the people who follow this club down," he said.

"You have embarrassed them and you have embarrassed me." And on he went. We kept our heads down and our mouths closed. We didn't look at him.

Stan stood up. He apologised to Martin, and to the rest of the lads. It was his fault, he said. It was a stupid mistake, he would accept any fine and he would never do it again. It was the decent thing to do.

If he was hoping that might take the angry wind from Martin's sails, however, he was in for a shock. Martin tore a strip off him. Stan was fined two weeks' wages. He carried on. "You'll report to my office first thing tomorrow morning," Martin told Stan.

Then his eyes fixed on Marshy. "You, pal, have not earned the right, you have not done enough in the game, to call me at 1am in the morning." Marshy looked sheepish.

He moved on to Walshy. "And you – my captain – were you dancing on a table with your trousers round your ankles? Is that the kind of behaviour I want from my first-choice centre-half?"

Walshy shook his head. "Not me, boss. I didn't do that."

Martin didn't believe him. He shook his head and moved on.

There was another 30 minutes of shouting and swearing. He waved the copy of the *Mercury* around.

"They're right," he said.

"You're a fucking disgrace. Every. Single. One. Of. You."

The next day at training, he was still furious. He came into the training ground with another newspaper, another picture, another story – a picture of Gerry, flicking the Vs to a photographer.

Oh no. I recognised it immediately.

It didn't look good.

"What did you think you were doing here?" he said to Gerry.

"That's not me, boss," Gerry said. "It's not me. You can't blame me for that."

"So – who is it? If it's not you – TELL ME WHO IT IS…"

Gerry looked away, away from the gaffer's piercing gaze. "I can't tell you boss, I can't do that."

I heard what was going on. Everyone heard it. It would have been impossible not to hear it. He was furious, again. I waited until he had calmed down and I approached him.

"It wasn't Taggs who did that, boss," I said. "It was me. I did it without thinking about it. I'm sorry."

He stood in front of me. The paper in his hands. He sighed.

"I thought you had more fucking sense than that," he said, and he walked off, shaking his head.

For a week, the story limped on; not just in the local paper and media but in the national press. It turned out the bloke who owned the La Manga bar, Tony Coles, was originally from Leicestershire. The *Leicester Mercury* were all over that. "It was a shameful spectacle, a bunch of well-paid professionals having too much to drink and behaving like hooligans," he told them.

Martin kept the disciplinary action in-house. He spoke to the press and he was frank, as he always was.

"I signed Stan because he is a talented player who has been wasting every Saturday of his life for the last 12 months," he said.

"These events suggest I need my head examining but I still believe he was a risk worth taking. This is his last chance and there is still an opportunity for him to prove everyone wrong."

The club held "an internal investigation", basically, I think, to show the media and supporters they were taking it all very seriously.

They let it be known that the bill for damages at La Manga – which came to £700 (frankly, I'm amazed it wasn't more) – was paid for by the players, as were the emergency flights home. Stan was fined £30,000, a club record.

What it all did, though, was create a siege mentality. Us versus Them. We stuck together like a band of brothers as we read the barbed comments in the media and the snide opinion pieces.

We played Tranmere in the final of the Worthington Cup on Sunday afternoon, February 27. We won 2-1, thanks to two set-piece headers from Man of the Match Matt Elliott.

They were a decent side, Tranmere, and they deserved to be in the final. But, really, it should have been three, maybe four. Emile put me in midway through the second half. I should have scored, but I hesitated and missed. Still, we won comfortably.

A week later, we played Sunderland at home, Stan's Filbert Street debut. We won 5-2, the best game I played in during my eight years at City. In Stan and Emile, we had two top-class strikers.

They tore Sunderland apart that day.

And La Manga? After a few weeks, after winning the League Cup and after that Sunderland game, everything seemed to calm down. After a while, people started to joke about it. Martin said he would never take us away again. We hoped he was joking. Nothing like that would happen again, we said.

Not as bad as that...

THE MAGIC OF MARTIN

All the best managers had it. Clough. Shankly. Busby. Ferguson. An air of natural authority. An attitude that said: 'I am right, even if I am wrong. And you, sunshine, you will get to know this.'

*Martin O'Neill had it. And everyone at Leicester City – from the players, the board, the journalists who covered games, the fans, the tea lady, **everyone** – knew. He was the boss. He'd do things his way.*

For four-and-a-half brilliant years, Leicester were a club moulded in the image of their charismatic manager. They were his team.

How did he do it? We're about to find out – well, find out as best as we can because, truth be told, you can write it down, you can analyse and scrutinise it and say confidently that it must be this or that but for those four-and-a-half years, Leicester City were a very rare thing in football – they were a club that was more than just the sum of their parts.

There was all sorts going on at Filbert Street in those heady days between 1996 and 2000. We could strip it all down and list them like ingredients in a cake, but we still wouldn't get it. It's not that simple.

There was a sort of alchemy; an alignment of the footballing planets that turned a small, underachieving East Midlands football club into Wembley play-off winners, double League Cup winners, League Cup runners-up (once), twice UEFA Cup qualifiers, top-10 finishers in the Premier League (for four seasons running).

Leicester City did this on a meagre budget, with a team fashioned from senior players with a point to prove, and youngsters eked out from the lower leagues by O'Neill and John Robertson. They had a work ethic and they had a camaraderie.

They seem like halcyon days now.

Back then, says Muzzy Izzet, it was what it was. They took it for granted, almost. It's only when you look back that you can see it for what it was really was: something rare, something special.

It's the question I'm asked most these days, more often than: 'How are you, mate?' or 'What are you doing now?' or 'How about that overhead kick at Grimsby, eh?' The most recurring question is: 'So – what was Martin O'Neill *really* like?'

And I'll smile, usually, and say he was a genius or something – and he was, and most people seem happy with that. But it doesn't cover it, because it was more than that – and it wasn't just Martin, either. There were three of them. The Three Wise Men of Leicester City. Because when people talk about Martin O'Neill they often overlook John Robertson and Steve Walford, his coaches. I don't. The other players who were there, the lads who played for them, they don't either. We know how important they were to the team's success.

Martin was brilliant, the best manager I have ever played for

– but Wal and Robbo were every bit as important. Together, they were a brilliant team. How did it work? I wish I could tell you. I wish I could boil it down and lay it out, simple, straightforward, this is what it was.

But I can't – because I'm not entirely sure how they did it. They were three different characters. O'Neill and Robertson were better known for what they'd achieved 20 miles up the A46 at Nottingham Forest. Wal had been a pro at Arsenal, Norwich and West Ham.

City were also a small, underachieving club in the East Midlands with not much money and a well-earned reputation of being something of a yo-yo club, bobbing between the top two flights. It shouldn't have worked. And yet it did.

It worked like magic. If you're reading this, and you're a Leicester City fan, you know that much. Being at Leicester City from 1996 to 2000 was like being a member of the biggest, happiest, strongest and most supportive family you'd ever known. It was a privilege and I loved it.

The manager and the coaches had your back. Your teammates had your back. The fans in this big Midlands city with just one club were right behind you, too. It was a magical, brilliant time; the best of my footballing career.

I have friends who say, if you could have one day again from your career, what would it be? And I can't choose. There are so many. I think about that goal against Watford at Vicarage Road at the end of that 1995/96 season, my first goal for Leicester, six, maybe seven thousand fans going mad in the away end.

The play-off final against Palace and the party that started the moment Claridge shinned that ball beyond Nigel Martyn, and carried on all the way up the M1 and lasted until the early hours at Sketchley Grange. Then there's the three League Cup finals, winning two of them.

I remember a warm September night at Filbert Street, City versus Atletico Madrid, walking off the pitch after losing 2-0 but Martin putting his arm around my shoulder and saying: *'Son, you were world class tonight'* and even though we'd lost, that feeling, that confidence, staying with me for weeks. He made me feel like a world beater.

Turning up at Old Trafford. Anfield. Stamford Bridge. Goodison Park. Villa Park. St James' Park. Elland Road. All these places where no-one gave us a hope and yet climbing back on to the bus for the trip home with a crate of beer and three points in our pocket; singing and drinking and laughing and joking all the way home to Leicester.

Can I have one of those days again? Just one? I want them all again. They were *magniff*.

Three men were responsible for all of that: Martin O'Neill and his two deputies, Robbo and Wal.

So what was Martin like? How did he make it work? I'll have a go at telling you but, frankly, I'm not sure I'll get close. Partly that's to do with the fact that I just floated through those four years at Leicester, thinking football would always be like that, taking this magical atmosphere for granted.

It wouldn't, of course – and it was a shock when Martin left and it all started to unravel. But mainly because, even if I could list everything he did and forensically examine the exact way he did them, I wouldn't come close. Because there was an 'X Factor' involved at Leicester City at that time; an alchemy, something I don't think it's possible to describe.

I've played football all my life. I've been in and around football clubs since I was eight. Few had the authority, or the charisma, that O'Neill possessed. I didn't know anyone who could inspire players in the same way Martin, Robbo and Wal did. I never played for a manager who had the total devotion of his players in the same way Martin had at Leicester. It was like we were his orchestra and he was the conductor. He just had to wave his hand and we were there, dancing to his tune. It was magical.

So what did he do?

Firstly, and most importantly, he made you feel wanted. Not just O'Neill, but Robbo and Wal, too. I don't care who you are or what you do, you want to know that the work you do is appreciated. I felt that from the first day at Leicester. I remember John Robertson walking off the Belvoir Ground training pitch with me one morning. I'd been there a week. I was still wide-eyed and nervous, ridiculously keen to impress. And we walked off and he said: "Thanks for coming up here to help us out, son."

He said this to me as if I, this skinny little Turkish kid from the East End, was somehow doing him and this club a favour. He valued me. And he wanted me to know that I was valued. It was a simple thing, a small thing – but it meant so much to me in those early days and weeks. I'd never had that at Chelsea. I never felt valued. I knew right then, in my first week at Filbert Street, that I wanted to stay at Leicester.

Martin extended my loan: I had one month, then two. I knew, even if we lost at Wembley and we stayed in the old Division One, that my future was here, not at Chelsea. People are sometimes surprised when I say that. I don't know why. You go where people want you. I was wanted at Leicester.

After the Crystal Palace play-off final victory in '96, I went on holiday to Turkey with a few mates. Before I left, Martin took me to one side. "Don't worry, lad," he told me, "I will do everything I can to sign you. I will sort it out. Go on your holiday, relax and don't worry about this. When you get back, you'll be a Leicester City player."

And when I got back, true to his word, it was done. I signed for £650,000, rising to £800,000 depending on appearances. How many, I don't know. I don't think I ever did. I know they had to pay the full £800,000, though. I never asked him about the money I would get because I trusted him. He didn't let me down. I don't think he ever did. What I didn't expect was that Chelsea manager Glenn Hoddle was about to leave and become England boss. Ruud Gullit took his place.

I liked Gullit. He liked me, too. Maybe I'd have got a chance at Chelsea under him. It's possible, I don't know. I didn't wait around to find out. I had a new home. I had no regrets about leaving Chelsea. None at all. I wanted to play for Leicester.

They looked after me, too. I went from £500 a week as a Chelsea reserve to £2,000 a week with Leicester. I got a £25,000 a year signing on fee – that was £25,000 every year, for four years – and great bonuses. We got ridiculous amounts in bonuses at Leicester because we always overachieved. We won things. We did well. They paid us well for it.

For staying up in that first year, they gave me £40,000, £40,000 for winning the Coca-Cola Cup and another £30,000 for getting into Europe. A total of £100,000, in my first season, in bonuses. For playing football. I'd never had so much money.

After my first year at Leicester, Martin called me in. I wondered what he wanted. "You've done well for us, Muz," he said. "We would like to double your wages."

They did more than double my wages. They put me on

£5,000 a week, just like that. I didn't ask for it. They just did it. I suppose there might have been some sides sniffing around and they wanted to keep me happy and keep me at the club. I'm only guessing at that. No-one ever told me that other clubs were interested. Not at that stage. It wouldn't have mattered if they were. I wanted to stay. I was even happier to stay when they doubled my money.

A year later, another call: £10,000 a week. Again, just like that. I hadn't asked for it. Martin made sure that he saw me right. I like to think I was doing the business for them and they wanted me to know they appreciated it.

Martin liked to play 3-5-2, mainly, at Leicester. That was our system. We played to our strengths. Three big centre-halves. Two industrious wing-backs. Three midfielders, who were expected to get forward, join the attack, track back, put in tackles, press constantly, work, work, work – and then two strikers.

Martin didn't worry too much about tactics. He didn't worry too much about the opposition. Occasionally, he would detail a player to man-mark someone, like Pontus Kamark did to great effect against Junhino in the League Cup final. But, usually, he wanted us to concentrate on our own game.

I knew, always, where I should be when we didn't have the ball. If Mike Whitlow or, later, Steve Guppy got the ball deep in our own half on the left, I knew where I had to be. I knew where Lenny was. And Parks. And Sav. I knew where Emile would be. I knew where everyone was and what was expected.

We were well-drilled. We knew what to do. And Martin made sure he had a team of round pegs for round holes. We had a job to do and we did it. It wasn't rocket science. It was simple.

Football is a simple game made needlessly complicated by idiots. We played it simple, just how it should be. We didn't spend a long time discussing tactics and going over moves, endlessly, again and again.

But every player knew what he had to do and where he should be. And we stuck to it. We worked hard. We pressed and we harried. When the opposition had the ball in their own half, we were all over them. We didn't let them rest.

Martin also liked us to lay traps. How did that work? Well, let's say their 'keeper had the ball. We would actively encourage him to throw it out to one of his full-backs. We'd hang back, hands on hips, blowing, looking tired, and then as soon as he rolled it out, to the right-back or the left-back – *bang!* – we'd spring into life and press them. We pressed teams high up the pitch, trying to force an error.

It was obvious, really; school ground stuff. But it worked. We couldn't do it constantly. And some teams were sharper than others, and they worked us out. But plenty of teams didn't. We did that for four years under Martin O'Neill. Even the teams that did work us out, they couldn't match our drive, our work rate. We were quite often too much for them.

We did a lot of pressing in training. Steve Walford would have us in a small, constricted area – one team trying to keep possession, another trying to nick the ball off them. It was just a simple pressing and passing game. Passing under pressure. Working on your touch, keeping the ball. But because of the players we had at Leicester and the spirit at the club, it was always a laugh and always competitive. I loved it.

We ran and ran and ran. I was fit when I was at Leicester, the fittest I've ever been. It was vital we were fit. The way we played demanded it. Look at the results. It was the same in every one of those four seasons. We started off well – and then we would tail off some time after Christmas. Every year it was the same.

Why? We just couldn't maintain that kind of intensity. You can't play like that all season. It's physically impossible. So come February and March, we'd start losing or drawing more games, dropping points. Some seasons, by April and May, we'd pick up again. I guess that's when other clubs, other players, were tiring too and suddenly, as the season neared its end, we found a new level playing field.

Martin was no different with us when we were promoted to the Premiership. He was exactly the same as he'd been in Division One. He didn't fear any other teams. We continued to concentrate on what we did – not what they might do.

We might have gone to Arsenal or Man United and played 4-5-1 occasionally – an extra man in midfield, making us harder to beat – but mostly we concentrated on our game. We didn't worry about the opposition, whoever they were.

Was that wise? Yeah, I think it was. If you spend too much time talking about the opposition and how you might play them then you build them up in your mind. They become something they're not. We concentrated on what we could do.

We were good at set pieces but we never practised them. People don't believe me when I say that, but it's true. I can still remember the feeling if we got a corner at Filbert Street.

The stamping on the floor, fans thumping on the ad hoardings, the lads at the back of the Kop banging on the corrugated iron at the rear of the old stadium, the whole ground alive with this expectation that something might happen. It was almost gladiatorial.

That didn't just happen, that sense of expectation. It happened because something usually did happen. We scored lots of goals from corners. We created that expectation. We all enjoyed that feeling – that sense of expectation – when we won a corner. The opposing team hated it. But we never worked on it.

Steve Guppy would whip balls into the box at the end of training, all of them in or around the six-yard area. There wasn't a better crosser of the ball in the Premiership than Gupps. He had a reliably brilliant left foot. If he could do that, then we knew that we'd got players who could head the ball – Steve Walsh, Matt Elliott, Gerry Taggart, Emile Heskey, Ian Marshall, Frank Sinclair – who would all be in and around the edge of the six-yard box ready to attack the ball.

Imagine that, if you're the opposition centre-half. You don't want to look down the field to see three centre-halves like Walsh, Taggs and Matty coming down the pitch for every corner. And if they missed, then we had enough players – Claridge, Cottee, Collymore, me, Lenny – who would happily pick up the pieces. I was always on the edge of the box, lurking, picking up the scraps. If it came to me, I'd have a go.

Martin wanted us to work hard closing teams down. Pressing. Harrying. Working for each other. We did that well. As a midfield, we didn't let teams play through us. We knew we had three strong, tough centre-halves but we also knew they weren't the fastest, either – so we would work to make sure that wasn't exposed. That was the way O'Neill liked us to play. We understood that. Players who didn't understand that generally didn't last long. Players like the Greek international, Theo Zagorakis.

I don't think I played with a more skilful, composed midfield player than Zagorakis. He was a brilliant footballer and a decent, easy-going bloke. But, culturally, he couldn't get the hang of life at Leicester City or the English game. He didn't have the work ethic to be part of a Leicester City team.

O'Neill's City was built on hard work. We couldn't afford to carry anyone. We all had to work. And if Theo was in the team, for all his great touch and vision, we had to work harder. I knew that. I felt it. When we had the ball, there wasn't a problem. When we didn't – there was. And that's why, for all his ability, his career at Leicester was short-lived.

If you made a mistake, you admitted it. We were an honest team. We all knew how we should play. So if it went wrong, we all usually knew why or how it had gone wrong. There was a culture of honesty and openness. O'Neill encouraged that.

I remember Kasey Keller coming in at half-time during one game. He'd let in a soft goal, a long-range shot that had squirmed under his body. He blamed everything and everyone but himself.

There was a bobble, he said. Someone should have closed him down. It wasn't his fault, he said repeatedly when, clearly, we could all see that it was. No-one liked that.

Leicester City were a team built in Martin O'Neill's image. Did we fear him? We absolutely did. We respected him, certainly. He wasn't the kind of boss who walked around the place smiling and cracking jokes, trying to be everyone's best mate. He didn't have to do that. He had our respect for the things he did, his achievements. He was never 'matey' with anyone. There was a distance between us; a line between us, the players, and him. We knew where that line was and we didn't cross it.

He could walk down a narrow corridor at the training ground, and I could walk past him and if we'd lost the Saturday before, he wouldn't acknowledge me. He wouldn't speak. And I'd know why he wouldn't speak. It was because we'd lost. We'd upset him. I'd upset him. No-one wanted to upset Martin.

He didn't lose his temper often but when he did, you didn't want to be around. You certainly didn't want to be on the receiving end of it. It was fearsome. He would blow at half-time, on occasion, or sometimes at the end of 90 minutes. And when he went it was a sight to behold.

What made Martin mad was if we hadn't tried hard enough, if we'd let ourselves down. That was his biggest irritation. He could stomach being beaten by a better team. But if we were beaten by a better team and we hadn't tried hard enough, if he thought we hadn't put in enough effort, if we were flat – and it did happen, it happened a few times – then he'd be furious.

He had a right go at Lenny once. This was rare because Lenny was his favourite. We all used to say that. And, yet again – this just goes to show how great he was – Lenny still got it. Both barrels. He did this without fear or favour. And you know what? As much as I might have sat there, head down, looking at my boots, not daring to meet his gaze, he was nearly always right.

He was never one of those managers who might have an undeserved go at someone just to try to fire them up. I don't ever remember him doing that, in the way that football writers used to say that Brian Clough did. If he had a go at you, there was usually a reason. And he was usually right.

The reason I remember him having a go at Lenny was that Lenny tried to have a go back, which was naive.

You didn't answer back. It wasn't a debate. You took it. You took the bollocking, said nothing and moved on. Having a go back just made him more angry. You didn't want to make him more angry. In an argument with Martin, there was only ever one winner.

Did he ever have a go at me? Not really. And if he did, I didn't have a go back. I learned early on there was no point. There was a game at home to Arsenal, August 1997, the famous one we drew 3-3, when Bergkamp scored a hat-trick but we pulled it back when Walshy scored in the 96th minute.

Their midfield outclassed us for most of that game. Arsenal weren't just a skilful team back then – they were strong, too. They were physical. They had Vieira, Petit and Parlour, with Wright and Bergkamp up front.

I came in at half-time and I knew I hadn't played well. I couldn't get near them. They were too good. There was a gulf in class and I knew it. I felt it. I came in at half-time and hoped the boss hadn't noticed. Some chance.

"What the fuck is up with you today?" he said.

I shrugged.

"Wherever the ball is, you're not. What's going on? Sort it out. And sort it out quick – or you're off."

I nodded. I had every intention of sorting it out. But I didn't.

Early in the second half, the board went up. Come in number 6. Martin took me off early. I walked past him and sat on the bench. I said nothing. He said nothing. I hated it. I hated being substituted, especially when I knew it was deserved. I'd let him down and we both knew it.

When things like that happened, it was a wake-up call. I needed to up my game. I stayed late in training for weeks after that match; I got Steve Beaglehole, the youth-team coach, to knock balls in to me. Just for half an hour or an hour, working on my touch and my passing. I wasn't alone. We all did that. We didn't want to let anyone down. That was the spirit that Martin O'Neill built and nurtured in the camp.

He was a master at psychology. After we lost to Spurs in the 1999 Worthington Cup Final in a dull but tetchy game, there were all sorts of headlines in the nationals about the tension between the two teams. Typically, a week after the final, we had Spurs away at White Hart Lane. We were fired up. We wanted our revenge. They would have been fired up, too.

We warmed up before kick-off and they were playing the winning goal and the highlights of the final on the screens. We could feel the fans getting more angry, more agitated.

In the changing room before we ran out, Martin announced that he wanted us to form a guard of honour and clap the Tottenham players onto the pitch. It wasn't something we were that enamoured about, to be honest, but we did it because the gaffer wanted us to do it. We just thought he wanted us to do it because it was nice gesture.

It was a nice gesture – but it completely threw them; their manager, George Graham, the players and the fans, too. They didn't know what to do. You could see it on their faces. The fans didn't know whether to boo us or applaud us. It neutralised the atmosphere immediately. It took the sting out of the game before we even kicked off. We outplayed them that day, winning 2-0 with goals from Matt Elliott and Tony Cottee. It was the first time Spurs had lost at home for six months. We'd got 'em back – and it was all due to Martin and his guard of honour. We went unbeaten for the next five games.

If we won, we celebrated. It didn't matter if we were battered, if we won, if we got all three points, then that was all that mattered. We went away to Leeds once, early in the 1997/98 season. We won 1-0. Walshy scored. It was perhaps the only attempt we had on target. They battered us, absolutely battered us that day but, somehow, we clung on.

Afterwards, it felt like we'd won 5-0 and played them off the park. There was no inquest in the changing room. We got on the bus and we sang our way home. We always did that at Leicester. We celebrated success.

Martin loved to win. When we'd won and you'd played well, he'd drape his arm round your shoulder and he'd fill your soul with confidence. It was emotional nourishment. It felt good. And that would last all week. John Robertson would do the same thing, too; over and over again, in your ear, telling you how good you'd been, how you'd bossed it in midfield, how you'd "won the game for us."

You show me a footballer who doesn't want to hear something like that. It was brilliant. And it made you want it every week. I wanted Martin or Robbo to tell me every week I was the best midfield player in the Premiership because when they did, it made me feel 10 feet tall. He did that to me. He did that to 10 other players, too. We all wanted to please him. We played for each other, we played for the fans, we played for ourselves – but mainly we played for Martin, Robbo and Wal.

When we won, we went out. After a good win, we'd climb back onto the bus and, at some stage, a crate of beer would appear. We'd crack them open, get the cards out. Sometimes, after special games, great victories, Martin would come to the back of the bus and play cards with us, too, and Robbo, although someone would usually have to lend him some money. So someone would give Robbo £50 and he'd sit there, smoking and drinking with us, and he'd lose that £50 inside 10 minutes and he'd throw his hands in the air, call everyone a wanker and go back to the front of the bus.

We played Burie, which was like a shortened version of Knockout Whist. It was £10 a man usually – and the pot would get to £500, £800, £2,000 sometimes – and we'd all be laughing and joking, singing and drinking, taking the piss out of each other all the way home. We'd be buzzing. And then someone would say: "Are we out then?" and usually we were. We all went out.

Martin loved his trips away with the lads. Cloughie did it during his time at Forest, and he carried it on at City. We didn't mind that at all. I remember one trip to Tenerife, we were due to play cricket on the beach. Martin liked his cricket and a big team game would be a good laugh, he used to say. It's fair to say Martin enjoyed the cricket more than us, I think.

His idea was that everyone would get a bat. It took ages. I think some of the lads were getting a bit tense because it was dinner time and it was starting to cut into our drinking hours.

The last man to come in was The Gaffer. He fancied himself as a batsman. So there he was, marking out his crease, making all the defensive shots, leaving a ball if it went wide of the stumps, putting his front foot out and lifting his bat. All of that. All very serious, like he was bedding himself in for a long knock.

I forget who bowled but a ball came down, he played at it, missed, clipped his foot with the bat and the ball came through to me at first slip. I caught it. I didn't appeal. I knew he hadn't hit it. Walshy was standing next to me. He went straight up, hands in the air. "HOWZAT!!??!" Everyone else joined in. He wasn't out. He hadn't hit it. He was nowhere near it. But there we were – a dozen grown men all shouting HOWZAT loudly on a public beach in Tenerife.

Robbo was umpiring. He put his finger up. "I think you were out, Gaffer, all the lads think so, too," he said. Martin threw his bat down. He was furious. He moaned about it for the rest of the trip. We went back to the hotel, showered, changed and went straight out on the piss.

But that was Martin. He was ultra-competitive in everything he did. They had a staff versus media game in Madrid, the night before we played Atletico in the UEFA Cup. Most managers would have been back at the hotel, preparing for this enormous European game the following day.

Martin and his staff were taking on the press guys in a game that was anything but friendly. It was supposed to last until the team coach came to pick them up. They'd been playing for an hour when the coach arrived, but the staff side were losing 5-3. So Martin ordered the game to go on – until they'd won. Which, eventually, they did.

For four years, we overachieved at Leicester City during Martin O'Neill's time. We went to places and got results that we had no right to get. It was an honest club full of old-fashioned, honest footballers, steeped in good values like hard work, determination and camaraderie. We liked and respected each other and we liked and respected the boss.

Just getting one of those things right – effort, determination, camaraderie and the confidence that brings – is something. At City we had all four. I look at most teams in the Premier League now and I think: 'We could have had 'em.'

Seriously. On our day, we could.

Can you tell me, really, that the Manchester United of today is better than the United that won the treble in 1999? I don't think it is. And we beat them. Today's Liverpool team? Better than they were in the late '90s? Not a chance. We beat them, too. And Arsenal. And Newcastle. And Spurs. And Leeds.

Leicester City, as a team, were more than the sum of its parts. We played with no real pressure because still, regardless of the top-10 finishes and cup triumphs, people still wrote us off. We were perhaps two or three players short of being a genuine top-six team. We needed a top class 15-goals-a-season striker. Doesn't every team?

I often wonder what would have happened if Martin had stayed, Heskey hadn't gone to Liverpool and his partnership with Stan Collymore was allowed to blossom. That 5-2 victory against Sunderland – Heskey's last game – was one of the finest 90 minutes I've ever seen, definitely one of the best games I played in during my eight years at City. It should have been the beginning of a bright new era at Filbert Street. Instead, it was the beginning of the end.

Martin had resisted offers from Leeds and Everton. There may have been others that we never knew about. But when Emile left, and then when Celtic came in, we knew, really. We knew that was the end.

At the culmination of that 1999/2000 season, Martin took all of his staff to London. A show. A few drinks. Staying over at a nice hotel. He did it every year. They all loved him for that. But that night, after the show, Martin didn't show up. He'd gone to meet someone from Celtic.

And that was that. The end of an era.

No-one saw him again.

THE 7m DOLLAR MAN

In the spring of 2000, after passing his driving test a few weeks earlier, 25-year-old Muzzy Izzet bought a new car – a blue Jaguar XKR.

The insurance cost more than the little red Fiesta he'd been driving from his home in Markfield to Leicester's Belvoir Drive training ground – an L Plate in the back window, City striker Graham Fenton looking on anxiously in the passenger seat.

"Nice car, that," said Martin O'Neill one morning, casually, after training. "I'd like a drive in that."

So, after training, the Leicester City manager climbed in and Muzzy took him for a quick spin around the Aylestone district of Leicester.

Martin O'Neill didn't want to see his car, of course. He wanted to get Izzet by himself.

There were all sorts of rumours, all kinds of talk in all sorts of papers. Muzzy for England. Muzzy for Leeds. Muzzy for Blackburn. Muzzy for Chelsea. The City midfielder was a wanted man. The City manager didn't want him to leave.

Izzet was on a decent contract: £10,000 per week, plus bonuses.

O'Neill offered to virtually double his money. A pleasantly-surprised Izzet agreed with O'Neill's suggestion that they'd sort out a new contract in the summer. That day never arrived.

A few months later, Martin O'Neill was made an offer he couldn't refuse. He left Leicester City for Celtic.

A new manager was appointed. Peter Taylor. A Londoner. He seemed like a nice chap, Izzet thought. Friendly. Easy-going. He wanted to be the players' mate. They weren't used to that. There were contract talks that summer – not with O'Neill, but with Taylor.

By now the rumour mill was in overdrive. A queue of clubs wanted to sign the City number 6. At the front of the line were his old team, Chelsea, now managed by Gianluca Vialli.

Chelsea, who had let him go for a pittance under Glenn Hoddle, wanted him on a free transfer at the end of the season. "If we can get him on a free," they told his agent, Jonathan Barnett, "then a £40,000-a-week contract shouldn't be a problem."

It came to a head one afternoon in the manager's office in the summer of 2000. Peter Taylor and club secretary, Andrew Neville, on one side; Muzzy Izzet and his agent, Jonathan Barnett, on the other.

The Leicester City number 6 didn't say much. He didn't have to.

He was holding all the aces.

Everyone in the room knew it.

If Leicester City wanted to keep him, they'd have to dig deep.

Meanwhile, in a twin narrative that no-one had yet foreseen but

was now looming ever closer, the club was on the verge of the darkest
period in its long history.

It's October 1, 2000. A Sunday. Leicester City come away from
Sunderland's Stadium of Light with a grim 0-0 draw, which
makes it 16 points from the first eight games of the season. And
with that, and for the only time in Leicester City's history, the
Foxes climb to the top of the Premier League table.

"ON TOP OF THE WORLD!" said the jubilant back page
of the *Leicester Mercury* the next day, and the paper rolled out
a feature about the last time City sat at the top of football's
top flight, way back in August,1963, after beating Arsenal 7-2
(although, the season before, City had topped the table in April
with only five games left, odds-on favourites to be champions.
They lost the last five and finished fourth).

The season had hardly begun but the city of Leicester was
awash with excitement and expectation. Great work by Peter
Taylor, everyone agreed. He was voted as the Premier League's
Manager of the Month. Well done, Leicester. Well done, Peter.
A year and a day later, Peter Taylor was out of the door and
looking for a new job.

Everywhere we went that week, people wanted to shake my
hand and pat me on the back.

"Well done, son."

"Top of the league."

"Let's keep this going all season."

All of that, everywhere I went. And I smiled and said nothing.
Because, secretly, it made me feel a bit queasy. I knew the truth. I
knew what was really happening and what was about to happen.
I was seeing it from the inside. I could see it was starting to

unfold. Taylor may have managed to do what Martin O'Neill never did – guiding City to the top of the Premier League – but the truth was he, we, Leicester City, had fluked it.

Look at the figures, look at the games. Scratch the surface – and you don't have to scratch very hard, either – and an inconvenient truth emerges. Our second game of the 2000/01 season was away at West Ham. We won 1-0. I remember that game vividly because it was one of the most one-sided matches I'd ever played in. West Ham battered us, absolutely battered us, that day. It was embarrassing.

Darren Eadie scored a few minutes into the second half. Perhaps the statistics say otherwise, but I'm sure it was the only attack we had all game. West Ham took us apart that day and I remember getting back on the coach and thinking: 'How the fuck did we win that?' I dug out those fixtures the other day.

First game: Villa at home – D
Then West Ham away – W
Bradford City away – D
Ipswich home – W
Southampton home – W
Chelsea away – W
Everton home – D
Sunderland away – D

So, yeah, we were on top of the league, unbeaten, the best team in the country in October 2000. But with the exception of Chelsea away, it wasn't the toughest of starts, was it?

It wasn't that we were a bad team. We hadn't turned, overnight, into a bad side, despite the loss of some very important players who, I still think, were sold off or shunted out too quickly. The nucleus of Martin O'Neill's team from 1999/2000 was still there. And he seemed all right, Peter Taylor. A nice bloke. He liked a laugh and a joke. Training was a bit more relaxed, not quite as intense as it had been with Steve Walford and John Robertson, or as varied, but it was ok, good enough. And there we were. Top of the league. But I knew we'd fluked it. I knew we didn't deserve to be there. And I knew it wouldn't last. Sure enough, it didn't.

We carried on, briefly, flattering to deceive, picking up good points here and there as we slid down the table. And then, on Boxing Day 2000, we went to Highbury to face Arsenal. They beat us 6-1 that day. We were dreadful. We won four of the next 18 Premier League games; 12 points in the next five months. It was relegation form.

People talk about the wheels coming off for us that season when we lost 2-1 at home to Wycombe Wanderers in March in the FA Cup. And it was bad, that afternoon, sure. I pulled my calf muscle early in the second half. We'd used all three subs so I couldn't come off.

I limped around the pitch for the remaining 35 minutes. It wasn't the most serious of injuries but, because I played on, it became more of a problem. That was it for me. My season was over. I spent the rest of that campaign watching from the sidelines as our season drifted away, defeat following defeat. I'm not a great spectator at the best of the times, but it was awful, absolutely awful to watch.

It wasn't true, though, that the wheels came off for us during that Wycombe game. The wheels came off before then. That game was an embarrassing, high-profile failure – out of the quarter-final of the FA Cup, in a game against unfancied, lower league opposition. Wycombe were two leagues below us. It doesn't get much worse – although, it did get worse than that.

That night, we had arranged to go out with some of their players in Leicester. Steve Guppy knew a few of them. "They're nice lads," he said. I don't think anyone had contemplated the prospect of going out with them, in Leicester, after we had lost to them. No-one had thought of that. So we went out with them, a bar first and then over to Baffone's. They loved it. I didn't. I hated it. I made my excuses and left early. I didn't want to be out, drinking, after a game like that. No thanks.

It's convenient to say it all started to go wrong there, in that Wycombe game, but it's not true. The truth is that it had started to go wrong long before then. And everyone within the club knew it. Even, I suspect, Peter Taylor. And yet, every month, as everything that Martin O'Neill built seemed to crumble a little bit more around me, I received a pay slip that contained numbers on it that were so astronomically huge, so ridiculously large, that I used to look at it and laugh.

I couldn't believe it. I was now earning £35,000 a week, £1.8m a year. Over the course of my four-year contract, I would earn £7.28m. Granted, I seemed to be paying more tax than Donald Trump but I tried not to concentrate on that. I didn't look at what the tax man was taking. I tried to concentrate on what was going into my bank account. It was astonishing.

I received £35,000 a week if we were winning or losing, if I was playing or if I sat on the sidelines, watching, nursing an injured calf muscle, which is what I did for the last three months of that season. How had this happened? How had this scrawny kid from Mile End become a millionaire playing football for

Leicester City? You need to put it in a bit of context. Let's go back a year. This is when it starts.

The 1999/2000 season began pretty well for us, me especially. It was our fourth year in the Premier League. We hadn't gone up and scraped by, as most experts predicted we would. We'd done well. We deserved to be there. We could compete with the big teams, home and away. We were there on merit. And by this stage, we were starting to believe it, too. Teams knew that when they faced us, we'd give them a game.

We lost at Highbury in the first match of the season, then again to West Ham three games later. Then we found our feet. We lost just two of our next 11 games, winning eight and drawing one. I was playing as well as I have ever played.

In September, they made me Carling Player of the Month. I still have that trophy at home, somewhere. I was the first City player to win the award. A year later, Tim Flowers won it, too. O'Neill kept saying I should be playing for England. Around the same time, I was receiving overtures from Turkey that they wanted me to play for them.

On the domestic front, Chelsea were interested in signing me. So were Leeds. So were Everton and Blackburn. I was playing well. I was fit. I was happy. The whole team were playing well and getting on well, too. It was a real purple patch, one of the happiest times of my career, and my life.

It was flattering to hear about the other clubs' interest, but I wasn't interested. Not really. All a footballer wants is to play every week and to feel wanted, to feel part of it. I had that.

My contract was up, though, at the end of the 2000/01 season and as I continued to play well – I seemed to be scoring for fun at the start of that campaign – the whispers grew louder.

Chelsea seemed more and more interested. They never spoke to me. They were in regular contact with my agent, though.

Would Muzzy come back? What would he want? Could we get him on a free at the end of the season? If we can get him on a free, we can pay him a bit more...?

We beat Tranmere to win the Worthington Cup in February. We were doing well in the league. We ended up finishing eighth, above Spurs, above Newcastle; our fourth consecutive top-10 Premier League finish.

Martin said good things about me – even if, even by then, I was never quite sure where I stood with him – and I liked him. I liked him as a man and a boss. I liked playing for him. I respected him. When he collared me after training and said he wanted a ride in my new car, a Jaguar XKR, I reversed it out of the training ground and we went for a spin. He wasn't bothered about the car, of course. He wanted to get me by myself.

"There are some clubs after you. I know that and I'm not surprised," he said. "You've done well for us. It was only a matter of time." I steered the car around Aylestone. I didn't know what to say, so I said nothing. He did all of the talking.

"I know what you're on," he said. "We'll try to improve that next season, shall we?"

I was earning £10k a week. Decent money, I thought. I was happy enough with that. The club had upped it virtually every season, and upped it without me having to ask for more. They just gave me more. Leicester City weren't one of English football's big teams. They weren't rolling in money. But they looked after me and I appreciated it.

"What would you say if I upped your £10k to £18k? That's an 80 per cent pay rise," he said. "It's not to be sniffed at."

160

He was right. It wasn't to be sniffed at. I was stunned.

"There aren't many people, in many professions, that get a pay rise like that. But you know what? I think you're worth it."

Silence. I waited for him to fill it. He didn't.

"Erm, right. Ok. That sounds good, boss," I said.

"Right," he said. "Good. We'll sort that out in the summer. You're an important part of this team. We all want you to stay."

"I want to stay, boss," I said.

And I did. I really did.

"Good," he said, again. "In the summer then, eh?"

I nodded. In the summer.

And then the summer came, and our day never arrived. Instead, Martin was made an offer he couldn't refuse. Celtic came in and he left. Frankly, I thought he might have gone a year earlier, when Leeds wanted him. He stayed. I don't know what he thought this time. Maybe he looked around and thought: 'You know, I don't know what else I can do here…'

I didn't blame him. He'd done a brilliant job at Leicester. His four-and-a-half-years at Filbert Street was the most successful period in the club's history. He never said goodbye, which was a shame, really. I think we all would have liked to have shaken his hand and wished him well. Steve Walford did, though. We turned up for pre-season training and Wal was there.

"I've just come to wish you all well and say thanks," he said. It was typical of him, really. We all loved Wal. We shook his hand, hugged him and wished him well.

I remember him turning his back, giving us a final wave and the tears welling up in his eyes. He cried. A few of us cried, too. We were a tough bunch back then, at Leicester. But that was how much we loved him. We knew he was a great coach. We just didn't realise how great. You don't though, do you? You don't realise what you have until it's gone. You only find out later. We were about to find that out.

The new Leicester City manager was appointed in the close season. Peter John Taylor was from Essex, a former England Under-21 manager who came to City from lowly Gillingham, who had just won the Division Two play-off final. The Gills had also enjoyed a good run in the FA Cup. He looked like a promising young manager.

My first impressions?

It would be easy to say he was a charlatan, a shyster and a con-artist and I knew it wouldn't work out, blah, blah, blah.

Easy, but not true. I liked him. He got us in early and gave us a talk; the usual stuff about everyone having a chance, how he wanted to carry on Martin's good work, how he wanted to establish a happy, relaxed camp and how his door would always be open. There was nothing for anyone to dislike there.

I was a bit worried about the contract Martin O'Neill had promised me. I wondered if that would materialise now that Martin had gone and a new man was in the big seat. Although, after what happened that summer, I have to say I was less worried than I might have been. It wasn't just paper talk about Chelsea. They were interested.

I was on holiday in Portugal in July 2000 with my wife, Carly, my brother, Kem, and my mum and dad. We were having a meal one night and my phone rang. It was a call which would change my life. It was my agent, Jonathan Barnett.

Chelsea had been in touch again, he said. They meant business. If they could get me on a free at the end of that season, then they'd be willing to pay me £40,000 a week, he said.

"You don't need to do anything yet," he said, "but have a think about it, eh?"

I put the phone down and laughed. It seemed incredible.

Pre-season, Peter Taylor called me in. We had a meeting; me, my agent, Peter Taylor and Andrew Neville, the club secretary. He'd heard that Chelsea were interested in me. Nothing like that stays secret in football for very long. He wanted to offer me a new contract, he said. I was still on £10k a week. "We want to pay you more than that," he said.

"What you need to know," said Jonathan, "is that Chelsea are *very interested* and are willing to pay him £40,000 a week so if you want him to stay then we need to be looking somewhere around there." He didn't mention O'Neill's offer.

The club couldn't match that, said Taylor.

I didn't say anything. I let Jonathan do the talking. I sat in the office and looked at my shoes. I was embarrassed. I wasn't at Leicester for the money. I didn't play football for the money. The money was nice, sure. But it wasn't my primary motivation. It never has been. Jonathan played it cool.

"Well, this is where we are, gentlemen," he said. " You need to have a think about that." And with that, the meeting ended. We all shook hands and me and Jonathan walked out.

I wondered if we'd done the right thing. I didn't wonder for long, though. We'd barely had the chance to talk about it when Peter Taylor caught up with us in the car park. He had a piece of paper in his hand.

"We can't match £40k a week," he said. "But we can offer you £35k a week."

This was the deal – £35k a week, if I played or if I didn't play, over four years. I tried to do the maths, quickly, in my head. I couldn't. All I knew was that it was more than £1m a year. "We want you to stay," said Taylor. "It's a good offer. Please think about it."

I knew what I was going to do instantly. I was going to stay.

I was flabbergasted by the offer. I was still on £10k a week. They had more than tripled my money. They'd offered me a pay rise of 300 per cent. It was ridiculous, absolutely ridiculous.

Jonathan Barnett was a top football agent. He had Joe Cole, Ashley Cole, Kevin Davies, a long list of top players on his books. At that stage, I was his highest-earning player.

Would I have accepted less? I would. I liked it at Leicester. I was settled in the county. Carly was pregnant. She liked it here, too. We wanted to raise a family here. How much less would I have accepted? I don't know. I didn't really want to go back to Chelsea. Would I have stayed for the £18,000 that O'Neill offered me? I don't know, but probably, yeah, I think I would.

I sold my house in Markfield – the one that I bought from Spider Kalac, the one with the extra-high door frames – and bought a new house in south Leicestershire. It was the first house we saw. We both fell in love with it. I still live there now. It's not a mansion, my place. It only has four bedrooms, but it's a nice house, with nice grounds and I like where it is, the village, the pubs nearby. We could imagine living there for a long time.

In the days after I was offered my new contract, there were more meetings. Matt Elliott was called in. His contract was improved. So was Lenny's. So was Sav's. Clearly, Taylor wanted to keep us at the club – and the best way to do that, he thought, was to offer us lucrative, long-term contracts.

I don't know what the others were offered. I still don't to this day. I suspect Lenny was offered a bit more than me. I don't know. We didn't talk about it. A changing room is no different to any other workplace. You don't bang on about how much you earn, do you? Well, apart from Sav. He was on about it relentlessly, forever trying to get me, Lenny and Matty to tell him. We didn't tell him, and it drove him mad.

Lenny wasn't himself around this time. He started the season fine, but his form dipped. He wasn't as bubbly, laughing and joking, around the training ground. It wasn't a massive difference, just a slight one. He was just a bit more subdued. However, even when he wasn't playing well, he was still better than most midfield players he came up against. Lenny rarely came off second best in any midfield battle. He could hold his own with anyone, at any ground.

I only found out later that he was suffering from depression. I think Martin's departure and the constant rumours – was he staying? was he going? – affected him. I don't know for sure. I'm guessing. I had no idea he was suffering like that and I roomed with him. If I had known, I wonder what I would have done or said. I like to think I'd have said something, but I was little more than a kid, really. I didn't know anything about the complexities of depression.

He left not long after that and joined up with Martin at Celtic. Lenny was embarrassed about how much he was earning at City, too, I found out later. He took a pay-cut to join Celtic. When he left, the heart of our midfield went with him. Taylor bought a few midfielders but they never filled Lenny's shoes. We missed him massively. I used to ask him about this. "You've got to fill that gap," I said. "He was so important for us." Taylor would nod along. "I will. I have a few players in mind," he said.

He never did. He never filled that gap.

Pre-season, our training was good. It wasn't bad training. It just wasn't as good as it had been under Wal and Robbo. Taylor took the training; Taylor and his coach, Steve Butler, a former Watford and Cambridge striker who had been Taylor's right-hand man at Gillingham. He was all right, Steve, a nice enough chap. But there wasn't the intensity, the competitiveness, the sheer enjoyment that we'd had with Wal.

As me, Lenny, Matty and Sav were given huge contracts to stay, Peter Taylor made his biggest mistake – he had a huge clear-out of Martin O'Neill's squad, a big name clear-out, too. Good players in important positions – players such as Steve Walsh, Tony Cottee, Ian Marshall, Stan Collymore – all left the club. Garry Parker retired and joined the coaching staff.

Emile Heskey had left the previous season to join Liverpool in an £11m move and, suddenly, the nucleus of Martin's over-achieving Leicester City side had disappeared. The spine of his side – with Lenny going to Celtic in December, midway through the season – was gone.

I don't think you can lose players of that calibre – and big characters in and around the club, at that – and not feel the difference. We felt it. We felt it in training.

Training with the likes of Walshy and Cottee was always competitive. That's how they are. And you might argue that they were getting on, that they might not have had long futures at the club, and you might have a point – but, still, losing all of those players in such a short period of time had a hugely detrimental affect on Leicester City. I didn't think then, and I still don't now, that they deserved to be treated the way they were.

It was a confusing time for me.

On the one hand, Taylor had come in and he'd bombed out

good players, good friends of mine, kicked out of the club they loved. They didn't deserve that. I had the hump about that for weeks. It made me cross. And yet, on the other hand, he'd given me a contract worth £35k a week. I used to drive in to training thinking: 'You fucker – but thanks.'

People still ask me, to this day: 'What was he like, then, Peter Taylor?' and the honest answer is that he was all right. He was a nice chap. He was personable. You could get on with him. As a bloke, I liked him. Plus, he offered me a bloody huge contract so, you know, on that front, I'm not likely to dislike him.

I would say, with hindsight, that his jocular, happy-go-lucky bonhomie didn't work. He wanted to be our mate. He was much more hands-on than Martin was and took most of the training sessions. That's all fine, and enjoyable – but when things started to go wrong, when he needed to dish the bollockings out, he couldn't do it. He didn't have that distance. He was too close to us. We didn't respect him.

I wouldn't say that we feared Martin O'Neill – but we were wary of him. He had an aura and he managed, somehow, to keep you guessing, to keep you wondering where you stood with him and, at the same time, to let you know precisely what he thought of you. I know how that sounds. It's a contradiction. But it's true. He was the boss. Full stop. You did what he said. I think footballers like that. He was the gaffer. We all knew it.

Taylor didn't have that natural authority. He couldn't be horrible to us. It was nice, in many ways but as we pissed games away, week after week, that's what we needed. We needed a kick up the backside. We needed an occasional bollocking. We fell into a rut. We needed to be told to pull our socks up, especially when it all started to go wrong, but it never happened.

Taylor's other big mistake, after letting all these big players leave the club, was that he didn't replace them with the same quality. He bought some players who weren't cut out to play Premier League football.

He knew he had to replace Lenny. He bought Matt Jones in December 2000, shortly after we'd beaten Leeds at Filbert Street 3-1. It was Lenny's last game at Leicester. Matty, a lovely lad, didn't play well that day. I'd not seen him play before. I remember wondering, on the back of that performance, if we hadn't made a big mistake.

Matty was unlucky with injuries. We didn't see the best of him but I think he also suffered with the comparisons to Lenny and the price tag. None of that was his fault.

A few months later he bought Junior Lewis. He'd bought three midfield players in a bid to somehow fill the one gap that Lenny left. He still didn't fill that gap.

We got Roberto Mancini on loan. That was an experience. He had some class touches in training. But he was in his mid-30s. He couldn't run. He didn't track back. He had vision and he could read the game, but I don't think I saw him put a tackle in. It just heaped extra pressure on the rest of the midfield.

Taylor bought some good players, too, like Jamie Scowcroft. Gary Rowett was a decent right-back. I liked Callum Davidson and Ian Walker did well for us in goal. It was just that too many of his high-profile, big-money signings didn't come off.

When I was a kid, I played with Ade Akinbiyi in the London youth leagues. Ade was a lovely lad and as hard as nails. Honestly, you wouldn't want to mess with Ade. He was the toughest lad at the club. Every day, in training, he was on fire. He was brilliant. He had the lot – pace, power, determination –

and he was clinical. Ade's problem – and, again, it was hardly the lad's fault – was the weight of expectation that came with him. He was Leicester's record buy. We bought him for £5.5m, plus he was Emile's replacement. I knew what Ade could do. I saw him do it in training. He was unplayable.

But there was so much pressure on his shoulders, a big price tag on his head and a constant expectation that he would deliver. When he started to falter, when the game started and he missed one chance, and then maybe another, and the cheers turned to groans, it got to him.

I didn't like it when the crowd turned on Ade. You're never going to improve the way a player performs by booing him. I understand why it happens. I've been a fan. I've stood on the terraces and I've heard it. I know it's part of the game. And you pay your money, you have every right to do what you want.

But I felt for Ade. Every time we lost, people pointed the finger at Ade, moaned about his missed chances. It all became his fault. It wasn't his fault. It was our fault. We lost because we weren't good enough, all over the park. We never saw the best of Ade at Leicester, that's for sure.

It was the same, to a certain extent, with Trevor Benjamin. He was only a young lad, a nice kid. He came from Cambridge, where he'd been dong well, for £1.5m.

Trev's eye-sight wasn't great. Matt Elliott was in the treatment room when Trev had his medical. He was having his eye test and was holding his right hand to his right eye and reading down the table of letters. It wasn't going well. He managed to read the first two rows and started to struggle.

"Ok then," the doctor said, "now let's try with your good eye."

"But that was my good eye," said Trev.

We all called him Clarence, after the short-sighted Ronnie Barker TV character. The jump, from Cambridge to Leicester City in the Premier League, was too much for him. It wouldn't have been such a big deal, perhaps, if Taylor had bought him for £300,000. But he was five times that. A lot of money. A lot of pressure – for the player and, ultimately, for Peter Taylor. There were others. Ade and Benjamin get the most attention because they were the strikers. But Taylor bought worse players.

Kevin Ellison, a winger, had been playing semi-pro before he signed for us. His first City game, I think, was Manchester United away. He came on and played on the left in front of Gupps. I don't think Guppy was that pleased. To be honest, I don't think many of us were.

I could see the difference at Belvoir Drive. There was a dip in quality. The intensity wasn't there.

There were a rash of stories and articles when we topped the Premier League in October 2000 and I remember thinking: 'Thank God we have those points. We might need them.' I knew, at some stage, we'd struggle. I knew we could have gone down that year.

After a week at the top, Manchester United came to Filbert Street. They annihilated us. They won 3-0, with Sheringham getting two and Solskjaer scoring the other. Our short-lived reign as the league's best team was over.

After that Arsenal game on Boxing Day, we picked up just 13 points out of a possible 54. It was relegation form. And we all knew it. What saved us that year was our early run.

Taylor started doing odd things in the dressing room. Under Martin, everything was kept deliberately simple. Under Taylor, all of that changed. There were drills in training and DVDs, posters on the dressing room walls with formations on them. He filled our minds with so much information, it was counter productive. Then, as our run of form grew worse, he started to go round the dressing room, trying to psyche us up.

"Come on," he'd shout. "We're gonna win this one, aren't we?" And he'd lean into your face and clap and clench his fists.

He used to get us running on the spot, getting us all to shout positive messages. Then he'd want us to form little huddles and start chanting. We all did it, too. We had to, although some of us did it more convincingly than others. I was a bit embarrassed by it. I thought it was a bit patronising. A good team shouldn't need stuff like that.

I started to feel a bit sorry for him. He was a decent bloke, he really was – but we could see he was struggling. He was out of his depth. In a matter of months, we lost our confidence. We lost our work ethic. And we lost some of that quality, too. It was a fatal combination.

We finished 13th that season, one point behind Spurs, six points above Middlesbrough. It flattered us.

The club gave Peter Taylor their backing and a new contract. A few of us were worried. If we started next season the way we'd finished that one, we'd be in trouble. We could see that. Surely we wouldn't do that, though?

It was the last season at Filbert Street. A brand new 32,500-capacity stadium was rising from the ground 500 yards further down Raw Dykes Road. No-one wanted to contemplate starting that season in a brand new stadium, in Division One.

I remember the fixture list coming out.

First game: at home and against Bolton Wanderers.

Phew.

THE COMFORT ZONE

He heard it initially as a first year pro at Chelsea, not much more than a kid really, playing occasional reserve-team games, mixing it up with the big boys.

Coach Eddie Niedzwiecki used the phrase so often at Chelsea, it almost became his catchphrase. 'Comfort Zone.' You won't win anything, he used to say, when you're in the Comfort Zone.

It was one of Eddie's bêtes noires. He was always complaining about players being in 'comfort zones,' first teamers, usually; senior players coming back from injury and having a tentative run-out, not breaking sweat or putting a foot in. Muzzy Izzet wondered what he was on about when he first heard it. One of his colleagues thought it sounded like a furniture warehouse. The Comfort Zone. It didn't *belong on a football field. Footballers slacking? Not trying hard enough?*

It seemed almost unthinkable to Muzzy. Why would you want to play football and not try your hardest?

How could you get this far, he wondered, a professional footballer at one of the country's top clubs and then kick back, just float through games, deliberately not giving it the best of your ability?

It didn't make any sense.

And then, one day in 2001, he realised – and he wasn't entirely sure how – that he, too, had slipped into this mysterious comfort zone. Not just him, but a few of his colleagues, too; men who, a year or two earlier, would have laid down and died for the cause. Now they were just floating through games.

How did this happen?

He's not entirely sure. He just knows it did.

He's never tried to explain it or analyse it before. But he knows how it began. It began with the systematic dismantling of one of the most underrated teams in the English Premier League.

It was exacerbated by a pay rise that left him, frankly, a bit embarrassed and it continued unabated as a new manager, and then another one, tried to rescue Leicester City Football Club from the footballing abyss. They all failed.

This is the story of a great club's demise.

Funny old game, football. For the most successful and enjoyable four and a half years of my footballing career, I genuinely didn't know from one Saturday to the next if I'd be in the team.

From March 1996 to the end of May 2000, the entire period I played under Martin O'Neill, I was constantly terrified of being dropped, of being found out, of being pulled to one side by the gaffer and told: *'It's all over, son. You're not what we want.'*

I'm not lying here. I'm not trying to say this because it would make this book more interesting. If I wanted to do that, I'd have started way before now, clearly. It's true. I was riddled with insecurity during those early years at Leicester.

I'd drive into training and I'd see these players in the changing room – players with a real sense of charisma and quality, like Walshy, Lenny, Matt Elliott, Cottee, Taggs, Parker, there were many of them – and I wondered: where do I fit in here?

I knew I could play. I knew I was all right. I knew I was fit and I could run, I could see a pass, I had good feet and I'd score the odd good goal – but, for those first four and a half-years at Leicester, I was insecure. I was worried; worried about losing my place, worried I might be dropped, worried I wasn't worthy of my place in the team.

Partly, that was down to my age. I was a young kid, in my 20s, in a team of slightly older players, too, which perhaps didn't help. It's not just footballers who are insecure in their 20s. It's human beings. I was riddled with self-doubt. It took me a long, long time to shake that off.

And then there was Martin. An inspirational man, a brilliant tactician and fantastic man-manager, this is how he *wanted* his players to feel. He could make you feel 10 feet tall with one choice word; one moment, away from the crowd, his arm round your shoulder, pouring gold dust in your ear. And yet, at the same time, he could take that away with just a look or a shrug.

It sounds like an obvious contradiction – and it is, it was – but that was the man. He was a complex character and I don't think any of us could really read him.

But that's what made him the boss and it kept you on your toes. You always wanted to please him while knowing, always, that he could take that away from you in a moment. I was terrified of that.

To the fans, they might have thought I was nailed on in that Leicester midfield. Number 6, Muzzy Izzet, one of the first names on the team sheet. It never felt like that. Although I knew he liked me and rated me, I knew I was only ever one, possibly two, bad games away from the chop. So I tried my best, in every practice session and every game. I gave my all, all the time.

And then Martin left and Peter Taylor arrived and that all vanished. At the same time everything started to go wrong, it all just became a little bit too easy, a bit too predictable.

On Saturday, August 18, 2001 – the final year at Filbert Street as a new stadium was being built 500 yards down the Raw Dykes Road – Sam Allardyce's Bolton Wanderers came to town for the opening game of the season. We lost 5-0: 5-0 at home, against Bolton. Not Manchester United or Liverpool. But Bolton, for fuck's sake. We were shocking, absolute horseshit.

I cringe when I think about that game. I remember walking off at the end and not being able to look up at the fans above the tunnel. I couldn't look them in the eye. I was too embarrassed. We'd lost before at Filbert Street. But we'd never lost like that.

We gave in. We rolled over and died. Leicester City teams never did that. It was the beginning of the end. A week later we went to Arsenal. We lost 4-0. Played two, lost two, goals for none, goals against nine.

We were playing differently. Under Martin, we would press constantly, put good players under pressure, not let teams settle. Why should we sit back and let them play their game? We weren't there to admire them. We were there to beat them. We were a pain to play against because we never let the opposition settle. Other players told me that afterwards, but we knew it. We didn't give them a minute, we were all over them – especially high up the park, when they had the ball in their own half.

Under Taylor, this stopped. He wanted us to sit back and invite teams to come at us. We did this, but it's fair to say that we didn't do it particularly well and we didn't like it. Frankly, we weren't a good enough side to play like that. It was too risky. You play like that and the simple plan is that you hope to win the ball in your own half and launch a quick counter-attack, hitting them on the break. We didn't have the nous to play that game. Or the pace, not all over the park. We were used to working hard, setting traps, pressing teams, putting them under pressure. Now we were being told to do the exact opposite of that.

The intensity we had, our competitiveness, our very essence – the *'Foxes Never Quit'* spirit that we were proud of, a spirit that pulled us through games when our quality didn't always deserve it – all of that disappeared. We started losing. And when you start losing, it's hard to stop.

There was a temporary reprieve when we beat a poor Derby side 3-2 – they were relegated that season – but the slide continued. We lost against Middlesbrough, Newcastle and Charlton. By the end of September we had played eight, won one, drawn two, lost five. We had five points and were bottom of the league. A malaise that had started nearly a year ago – long before Wycombe knocked us out of the FA Cup – had continued, unabated. It had continued – and it had got worse.

Peter Taylor was sacked the day after the Charlton game, the end of September 2001. By then, we were doomed. He gave a press conference at the ground the day after he was sacked. I don't think I've ever seen a manager do that. It was a disap-

Leicester best: Of course I meant it! Celebrating in front of the travelling faithful after my overhead kick winner at Grimsby Town, November 2002

Annoyance: (Right) Closing in on Tim Sherwood during the top-of-the-table clash with Portsmouth, February 2003

Sealed with a kiss: Paul Dickov is the lucky recipient after the 2-0 victory over Brighton two months later which secured promotion back to the Premier League

Thumbs up: Perhaps feeling a little worse-for-wear during our open-top bus parade around the city following promotion

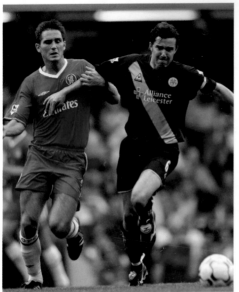

Back in the big time: (Left) Holding off Chelsea's Frank Lampard, and (below) leading City out alongside opposite number, Manchester United's Roy Keane

In the eye of a storm: As captain the press attention was fierce following our return from La Manga in March 2004

Pulling together: Relief all round as our first game back after La Manga ends in a 1-0 victory at Birmingham City, our first win in nearly four months

Down – and nearly out: Frustration after a late chance against Liverpool goes begging

Final acts: (Left) My final goal for Leicester, a 3-2 defeat at fellow relegation rivals Leeds, April 2004 and (above), saluting the fans following the final home game, a 3-1 victory over Portsmouth

New challenge:
(Above and left)
Pre-season training in
new surroundings – with
Birmingham City

Blues goal: My first goal
for the club, at Bolton
Wanderers in September
2004 – unfortunately, it
would be my last goal in
professional football

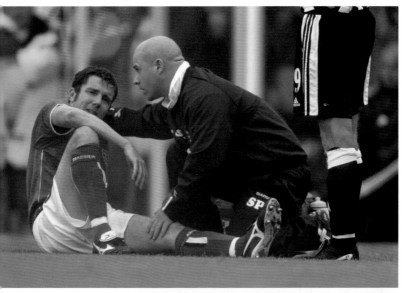

The beginning of the end: Feeling the pain of Olivier Bernard's challenge that would eventually cut short my career in October 2004

Stand aside: (Right) Letting Robbie Savage try his luck from a set piece, against Everton – I was later sent off for handling on the goalline

All over: Another dismissal – the second booking an apparent dive – in a 2-0 Boxing Day defeat at Spurs in 2005; (below right) my final game, a drab 1-1 draw at Wigan the following April

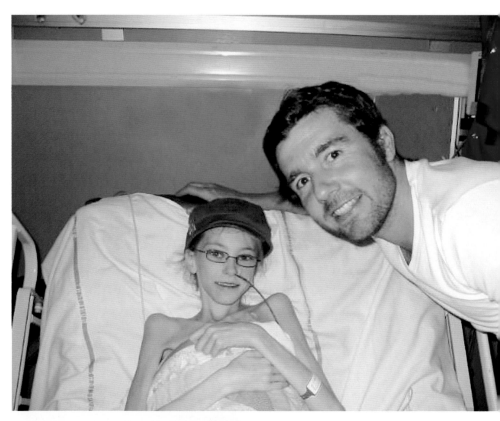

Forever in my heart: (Above) Louise Moon, one of the bravest people I have ever met

Still got it: (Left) As a favour for the builder who renovated by parents' house, I turned out for Sunday League side Thurmaston Town; (below) preparing to volley, for the Leicester Legends side in 2014 – recovery takes a lot longer these days...

Look at dad there, son: Proving that I really was a player once – with Dylan in 2008

Summer school: Me and Walshy pose for a picture with some of the coaches and kids in the early days of our football Academy

It's an education: On the whiteboard during a session with myself and Walshy's Football Academy at Castle Rock High School in Coalville

Family Izzet: The full clan (left to right) me, Dylan, Lyla, Ella and wife Carly

pointing start, he admitted, but he could have turned it around: "If the club had given me a bit more time, I'd have done it."

I watched the interview on Sky Sports that night. There were a lot of 'could haves' and 'would haves', a lot of 'ifs' and 'buts'. The table didn't lie. We weren't good enough. We were where we deserved to be. He might have thought he could have rescued us, that he could have turned it around. But he wouldn't. We all knew it wasn't going to happen. He said he would prove Leicester wrong for getting rid of him. He didn't do that either.

I spoke to a journalist at the *Leicester Mercury* who interviewed Peter Taylor not long after he'd left City.

"Were you out of your depth in the Premier League?" he asked him. Taylor responded by launching into a foul-mouthed tirade for having the temerity to suggest he may have been operating at a level that, possibly, was above his ability. What happened at Leicester – and what happened next – tells us perhaps he was.

Peter Taylor spent just shy of £25m during his 14 months in charge. When we lined up that season, 2001/02, we were the most expensive Leicester City squad in the club's history.

In the summer, he'd bought Dennis Wise (£1.6m), Ian Walker (£2.5m) and Jamie Scowcroft (£3m) – who were added to players like Ade Akinbiyi (£5.5m), Matt Jones (around £3m) and Trevor Benjamin (£1.3m). It was a big outlay.

"Europe is the target," Taylor told the *Mercury*. "I look at the top-five teams and, with the players they have got, they should finish above us. But when I look at the rest of the division, I think we are as good – if not better – than all of them."

It was bollocks. We weren't. He was kidding himself. The fans knew. We knew. The only person who didn't was Peter Taylor.

I think he genuinely believed we were good enough. It was probably why he seemed so surprised when he was sacked.

The season was just two months old. But we were as good as relegated then. Gone by October. You could almost smell it around the training ground. Previously a jolly place, full of banter, piss-taking and laughter, it was suddenly soulless. It was awful. This was a new feeling for players like me, who had known success and good times under Martin O'Neill. I hated it.

Peter Taylor wouldn't have saved us.

By that stage, even after just eight games, I don't think anyone would have saved us. Frankly, I didn't hate the man but I was relieved to see him go.

We didn't know who we were going to get next. I vaguely remember talk about George Graham possibly coming. I'm not sure if we fancied that. He was a strict disciplinarian. No player fancies that but, in hindsight, that's perhaps what we needed.

After a brief spell where Garry Parker took charge – we lost 6-0 against Leeds, no-one blamed Parks – City announced that Dave 'Arry' Bassett would be the new City boss, with Micky Adams, then boss at Brighton, joining as his assistant. In a strange kind of footballing symmetry, Peter Taylor filled Micky's shoes at Brighton. It seemed like a fair swap.

Bassett came with a reputation for keeping struggling teams up. He had also been out of work for the best part of a year after leaving Barnsley, his last club.

"If Leicester were up at the top, I wouldn't be here," he told the *Mercury*. He was right, too.

He gathered at the training ground and said the things all new managers say. New starts. Clean slates. Seven months left, 30 games still to play. We can still do this. "Let's not walk around as if we are in a morgue," he said. "We can still do this."

There was a momentary lift. I liked Dave. He was a decent bloke, a real straight-talking, old-fashioned football boss. If you played crap, he'd single you out at half-time and he'd tell you. "What the facking hell is that, son? What are you doing? You better sort that out in the second half or I'm taking you off."

He dished out a lot of bollockings that season.

"You're playing like a bloody idiot."

"No, son, no, no – we don't do it like that, do we? Is that what we've been doing in training? It's not, is it?"

You could see him on the touchline, his head in his hands, tearing his hair out.

It was refreshing to hear the boss rip into us a bit. We needed that. Taylor was too close to the players. He didn't tell anyone off, even when they deserved to be told off. 'Arry was a breath of fresh air and, for a month, we seemed to rouse.

We won at home against Sunderland, with Ade Akinbiyi scoring. Ade whipped his shirt off and ran around the perimeter of the pitch, ecstatic. We were ecstatic for him, too. We hoped it might begin a glut of goals. It didn't.

We lost away at Manchester United, drew against Everton and then went to Villa Park, where we won 2-0. I wasn't playing that day. I was at home, injured, listening to it on the radio. I hoped, finally, that we'd turned a corner, that this could be the start of our revival. So much for that.

After that victory at Villa we didn't win again for three months; a total of 17 games. We came close. There were games we deserved to win, but didn't. We played Chelsea off the park at home in February. We led 1-0, then 2-1, only for Zola to come off the bench and equalise with a brilliant free-kick before Jimmy Floyd Hasselbaink scored the winner with the last kick. Unbelievable.

Micky took the training at Belvoir Drive. He was good, and good with us. He reminded me of Steve Walford. Training was varied, interesting and competitive. We liked him. Micky was a good laugh, a decent coach and a nice bloke. He got involved and made training fun again.

But something was missing. The fire. The spark. The quality. The camaraderie. The extra 10 per cent that Martin always managed to get out of us.

I was 26, nearly 27. I'd been at Leicester for five years. I was on £35,000 a week. I had been playing well – I was playing regularly for Turkey now, too, and the national coaches were all concentrating on the World Cup the next year. I was looking forward to that. In difficult circumstances, I did okay. I didn't play badly. But I couldn't shake the voices in my head telling me I should be doing more, trying harder, playing better. I was sliding, coasting, not giving it my absolute best. I didn't like it.

I found that hard to take, a truth I found hard to digest and I couldn't hide it, either. I felt I was letting people down, letting myself down. Somehow, somewhere along the way, I'd lost something. I'd gained all sorts of other things. I was more experienced. My positioning was better, my vision, too. I knew where to run, how to time that run and where not to run. As a midfield player, I could spot the game opening up around me. In many ways, I was a much better – a much smarter – player.

But I didn't feel as though I was playing as well as I used to play. My intensity had gone. And that's when the ghost of Eddie Niedzwiecki appeared.

"You're in the comfort zone, son,"

"You'll never win anything when you're in the comfort zone."

I knew it, too. I don't think I was particularly unusual at Leicester around this time, languishing in this comfort zone. Looking back, there were a few of us in it. You could argue Dennis Wise, in the latter stages of a fine career, came here just for the comfort zone. He was a good player, Wisey, but it could be said – and I wouldn't necessarily disagree – that when you're scrapping for points, desperate to eke out whatever you can at the foot of the table, you don't go and buy a 35-year-old ex-Chelsea player and expect him to scurry around in midfield for you. Wisey was never going to do that.

Wisey was like Marmite. Some players liked him. Some players hated him. Most of this was down to the fact that Wisey was always deliberately blunt. If he thought you were being a prick, he'd look you in the eye and he'd call you a prick.

Sav didn't like Wisey, mainly because Wisey didn't like him. He didn't like his flash, his brashness, the brightly-coloured sports car and the fake tan. We were used to it. It was just the way Sav was – and is. He didn't mean anything by it but Wisey, I think, thought that Sav hadn't done enough in the game to go around doing that. And he told him so.

At the end of October 2001, with Taylor gone and Bassett in charge, I put in a transfer request. I'd heard that other teams were interested in me and I thought, maybe, my time at Leicester was over.

I wanted to play in the top flight. I wanted to play for Turkey in a World Cup. I was worried that staying with Leicester would mean the death of both of those dreams.

I stood in the car park at Belvoir Drive one day in October and looked around. In these familiar surroundings, a happy home for five years, I felt like a man out of place. Lenny had left, Walshy, TC and Marshy as well. Parks had retired, Martin had moved on, Emile had signed for Liverpool. It seemed like a new dawn at the club. I preferred the old one.

I still liked it there. I liked nearly all the players, all the backroom staff. I was settled in our new home in south Leicestershire. Carly had just given birth to Ella. We were happy there. But my game wasn't right and I felt, for the first time since I'd left Chelsea, that it was time. It was time to go.

I had shed my self doubt – experience and a £35,000 a week pay cheque does that for you – but I didn't feel as though I was playing well, or as well as I should have been. It concerned me. It got to me, too. Mentally, I let it affect my game. I was preoccupied by it. I thought about it and I decided I was getting itchy feet. I handed my transfer request in to Dave Bassett.

I don't think he was cock-a-hoop about this but he never, ever stood in my way. At the time I thought this was decent of Dave and decent of the club although maybe they were already looking at their accounts and thinking they needed to offload some of their higher-earning players – so I started being courted by other clubs.

Middlesbrough were first. I drove up to the North East in my car. It was cold. I remember setting off in Leicester and seeing the temperature gauge in my car falling steadily as I headed further north. I'm sure there are some lovely areas around Middlesbrough. I didn't see any of them on that drive up. I think that long journey made my mind up before I even heard a word from Boro boss Steve McClaren.

When I eventually got there, McClaren was decent. He was friendly, likeable, honest. He told me he'd always been impressed with me, that he thought I could do a job for him in their midfield – and he promised to pay me more than I was on.

I liked all of that. But I just didn't feel it. It didn't feel right. Middlesbrough were building a decent team. He had Gareth Southgate at the back, Paul Ince and Robbie Mustoe in midfield. He had money. He was going to buy more players, he said. Middlesbrough were going places, and he wanted me in.

"You'll like it here, Muzzy," he kept saying. "They'll love you up here, you'll see."

He showed me round. I walked into their training room and they had the line-up scribbled down for that weekend's game. My name was in centre midfield. They seemed confident, I thought to myself. I wasn't sure that I liked that. We had a good chat and I came home. I knew I wouldn't sign.

The money was good – and it was a long contract, too. But it wasn't about the money, it never has been. It just wasn't right.

Aston Villa were interested. Under John Gregory, they had an ageing midfield of Ginola, Merson, Ian Taylor and Steve Stone. They made contact with my agent but, despite assurances that they were going to make an offer, it never arrived.

There were constant rumours that I was going to sign for O'Neill at Celtic. There was talk, again not involving me, with their people/my agent, but it never materialised. I think that Martin thought I wouldn't want to move up to Scotland. I think, too, he might have been right.

West Ham were reportedly interested at one stage. I think that would have been a genuine pull for me. They were the club I supported as a kid. Nothing happened. And then Leeds.

Managed by David O'Leary, no-one was spending as much money as Leeds were around this time. They were throwing a lot of cash around on players like:

Darren Huckerby for £4m from Coventry City;
Michael Bridges from Sunderland for £5.6m;
Danny Mills from Charlton Athletic for £4m;
Michael Duberry from Chelsea for £4.5m.

In four years, O'Leary spent £100m. Leeds didn't have this money, of course. They gambled it. They speculated to accumulate, risking their future success and expansion on money they expected to receive from Sky, ITV Digital and ticket sales. It was a risk Leicester repeated. In both cases, the gamble failed. In late 2001, Leeds made several enquiries.

"Sit tight," my agent, Jonathan Barnett, said. "They're interested. It will happen."

It never did. It wasn't anything to do with me as a player. Football had nothing to do with it. It was something that I had no control over.

In 1999/2000, Leeds had finished third in the league and were beaten by Galatasary in the semi-final of the UEFA Cup. In the first leg in Istanbul, two Leeds fans were stabbed and killed by a gang of Turkish fans. I remember seeing it on the news. Two lads, following their team in Europe, who never came home. That should never happen. I didn't know it then but this would scupper my move to Elland Road.

Leeds were putting together a £7m-£8m bid. Leicester would have accepted it. It was 10 times more than what they paid for me. It seemed like a good move for both clubs. Terms wouldn't be a problem, my agent told me. Leeds will give you what you want, he said. That's what Leeds did.

There's a famous story about Peter Ridsdale which was well-known in football changing rooms around that time. Leeds signed Seth Johnson from Derby. Before they went in for the meeting with the then Leeds chairman, Seth and his agent set their stall out.

"You're on £5,000 a week at Derby. We'll ask for £18k, but we'll settle for £13,000," said Johnson's agent. "It's still nearly double your money. Agreed?"

They agreed.

After a few pleasantries in Ridsdale's office, negotiations started. The Leeds chairman got straight to the point.

"Right, let's cut straight to it shall we – no messing about. How does £30,000 a week sound?"

Johnson and his agent said nothing. They were gobsmacked.

The shocked silence continued.

"Ah. Right. Okay then," said Ridsdale. "Let's make that £35,000 a week shall we? How does that sound?"

Seth Johnson couldn't sign quickly enough.

Peter Ridsdale insists that story isn't true. Maybe it isn't. If nothing else, though, it serves to illustrate just how much – and with such carefree abandon – Leeds were reportedly spending: £70,000 on private jets for directors, even £20 a month on goldfish food just in the directors' offices.

In 2004, Leeds were relegated with debts of £80m.

I never did speak to them. There was no contact with David O'Leary. It was all done through my agent. There was interest, a transfer fee that was virtually agreed, a handsome contract for me – and then it all seemed to go quiet.

I expected a call from Ridsdale or O'Leary. There was no call.

This saga limped on for weeks.

Sit tight, my agent kept saying.

Leeds were telling him all the right things.

The move never materialised.

I didn't find out until years later that the reason they went cold wasn't about me, how I played, where they thought I might fit in – but because I was Turkish and my name was Muzzy Izzet. They didn't think the fans would like that. So that was that.

A few years later, David O'Leary, as manager of Aston Villa, came in for me again. I remembered what happened and I turned him down flat. I didn't want to play for him.

We were relegated on a sunny day in early April, a home game against Manchester United. We lost 1-0, a Solskjaer goal. When it came, it wasn't a surprise. We'd been bottom since Boxing Day. You know what they say about teams at the bottom of the table at Christmas. They rarely escape.

It was Dave Bassett's last game.

He was presented with a trophy marking his 1,000th game as a manager. I remember the fans clapping politely and then launching straight into a rousing chorus of *'Micky Adams' Blue and White Army.'*

Late in the second half, 1-0 down, relegated, another chant started: *'Stand Up If You Love Leicester,'* the fans sang. It started in the Kop and then rolled and crashed, like a wave, right around the old stadium. I don't know how long it lasted but it seemed like everyone was singing it. I remember looking round and smiling, the hairs on my arms standing up, a shiver down my spine. It was a genuinely magical, moving moment.

We were down – but we weren't out.

On May 11, 2002, Leicester City played Spurs in the final

game at Filbert Street. On a day heavy with emotion and sentiment we won at a canter, 2-1, my old mate Matt Piper scoring the last-ever goal at Filbert Street.

Pipes had been on the edge of the first team under Martin O'Neill. He'd brought him with us on away games. He let him train with the first team. O'Neill rated him. He could see he had something – and so could we. He didn't play once under Peter Taylor. He made his debut the night Garry Parker took control against Leeds. Everyone liked Pipes.

I'd been on the transfer list for six months. Four or five clubs had been sniffing around, making enquiries. Leicester – saddled with a huge debt from Peter Taylor's well-thumbed chequebook, and the emergence of a fancy new stadium appearing just a few hundred yards down Raw Dykes Road – were not standing in my way.

In the 89th minute, they held a board up. Come in number 6, your time is up.

I remember walking off and the cheer started, the Kop first and then, like that chant before, washing all around the stadium; people on their feet, clapping me off.

I knew why.

They knew why.

It was my last game.

They were saying goodbye.

I walked off, my hands raised, clapping them back.

And I walked into the tunnel, into the dressing room for the last time, my last time at Leicester, and my eyes were full of tears. What was I doing? This was my home…

ON THE RIGHT

When it happens, when it finally happens, Muzzy Izzet is not expecting it.

The 2002 World Cup semi-final between Turkey and Brazil, an open and far more even affair than most experts had predicted, is midway through the second half.

On the Turkey bench, the Turkish manager, Senol Gunes, calls the Turkey number 13 over. He puts his arm around Izzet's shoulder. He says three words to him in English. They are the only words he has uttered in the past two months that Muzzy Izzet has understood.

In the 73rd minute, with Brazil 1-0 up thanks to a moment of individual brilliance from Ronaldo, Gunes leans into the number 13.

"On the right," he says.

The board goes up. Umit Davala comes off. Muzzy Izzet, aged 27, born in the East End of London, a hero at his club, Leicester City, is about to play in the biggest game of his life.

He's in his shorts and a training top. He is not wearing his shin pads. His boots are untied. He is utterly unprepared.

Unbeknown to his team-mates, the crowd, the watching audience of millions, Muzzy Izzet has mixed emotions. He wants to be there. It's a World Cup, a semi-final no less. Of course he wants to be there. He is thrilled, finally, to be given his chance.

But he's had enough.

He doesn't know what he's supposed to do, who he is marking, where he should stand at a corner, all the simple things he takes for granted when he plays for Leicester City.

Just "on the right." That's it. "On the right."

He glides on to the pitch.

He has 17 minutes to make his mark.

When the World Cup started I was 27 years old. I was living with Carly and we had a one-year-old baby girl, Ella. I played centre midfield for Leicester City. We'd just been relegated. Manager Micky Adams substituted me a minute or so before the end of the last match at Filbert Street and I got a standing ovation. Everyone – fans, media, players, the staff – assumed I was leaving. Leicester needed the money, I was told.

I wasn't sure I wanted to go. I liked it at Leicester. I felt settled. So with a lingering uncertainty, I left for the heart-sinking ritual of Heathrow Airport – check-in, departure lounge, flight, Istanbul – and joined the squad. It was May 2002, two weeks before the start of the World Cup.

It was a good Turkey squad with some fine players – Tugay, who'd been at Rangers before moving to Blackburn Rovers the previous summer; Emre, the hard-as-nails centre-half; the Galatasaray winger, Hasan Sas; striker Hakan Sukur; midfield-er Umit Davala, who played for Milan – and they seemed like genuinely nice fellas, too.

We would smile at each other and they would say odd words in English, and I'd struggle to say an odd word in Turkish and that was about the extent of my relationship with them. No-one was nasty or mean. They were decent. They accepted me and my circumcised Turkish penis. I was one of them. But no matter how hard they tried, there was a chasm between this East End boy, a second-generation Turk, and them.

On the last night of our training camp before we left for South Korea, manager Senol Gunes gathered us together at our training camp in Istanbul – players, coaches, medical staff and all the wives – and we had a huge farewell meal. Carly was in Leicester with Ella. I don't remember who I sat with. I just remember they all had their wives while mine was at home with a daughter who was just beginning to get to know her daddy.

They tried not to leave me out. And I appreciated that. But I was the odd man out, the one who didn't quite fit in. Everyone could see it. I tried to shake it off, but it was a coat I wore for the next six weeks. The World Cup hadn't even started.

I'd come from a dressing room at Leicester City where we all knew each other, where the joking and banter was relentless. There was banter in this dressing room, too. It was just that I didn't get it. I wasn't involved in it. It's hard work, that – when everyone is laughing at a joke you don't understand.

A dressing room – a successful dressing room – turns on the camaraderie of its playing squad; the craic, the piss-taking, the in-jokes. All the good teams have that. It brings a squad closer together. It creates a bond. You could see they had it. It was just that I didn't get it. Whose fault was that? It was my fault.

My biggest regret with Turkey is not the games I missed or any of my performances on the pitch.

It was that I never learned the language. I should have done. It would have shown a bit of willingness on my part, and it would have helped me to settle in.

Tugay, who was one of the finest players I ever played with, spoke a bit of English. He was a nice bloke and a decent player. I stuck to him so much at first that I had to prise myself away.

'Bloody hell, man, he doesn't want you clinging to him like a lost schoolgirl for the duration of the trip,' I had to tell myself.

I thought I'd better give him some space. No-one else spoke English. So that was that. I would walk the streets of South Korea and, later, Japan, where we were based in the latter stages of the competition, and go into shops and buy DVDs. I watched more films in those six weeks than Barry Norman. I don't remember any of them.

Most days, the squad would get together and go to a local mosque. Most of the team were Muslim. I'm not a Muslim. So I didn't go. I didn't pray. I stayed in the hotel. That gap – the gap between me and them – grew wider. Well, it did in my mind. And, by now, my mind was all over the place.

It was like living on another planet where I communicated with my feet, not my mouth. That was the only time the misery seemed to slip away – when I was playing football. When the football stopped, I started to feel not so much depressed, as such, but low, definitely. Isolated. Lonely. I didn't cope very well. I used to train and run and train and run, and then come back to the hotel and run more, just to try to sort my head out. My head was a mess.

I was tired. I wasn't sleeping. I had no energy, but I forced myself to run and to train because running and training were the only things that made me feel better. I couldn't bear to do nothing because my mind would drift back home and I'd start wishing I was there instead of here. So when I wasn't running or sleeping fitfully I'd watch DVDs, more films.

My memories of that World Cup are me, in a hotel room, by myself, the curtains closed, lying on my bed, watching another film, trying not to think of home. The football – and it seems crazy to say this, ridiculous to read it in black and white – started to seem almost secondary.

The group stages were difficult. We were in Group C – us, Brazil, Costa Rica and China. I watched each game from the bench, as players and coaches discussed tactics and shouted instructions about who should be doing what in a language I didn't understand. It all went over my head. We came second to Brazil, and were due to play Japan in the second round.

We flew from our base in South Korea to Japan. En route, our chartered plane encountered some mid-air turbulence and dropped like a lead weight. There was no warning. One minute the air hostess was fixing me a drink – the next I was watching her head smash against the plane roof as it plunged downwards.

It lasted for 20 seconds, maybe a bit longer. It felt like longer. It felt like imminent death, played out in slow motion to the soundtrack of grown men, the heroes of a nation, screaming. It was terrifying.

Somehow, the pilot regained control and the plane steadied and, eventually, we landed. As I walked off the plane – ashen-faced, shaking like a shitting dog – a delegation of players and coaches were banging on the pilot's door, demanding to know what had happened. The pilot refused to come out. I didn't blame him. Frankly, I wouldn't have fancied his chances.

We had a training session later that day. I'm no expert in body language but I can tell you categorically that no-one wanted to train that day. No-one. I was never scared of flying before that incident. Today, I'm like Dennis Bergkamp. I do it, I have to do it. We wouldn't go on holiday otherwise. But I hate it.

We beat Japan, the hosts, 1-0. For the first time in our nation's history, Turkey were in the quarter-finals of the World Cup.

Four days later in Osaka, we defeated Senegal 1-0 with a golden goal in extra time. I watched it all from the bench. I wanted us to win. I was proud to be there. I was desperate for us to get through. Brazil in the semis. One match from the final. *Come on!*

And yet... I hadn't kicked a ball. I had played no part in our progress. I watched our campaign as a spectator. I'm awful at that, too. I hate watching. I want to play. All that training, all that running, all that preparation and then five World Cup games, the biggest footballing stage in the world – and I watched them all from the bench.

Nobody ever said: 'We don't fancy you for this match, Muzzy' or 'We're going with Umit Davala in midfield because we think he's a better player' or 'He's more suited to this kind of game.' I could have handled that. I might not have liked it, but I would have a reason. All footballers need a reason. Instead, I took my place on the bench and watched as this young Turkish side made footballing history. Brilliant – but frustrating.

I'd call home sometimes. It was nice to hear Carly's voice. But every time I spoke to someone at home – Carly, my parents – it just made me feel worse. I called less often. It was self-preservation. It was after one of those calls that I asked to leave.

Fuck this.
I can't do it.
I can't get in the team.
I don't know why I can't get in the team.
I'm as good as them, aren't I?
My daughter doesn't know who I am.
This is shit.
I can't sleep.
What am I doing here?
This is a mistake.
I can't bear to watch one more film.
I'm going home.
Home.
I just want to go home.

I'd had enough. I rang Carly and told her I'd had it. My mind had gone. I wanted to come home. I threw a few things in a bag. I would leave that night. Yep, that night. I went to break the news to the management. I sat down and spoke to the PR guy. He was all right. He spoke a little bit of English.

"I can't carry on," I said.

"I feel like I'm going mad. No-one is speaking to me. I'm not playing – I don't know why. I don't know any Turkish. No-one knows any English. It's mad. I have to go home."

He listened to me. He nodded in all the right places. He said he understood how I felt. I was halfway home, I thought. I didn't feel happy about that. I felt relief.

"But if you leave," he said, shaking his head, "how will it look? It will look bad. It will look bad for you."

I didn't care about that. I needed to go home.

"But it will look bad for the team, too," he said.

"It will show the team in a bad light. Look how well we are doing. Turkey have never got this far in a World Cup. Everyone back home is behind you. You are a part of it. You must stay. Turkey needs you. Turkey needs you to stay."

I didn't want it to look bad for the team. I hadn't thought of that. I nodded. His argument was better than mine.

I turned and went back to my room. I closed the curtains, sat on the bed and watched another DVD.

Football was the only thing that could raise me from this stupor and, as the semi-final approached, my mood lifted. A semi-final of the World Cup. *A semi-final of the World Cup.* It is a big thing. How many players get that, I kept saying to myself. Not many.

We trained hard for the game. Brazil were the favourites, not just to beat us but to lift the World Cup. This was 'Big' Phil Scolari's Brazil, with Ronaldo in his prime, Rivaldo and Roberto Carlos. They were a special team. But, you know, so were we.

We went into the game thinking we could win it. I think that was the feeling, I couldn't be sure. Everyone seemed very positive, anyway. That was the vibe I was getting. I was on the bench. Again. I didn't expect to play.

It was a decent game, an open match considering the biggest prize of all – a place in the World Cup final – was at stake. Ronaldo scored in the 49th minute with a piece of individual brilliance: a shimmy, right-foot shot, no back-lift, the ball just beating the outstretched left hand of our goalkeeper, Rustu Recber, who was unable to stop the inevitable.

But we never gave in. We threw everything at them. The game was wide open and it was proper end-to-end stuff. It looked like they might get another. Then it looked like we might equalise.

In the 73rd minute, Gunes called me over. I don't know what happened. Maybe Davala was struggling? It didn't look like he was. He was a good player, Davala. I rated him. We all did.

"Get ready," someone on the bench said to me. "You're going on." I was sitting there in my socks, my shorts, my boots untied. Shit, my boots are untied.

I tried to tie them up. I couldn't. I couldn't tie my laces. I felt my heart begin to pound so loudly I feared it might explode out of my chest.

I'm going on.
Shit.
I'm actually going on.

Gunes put his arm around my shoulder and pointed to the far side of the pitch.

"On the right," he said.
On the right.
That's all he said. That was all he said to me in eight weeks.
On the right.
I didn't know where I was to stand for a corner. Who was I marking? Who was taking the free-kicks? Where was I supposed to be when they had the ball?

I knew none of that.

I'd come from a team where I knew *exactly* what I was doing. I knew what was expected of me. I always knew where Neil Lennon was. I knew where Garry Parker was. I knew which areas I had to close down. And I knew that if they got through me, they'd have to get through Matt Elliott or Steve Walsh. Here, now, for the biggest game of my life, I knew nothing.

But you know what? I didn't care. I was on.

It felt good.

For the first time in two months, I felt good, too.

I ran over to the right. I glided over to the right. My spot. On the right. I looked up. Roberto Carlos. Probably the finest left-back in the world. He didn't even look tired.

I wouldn't try to skin him. There would be no point. I'd come inside. I'd bring him with me. I'd create holes all over the back four. I would make endless runs from the right into the box.

Feed me. Give me the ball.

I played the most selfish period of football I think I've ever played in my life. I ran into the box, time after time after time. I thought: *'Well, I've got 20 minutes or so. I'm going to do everything I can to score a goal.'*

I'm not naturally a selfish player – but I was in that game.

It passed by in a blur. I vaguely remember I had a shot, and that I was in an even better position to score in the final few minutes as we pressed forward, but no-one found me.

I watched the clock tick down, the dream evaporate. I remember thinking that I wished I'd had more time to get into the game, to put my mark on it. To do something. And then I remember thinking I would soon be home.

I've never seen the game on video. There's a copy knocking around at home, somewhere – but I don't want to watch it.

The full-time whistle went. We shook hands with our opponents. I swapped shirts with Roberto Carlos. I gave that shirt away a few years later. A lad in the village called Martin Lynch was raising money for his son, who had a terminal illness. He knocked on my door one day and asked if I had anything he could auction off; some old shorts or some shin pads, maybe. It was for a good cause, he said.

I had a rummage around. I didn't have much. I haven't kept many shirts or memorabilia. I'm not very sentimental, although my spare Turkey shirt and World Cup medal is on show at the King Power Stadium. I found Roberto Carlos's shirt. I thought they'd probably get more for that than one of my old City shirts. So I gave it to Martin. I don't know how much it went for.

Officially, the Turkish players were not paid for playing in the World Cup. Unofficially, the players were meeting with the Turkish FA to sort out payments and bonuses. Someone came into my room and gave me a large brown envelope stuffed full of American dollars. I wasn't expecting that; playing against the best players in the world was enough for me.

Finally, it was time to go home. By now, I wasn't the only one ready to leave. We all were. It had been a long campaign. Two months, including the pre-competition training camp.

But it wasn't over. There was the irrelevance of the third place play-off, which we won, beating hosts South Korea 3-2. It was a decent game, apparently, although not for the first time, it mostly passed me by. I watched it from the bench and I do remember the first goal – the fastest-ever World Cup strike, scored by Hasan Sas after 11 seconds.

We flew home the next day. As we came into Turkish airspace, four F16 fighter jets guided us into Ataturk Airport. We stepped from the plane, the third best team in the world, to be greeted by 200,000 Turkish fans who had gathered to welcome us home.

The government had organised an open-top bus parade around Istanbul. Turkey was proud of its footballers and it wanted us to know it. It was nice. We went out in the bus which slowly inched its way around the busy Turkish city.

We waved at the fans. They waved at us. Thanks, we said. *Sağ olun* – thank you and good health to you. *Sağ olun*, they responded back. It was touching but then I looked at my watch. I longed to be home.

I left for London the next day. I was stopped at Heathrow with a bag of American dollars and a suitcase full of electrical equipment, which raised eyebrows at customs.

"I've been at the World Cup," I said. I showed them my medal and my Turkey shirts. They nodded and let me through. I exchanged some of my dollars for English pounds and hailed a cab.

"Fleckney, mate. South Leicestershire. Take me home."

I played for Turkey only once after that, in a friendly against Belarus in 2004. I was at Birmingham City by then, just before the injury. I never felt I had my best games in the red of my adopted home nation. I don't know why that was, only that it was.

Ironically, one of the few times I did play well – a home match in Istanbul against France, with their central midfield of Emmanuel Petit and Patrick Vieira, who I'd played against several times – they brought me off before half-time. I don't know why. I'd been playing well, against strong opposition. And the coach dragged me off, 37 minutes into the game.

I sat in the dressing room, as Gunes berated the players in a language I didn't understand and I didn't get it. All that way – to be taken off after barely half an hour. Jesus.

I was proud to play for Turkey, but I can't say I was unhappy when my international career ended. I was relieved.

ADMINISTRATION
& PROMOTION

*"If you can say I'm a bad owner and we're winning champion-
ships, I can live with that. But if we're not winning championships – if we're nowhere near winning championships – and we're
spending and losing money, then I have to look in the mirror and
say: 'You know, maybe I'm not doing this job properly'."*

Michael Jordan

*Dave Bassett told him first, followed by one of the directors. "There
may be trouble ahead," he said. "Big trouble. It's time for you to leave
– for your own good and for the good of the club."*

*Muzzy Izzet didn't know what he meant, but he could guess. He
soon learned, too, that they didn't necessarily want him to leave for*

his own good. They wanted him gone for their own.

There weren't many players in the Leicester City team in 2001/02 who would fetch £6m plus on the transfer market. In fact, there was only one: the club's Turkish midfielder, Mustafa Izzet. They wanted him out, they wanted his wages off the bill and they wanted the money in the bank.

When Micky Adams substituted Muzzy Izzet in the 89th minute of the last game of the season against Spurs, the final game at Filbert Street, there seemed to be an unspoken finality about it.

He wasn't taking him off because he was injured.

He wasn't saving him for another game.

He was giving this brilliant player and fine club servant a final bow; an opportunity for the fans to say thanks.

No-one expected Muzzy Izzet to still be a Leicester City player at the start of the 2002/03 season – least of all the man himself.

And yet it didn't happen. Robbie Savage left and joined Birmingham. Matt Piper signed for Sunderland in a move he never asked for or really wanted. But Muzzy, despite being courted by some well-known names and big-spending teams in the English Premier League, stayed at Leicester.

That summer, he played in a World Cup semi-final; him on the right, the world's best left-back, Roberto Carlos, on the left.

On the first day of the Nationwide League Division One season and with City in their new home, the Walkers Stadium, he ran out in the blue of Leicester City.

A storm was brewing. He knew it, he could smell it. The club wanted him to leave. He thought he wanted to leave. But still he stayed.

Why?

What was he thinking?

What really happened?

You're about to find out...

It was a beautiful summer's day on Saturday, August 10, 2002.
I got up that morning, got in the shower and wondered how it
had come to this: Leicester City, in a brand new stadium – playing in English football's second tier.

This would have been unthinkable two years earlier, under
the stewardship of Martin O'Neill, the man who pushed for
this new stadium as much, if not more, than anyone else.
Leicester City should have trotted out on to that pristine, virgin
turf at 2.55pm on Saturday, August 10, 2002 and faced Liverpool, Arsenal or Manchester United at the newly-constructed
Walkers Stadium, Filbert Way, LE2. But we didn't. It was Ray
Lewington's Watford, the first game of the new Nationwide
League Division One campaign.

City had been relegated. And although this should have been
unthinkable, it was entirely right. We were precisely where we
deserved to be. It wasn't as if this was a surprise. We'd been
nailed-on favourites for relegation since before October 2001,
before Peter Taylor was sacked. Anyone could see that.

But that morning – showering, driving to the ground, parking,
hanging my stuff on a new peg in a new changing room – it hit
home. It wasn't supposed to be like this. And yet there we were.

And there I was, too.

I was still a Leicester City player. If I didn't expect us to be
relegated, it's true to say that I didn't expect to still be at Leicester, either. I thought I was ready to go. Everyone thought I was
ready to go. So what happened?

Well, lots of stuff happened.

I spoke to Middlesbrough. I didn't fancy that.

There had been talks with Leeds, rumours about Aston
Villa, West Ham, Celtic, Blackburn, Bolton. I knew the club

wanted me to leave. I'd been on the transfer list for six months. I thought I wanted to leave, too. But deep down, I wasn't sure. I was settled in Leicestershire, I liked living there. I still do now. I was happy with my partner, Carly, and daughter, Ella.

I was 27 years old. I'd just come back from a World Cup in Japan and South Korea that had been exhilarating – but mentally exhausting. I felt a bit frayed. I don't think I've ever been as happy to be at home as I was in that summer of 2002.

I did a lot of thinking that summer. I wised up a bit. I looked around, at where I lived, at who I was – and what I meant to the people at Leicester. I liked it. I appreciated it.

Maybe, if I hadn't spent eight weeks away from home with Turkey, with players who I didn't understand, pining for home, then maybe all of this would have been different. Maybe I would have left. But what that World Cup campaign did, I think, was make me realise what I had.

There are lots of footballers who think the grass is greener somewhere else. I know that. I've played with them. I've trained with them. I've drank with them in players' lounges and pubs, at the back of coaches on long trips home. I knew there was a financial storm lurking at Leicester, but I also knew that I'd had good times at the club. I had friends here. I felt settled. I was on a good contract, too. Other clubs had said they could pay me more but, frankly, that didn't mean that much to me. I was on enough. I appreciated what I had.

Micky Adams took over as boss five games before the end of the 2001/2002 relegation season. It should have happened weeks, months before. Micky had been a great coach for us. Training was always varied and interesting, he liked a laugh and a joke. He was one of the lads. We loved him for that.

And then as soon as he got the main job, all that stopped. You have never seen a man change so quickly as Micky did when he went from being coach to boss. He became strict, really strict. He dished out bollockings. He was ruthless. There were players he fell out with, established first-team players who were banished from the first team and made to train with the reserves and the academy squad. He had them running around the pitch adjacent to ours, as we trained.

The lesson was simple: *Don't fucking mess with me.*

I wouldn't have expected Micky to do anything like that. But he did. And do you know what? He was right. He was right to do it. We were a better team for it, too. He needed to create some distance between him and the players. He needed to stamp his personality on the place; to let everyone know he was the boss. We respected him for that – well, most of us did – and we started that season well.

We ran and ran and ran that year. I didn't think I could have run any more than I did that season – until we came back the next season and he made us run again, faster and further. Micky liked to make us run.

By the end of August, with wins against Watford, Stoke, Reading and Gillingham under our belts, we were in the top three. We stayed there all season. And, because of all that running, we were fit. We hit our stride early and we found something that we'd lost somewhere along the way a season or a season-and-a-half, before that. We found our self-belief.

Confidence is such a mystical and hard-to-acquire ingredient in the game. But if you've got it – and this goes through every level of football, from kids to pub teams, Conference sides to the top Premier League outfits – you're halfway there.

People talk about tactics and formations. I've never thought they were that important. You need good players, who know what to do, who like each other and know how to play – and confidence. Get that, and you'll win. Keep winning and it becomes a habit. We got into the winning habit early that season at City.

We were in a first-class stadium. The facilities at the new ground were exceptional. The crowds were good. People came to see the new stadium – they came back because we kept winning.

The atmosphere wasn't as intense as it sometimes was at Filbert Street – but, still, it's a nice feeling to be playing in a big, full stadium, on a good pitch, and winning every week.

We had a good team. And for the first time in a long time, we could see it, too. Look at the nucleus, the backbone, of that 2002/03 promotion winning side:

Ian Walker in goal. There wasn't a better goalkeeper in that league. 'Walks' was better than most Premier League keepers. His form that season put him back into the England frame. We were all delighted for him.

Matt Elliott, Gerry Taggart and Frank Sinclair were at the back. How many opposing centre-forwards would have looked at our team sheet and fancied playing 90 minutes against those three? Not many.

We did play quite a bit of long ball that season, but we played to our strengths. We had Brian Deane and Jamie Scowcroft up front, with Paul Dickov scurrying around and picking up all the knock-ons. If all you knew of Paul was what you saw on a Saturday afternoon, then you might think that he was an argumentative little Scotsman with a chip on his shoulder and a permanent point to prove.

But he wasn't. He was a genuinely lovely, gentle, quiet man, who, at 3pm on a Saturday afternoon, was a man transformed. Dickov scored 20 goals that season. He was brilliant. We used to talk a lot, me and him. He was good for me and he improved my game, too, because he'd tell me about his runs, his decoys, where he was going. I knew his game inside out. We developed something of a telepathic understanding that season which we took into the Premier League the next season.

Micky brought Alan Cork in as first-team coach. Corky had played centre-forward for Wimbledon all the way through the whole Crazy Gang period. Corky, thankfully, was the sensible one. Like all good coaches, he kept things simple. He was a smart bloke, too. At a football club, the players don't moan to the manager. They moan to the first-team coach.

Corky got it in the neck some weeks, but it didn't matter who was moaning into his ear, he'd put his arm around their shoulder and nod along, say all the right things and promise to look into it. I doubt if he ever did, but he was brilliant at defusing situations before they grew into a major problem.

He never over-elaborated. He never concentrated too much on the opposition, either. He concentrated on us. "Do what you do and do it right," he used to say. "And that'll be enough." And, usually, that season at least, it was.

He loved his set-pieces, too, Corky, and we practised them relentlessly. We were good at set-pieces under O'Neill but we never practised them. Corky made us go over and over them. He drilled them into us, especially one which, for some strange reason and I never did find out why, he nicknamed 'The Mongo'.

Imagine a free-kick, on the right, 20 yards outside the box. Corky would line up four players on the edge of the box – 1, 2,

3, 4; they'd be, in this order – Jamie Scowcroft at the far post, then Brian Deane, then Matt Elliott, then Gerry Taggart.

I'd get ready to take the free-kick and from the back Scowie would make an early run towards me, towards the ball. I'd put my hands up and stop. Scowie would look annoyed, as if our plan had gone wrong, and then he'd fall back to his original position, at the back of the line-up. It just looked like an accident. He'd gone too early. But it was no accident.

Because then, as I ran up to take the kick, Scowie would drop further back again, losing his marker and right to the back post. I'd knock the free-kick long, to Scowie on the back post, who would head it back across the six-yard-box for Deane, Taggs or Matty to attack it. They'd be lining up to head it in. All I needed to do was hit Scowie at the back post. I could do that. It was ridiculously simple, obvious even, but I lost count of the number of goals we scored that season – and the season after in the Premier League – using that move or a variation on it.

In the middle of the park, Billy McKinlay played the unselfish, defensive midfielder role – he was a good player, too, Billy – which gave me more freedom to push forward. I loved it. I was playing well. I found my form but what was better was that I felt I was rediscovering my enthusiasm, too.

It wasn't a difficult league that season. We weren't chasing and pressing teams constantly and working hard for 90 minutes like we had been under O'Neill in the Premier League. We didn't have to. Our quality was enough, mostly. I enjoyed the telepathy I had with Dickov. I liked playing with him. I liked taking all the set pieces. I enjoyed that, too.

In the middle, Jordan Stewart took the left berth and The Funniest Man In Football, Nicky Summerbee, was on the right.

Nicky called himself 'The Option'. "When you're in trouble, son, just look over your right shoulder and ping it out to The Option," he'd say. And he said it so often, it stuck. We all called him The Option.

He was a genuinely funny bloke, The Option. He could slaughter you, absolutely slaughter you, for nothing at all in training and the whole team would be in stitches. He'd keep on at you until he found your weak spot – whether it was your hair, your clothes, your first touch, the music you liked, your missus and, believe me, nothing was off limits – and once he found it, he didn't let go.

Coming in to work every day with Nicky Summerbee was like being in the front row of a never-ending comedy gig. He was magic to have around. And even though we all felt the sharp end of his tongue, I don't think there was anyone who didn't like the guy. He took the piss, and he could be ruthless, but it was never evil. He sells cars now, apparently. I'm not surprised. He had such a gift of the gab that he'd be brilliant at that.

We lost the odd game that season, but not many. It really wasn't a good league. I noticed how teams would switch off against us; how some sides would visibly wilt 60 or 70 minutes in and we would lengthen our stride and pull ahead. The first touch of some opposition players wasn't great. I seemed to have more time on the ball. A lot of teams were fragile at the back and wasteful up front.

We were playing well and winning. There was only Harry Redknapp's Portsmouth keeping us off top spot. We were confident we'd get promoted. Everything was looking good – and then the whispers started to get louder; the club was in trouble. There wasn't enough money to pay the players. Bills were unpaid. Those whispers quickly grew louder. From something that seemed unlikely, far-fetched even, suddenly the dark clouds were gathering. Leicester City were in deep financial trouble.

We're sheltered from a lot of that, as players, but still, we read the papers. We heard the rumours There were copies of the tabloids at the training ground; the players bought the local rag, the *Leicester Mercury*. We knew something was going on.

One day in October 2002, Dave Bassett, who had stayed on as director of football although we rarely – if ever – saw him by now, called us all together at the Belvoir Drive training ground.

"The club is in a spot of bother," Dave said, "but with your help, we can avoid going into administration."

The club had debts of nearly £30m, he said. You didn't need to be a mathematical genius to see where that had come from: Peter Taylor spent £25m. The new ground was £30m. The money the club was banking on for being in the Premiership was gone, of course. Then the ITV Digital deal collapsed. The club was relying on that money, too. On top of that, there were players like me, Matt Elliott, Ian Walker and a few others on big contracts, which were costing the club millions every year.

"Don't worry, though," said Dave, "if you can agree today to defer 25 per cent of your wages – and if you get us promoted, you'll get that back at the end of the season – then the club won't go into administration."

A few of us asked questions: are you deferring 25 per cent of your wages, Dave? Are the directors? Is Micky? What happens if we don't?

I don't remember what he said but it must have been persuasive because we signed on the dotted-line. It would be a lie to say we were ecstatic about this but we did it because we thought it was the right thing to do, and we did, too, because we were confident of getting promoted.

What we were doing, essentially, was betting on ourselves. We were backing City to get promotion. It was October. We were either second or third in the league during October and yet, even though it was early days, I think we all knew – from what we'd seen and the quality we had in that side – that we could do it. We were gambling a quarter of our salary on getting the club back into the Premiership.

If we were promoted, we'd get that money back.

If we weren't, it was all gone.

Game. On.

And then I came in two, maybe three days later and there was another announcement. The club was in administration. So much for the wage-deferral idea preventing that.

I didn't know much about the financial side of the club. I knew that by going into administration, the club would take a hit to its image and a dent to its integrity – but it would also wipe out its debts. By that time, it seemed a fair swap. But then you got to hear of other things, and you started to see the ripples that administration caused both inside the club and around the city.

Administration meant that other people, good people who had done nothing wrong, wouldn't be paid what they were owed; people who were affected by the reckless way the club had been run would lose out.

It didn't seem very fair. Staff who had been at Leicester City a long time lost their jobs. Fans who had invested in the club when it was floated on the stock exchange lost hundreds, some-times thousands, of pounds.

People who did other jobs at other companies who had

done business with Leicester City got their fingers burned. I remember reading about a local printing firm who had done some work for City and were awaiting payment. They never got it. They went under.

People there lost their jobs, printers who perhaps came to see us play. City fans themselves were made redundant and forced to sign on – not because of anything they'd done wrong, but because of things Leicester had done wrong. I tried not to think about it because when I did, I felt sick. It was an awful time.

Dilly, the old girl who did our laundry, lost her job. She only came in a few hours a week. I don't know how much the administrators saved by making her redundant but it couldn't have been much. It seemed ridiculous. Dilly had been there for years. She was there, I remember someone telling me, the year I was born. She'd worked under 14 managers at Leicester City. We had a whip-round and got Dilly her job back.

It was a worrying time; worrying for everyone. The administrators ran the club. We heard various stories and read reports in newspapers but we didn't know what to believe. We didn't know what was going on behind the scenes, how grim it really was. Someone I knew high up in the business side told me we were hours from going bust; that there nearly wasn't a Leicester City. Imagine that. A club with a proud 120-year-old history – wiped out because of a year, two years' mismanagement.

However, there was an unexpected by-product of this financial uncertainty – and that was the camaraderie it created within the squad. There was a new kind of siege mentality at the club, a real *'us versus the world'* feeling that made us closer and kept us together. Micky noticed this and he played on it.

He used it in his speeches to us and in his interviews to the local press. 'Keep the Faith', Micky kept saying . *'Keep the Faith'*. He said it so often, it became his catchphrase. The club started playing Bon Jovi's *Keep The Faith* on matchdays. Little flags were printed, all saying 'Keep the Faith.' For the next few months – this season and the next – it was everywhere. *Keep the Faith*. They said it so often it began to lose its meaning.

I was still on the transfer list at Leicester City. But I didn't know why. I was, if you will, *Keeping the Faith*. I was enjoying my football again, almost as much as I was in the halcyon days of Martin O'Neill.

There were many reasons for that, but mainly because we were winning – and because we were winning, the fun was back. I was enjoying myself. With my 25 per cent pay deferral, I'd effectively made an investment in the side and in our future. I went to see Micky Adams.

"This is stupid," I said. "I don't want to be on the transfer list. I want to stay." He shook me by the hand and said he would be pleased to take me off the list.

By then, Leicester had one eye on the following season, a return to the Premiership. The news made the back page of the *Mercury* the following day.

"It's great to come off the transfer list after all this time," I was reported to have said. "I'm enjoying my football at the moment and I went to see Micky Adams first thing this morning to ask him to remove my name from the list.

"Although I've been on the transfer list for some time, I think everyone recognises I've continued to give 100 per cent to the cause. My decision allows me to concentrate fully on the important games ahead of us." Which it did.

I also had two years left on my contract. I'd been offered more elsewhere but, frankly, I was happy with the contract I had. We were playing well. We all thought we were nailed on for promotion. It hadn't been a difficult season. It was an easy league. We were playing for promotion and playing for our deferred wages.

The training ground was a good place to be again. There was a desire, a hunger, a real good vibe about the place again. I didn't want to leave that. I wanted to stay.

In November, we went away to Grimsby's Blundell Park. It was a grey, miserable, Saturday afternoon. We were second in the league. The game started slowly. I couldn't get into it. I'd been playing well, but I struggled that day. I don't know why.

It happens sometimes. You can have an early bad first touch, try something, perhaps, something that doesn't quite come off, make a few wayward passes and it messes with your mind. It affects you. It shouldn't. You should be better than that, as a professional footballer. But we're only human.

It was a scrappy game. Jamie Scowcroft scored early for us. Big Frank was sent off at the start of the second half, and almost immediately, John Oster equalised for Grimsby. Then it happened. If I could line up all the drinks that I have been bought for me by grateful, smiling Leicester City fans for what happened next, they would stretch from here to Canning Town.

Andy Impey – who came on to bolster the defence when Frank was red-carded – went on a run down the right. Their left-back lunged at him with a dreadful tackle which Imps managed to climb over. He looked up and crossed the ball into the box.

I'm sure Imps will tell you differently, but it wasn't a great cross. I was on the edge of the area, running in, and it came in behind me. I checked my run. I was facing away from goal.

I could let it float past me – or I could launch into an optimistic overhead kick. I did it without really thinking, instinctively. Somehow, I connected with it just right.

You can't aim for a corner or know where it's going to go with an overhead kick. You just hope you keep it low – they have a tendency to go sky high – and it's on target. I knew I'd timed my jump right and I'd hit it sweetly. It felt right. I knew that. But that was all.

By the time I landed on the turf, the cheers were ringing in my ears. So I knew I'd scored. My overhead kick flew past the outstretched hand of the Grimsby goalkeeper and into the top-right corner. It was a good goal.

I ran towards our fans behind that goal and celebrated.

"Now you see why that fucker is on 30 grand a week," Billy McKinlay told one of their defenders in the celebrations.

The *Leicester Mercury* occasionally run a *'What's the best Leicester City goal ever scored?'* poll – and it usually comes out on top. If I'm out in Leicester, people generally ask me three things:

What was Martin O'Neill really like?

What am I doing now?

And they want to know about that goal.

There were 7,310 people at Blundell Park that afternoon. Of those, maybe 1,000, maybe 1,500, were City fans. I must have met every one. You know what? It wasn't my best, either. I scored a better one than that (see my top 10 list).

We lost the odd game that winter but we didn't lose many. On December 14, Mark McGhee brought his Millwall team – featuring Steve Claridge and Dennis Wise – to the Walkers Stadium. Before the kick-off, the club's ambassador, Alan Birchenall, made an announcement on the pitch: Leicester City had come out of administration. There were nearly 32,000 in the ground that day. We heard the cheers, the relief, flood down the tunnel and in to the changing room. And even though Claridge opened the scoring in the first minute, there was only going to be one winner that afternoon. We beat Millwall 4-1. It was 11 days before Christmas. We were second in the league. The club would not be going under. Good times were here again at Leicester.

A couple of months later, we beat a mediocre Walsall team 4-1 at The Bescot Stadium, which left nine days until our next game – against leaders, Portsmouth. Micky took us away to Portugal for a midweek break.

It was like the good old days, under Martin. We started drinking in the departure lounge and we drank, constantly, for the next three days. We went for a light run in the morning, ate together at lunch – and then we'd start drinking. We'd start in the afternoon and we'd drink all day.

We drank in Figo's bar in Albufeira and although I remember very little of those three days, because we drank so much, I remember Micky taking me aside for a chat.

"Muz, I'm a bit worried – I think the lads are overdoing it. They're drinking too much," he said.

I put my arm around his neck and shook my head.

"Trust me, boss," I lied. "It probably looks worse than it is. They're going steady. No-one's going mad. This is just what we need – a bit of sun, some bonding, plenty of laughs.

"Trust me," I said again, patting him on the leg. "We won't lose against Portsmouth. Mark my words."

Micky ruffled my hair, grinned and went to bed. And we carried on drinking until the early hours.

There were some boozers in that team. There were the remnants of O'Neill's side – me, Matty, Taggs, Impey, Frank Sinclair; but then we had Ian Walker, Dickov, The Option. They didn't just drink – a few of them liked a fag, too. Matty smoked. Taggs and Dickov had the odd fag. Ian Walker smoked. Frank Sinclair smoked, but he was a case apart. Big Frank could do what he liked – and he usually did – but he was still an athlete.

Portsmouth was a night game. A freezing cold February midweek game. 'Arry Redknapp had a good team, but they were knocking on a bit. We didn't feel daunted by them. We were fitter, we thought, than they were.

By the end of that first half, we were blowing out of our arses. I was knackered. I remember coughing up at the side of the pitch, in the first half, my hands on my knees. It was awful. My mind flashed back to a drunken night in Portugal a week earlier.

"Don't you worry – we won't lose against Portsmouth."

We drew 1-1.

You could argue that those four days on the piss in Portugal had blunted our edge for that game. You might be right. I don't know. But we went the next 11 games unbeaten.

We beat Brighton 2-0 on April 19 and promotion back to the Premier League was secured. I scored that day, which was pretty much my final contribution to the season. I also gashed my knee in that game.

There was a problem with the pitch at the Walkers Stadium in the first year. It was, literally, awash with sewage. There was so much of it on the surface that some Saturdays, you'd run out at five to three and the crowd would be cheering, the old boy would be playing the *Post Horn Gallop* and you'd get to the centre circle, breathe in and it would sting your nostrils.

Sewage. Shit. I don't know what they used as fertiliser that year but it smelled ripe.

If any of the players had any open-wound injuries, they were cleaned up meticulously by the doctors to prevent infection. I got a cut in that Brighton game. The doc cleaned my wound.

"You should be all right there, Muz," he said.

I wasn't. The wound looked clean but that night, it started to swell up. The next day it was throbbing. It was hard to walk on it. I called the doctor and he came to my home on Sunday. He looked concerned.

"It's not good," he said. "I think you've got an infection there." Another one. There had been a few that season.

Sure enough, all the muck and fertiliser from the pitch had infected my leg. They took me to the local Nuffield hospital. I stayed there, on a drip, for three nights. I didn't play again that season. I didn't just miss the rest of the season, I missed Steve Claridge's testimonial game, too. I'd been invited to play and wanted to turn out for Steve at Fratton Park. I couldn't make it. I told someone at the club to let him know. The message never got through to him.

It caused a bit of bad feeling for a while – I think Steve was a bit pissed off with me – and I could understand that. I couldn't play, but I should have called him myself. I owed him that. I managed to explain that to him a few years later and we shook hands and he was okay. It was my mistake.

The final standings in the Division One table that year were Portsmouth, champions with 98 points; Leicester City, runners-up on 92 points and Sheffield United, who were promoted with us after winning the play-offs.

Leicester City Council organised an open-top bus tour of

the city. It would be fair to say we didn't really want to do it. "Whose fucking idea was this?" I remember Gerry Taggart saying, more than once, when we were on the bus, waving at the fans. We hadn't won anything. We'd come second. We were promoted, sure, and that was something to celebrate and be proud of – but a parade seemed a bit over the top.

We went out the night before, the whole squad and got battered. We were supposed to meet at 3pm the next day at the training ground. The bus would leave Belvoir Drive – two, three miles from the city centre – limp around a pre-ordained city centre route and then we'd get back.

It was a disaster. The players rolled in late, with hangovers, reeking of beer. There was a delay near the train station. I remember sitting on the top deck, grey clouds gathering, the rain starting. A woman in a high-rise block of flats waved madly at us and then hitched up her top to show us her flabby, white tits and there was Paul Dickov, waving, smiling, while all the time looking like he was about to throw up.

Still, the fans came out and waved and we waved back. "Good luck for next season," they shouted, and they stuck their thumbs up and we waved and smiled and stuck our thumbs up back.

And do you know what?

We all thought – fans and players alike – that we would be all right next season.

BACK IN THE PREMIER

"I don't like hope very much. In fact, I hate it. It hooks you fast and kills you hard. It's bad news. The worst. It's sharp sticks and cherry bombs. When hope shows up, it's only a matter of time until someone gets hurt."

Author Jennifer Donnelly

Finally, when the celebrations had died down, the open-top bus tour had ended and the promotion specials had been read and binned, Leicester City prepared to take their position in England's top flight.

The promotion was Micky Adams' third as manager (he'd previously been victorious with Fulham and Brighton) and he was rewarded with an improved, new three-year-contract.

Adams, an honest, hard-working manager, popular with players and fans despite his occasionally bemusing fondness for referring to himself in interviews in the third person – "Micky Adams doesn't get too carried away when we win and he doesn't get too despondent when we lose" – was bullish.

"We're in the Premiership, I feel terrific about myself, I feel terrific about my club and I'm confident," he told When Saturday Comes fanzine in the close season.

WSC took him to task.

This City team doesn't look that different to the one that was relegated two seasons ago. You need some new players don't you?

"Yeah," admitted Adams.

"I don't want to be disappointed next season because we've gone up and haven't competed. There has to be a significant investment in the staff and players."

He didn't want young, untried players. He wanted proven Premiership players but still hungry professionals, with time on their side. And they had to be good value.

Micky's best-laid plans were just that, it turned out. A dozen new players arrived at the Walkers Stadium in the 2003/04 close season. In total, they cost £370,000 (£120,000 for Derby's Lee Morris and £250,000 for Peter Canero from Kilmarnock).

The other 10 came on free transfers.

Unsurprisingly, perhaps, it wasn't enough.

City won six games that season, losing 17 and drawing 15.

Team captain Muzzy Izzet lost count of the number of games where his side took an early lead and then pissed it away.

It was to be the club's undoing. Leicester City finished 18th, relegated with 33 points. It was the start of a decade out of the top flight.

It was the final year of Muzzy Izzet's lucrative four-year-contract.

He didn't want to go. And however much staff and fans at the club

221

wanted him to stay, the club's creative lynchpin, the man who made the most assists in the Premier League that season – playing for a team that were relegated, too – it was obvious. He was on his way.

Where?

He didn't know.

Not yet.

Former team-mate Robbie Savage had been ringing him most of that season, urging him to come down the M6 and join up with him at Birmingham City. "It's good here," he said. "You'll like it."

But there were other clubs sniffing around, too.

As the campaign limped to a close, Izzet told his agent, Jonathan Barnett, that he didn't want to talk about transfers until the end of the season. And that's how they worked it.

Picture the scene. It's 3.50pm, Saturday, October 25, 2003. The away changing rooms at Molineux, Waterloo Road, Wolverhampton, WV1 4QR.

Eleven men in blue and white walk through the tunnel to greet their triumphant manager who is standing by the door of the away dressing rooms, smiling, trying not to look too chuffed, but failing. He can't hide it – neither can the players. They are smiling, too. Beaming, in fact. Everyone is beaming. *Magniff.* It is a good place to be.

Leicester City are away at Wolves – and 3-0 up, away from home, a local East/West Midlands derby in front of 29,000 fans and the talk is: How many can we get? Can we get five? Seven? Ten maybe? Ha, ha, ha. What a laugh. What a game. What a fucking hoot.

And why not? Wolves are woeful. The first 45 minutes are the worst I've seen from any team in the Premiership, ever, I think. They were that bad. Everything we did in that first half came off. They did nothing. Maybe we didn't allow them to do anything but, frankly, I'm not sure if that's right.

Three months and 10 games into the season, we had won just once – 4-0, a night game in front of the Sky cameras against a Leeds United side that were relegated that season, a Lilian Nalis 35-yarder that people still talk about today.

We hadn't been playing badly. We'd been unlucky. Losing by an odd goal here and there, drawing against sides we should have seen off. As 2003 turned to 2004 and points went begging every week, it became the story of our season.

The Wolves game came on the back of four straight league defeats – to Liverpool, Man United, Fulham and Spurs – and we were determined to stop the rot. We could do that. We could do that against Wolves.

That first 45 minutes, moving the ball quickly from defence to attack, pressing, pressing, harrying, pressing, busy, creative, quick feet, quick passes, clinical in front of goal, strong from set pieces – everything we worked at in training, it all paid off. It finally paid off.

Big Les Ferdinand, 17 England caps and by then 37 years of age but still quality, still deadly, still a good player, scored twice. Ricky Scimeca bagged the other. 3-0.

Game over.

Check us out.

We're back.

So there we sat in the dressing room, re-living this pass and that goal, barely listening to the gaffer Micky Adams, who is urging caution, stressing that we need to keep it tight in the first 10-15 minutes, not give anything away, not do anything stupid, and it struck me – and it must have struck a few others – that

Wolves could not possibly be as bad in the second half as they were in the first.

Micky continued to urge caution.

Be careful. Concentrate. Don't do anything daft.

It was all perfectly reasonable advice. None of it went in.

Micky didn't know what else to say. He was not accustomed to this; his team, his rampant team, three-up at half-time, laughing in the changing room, delighted with the way we had played. Our season hadn't been like that.

That game, the half-time team talk, the aftermath, has stayed with me more than any other during my time at Leicester. I don't blame Micky for our defeat. We threw it away. It was our fault. I wonder, sometimes, though, if he might have been a bit cuter there; perhaps if he'd have done something unexpected, created some kind of diversion, something which would have punctured our egos, it might have kept our feet on the floor.

Maybe he should have picked a player and torn a strip off him. It didn't matter who it was or what it was for. He needed to do something that would stop our premature jubilation and make us sit up and think: *Hang on, what the fuck was that about?*

If he'd have been really cute he could have taken me to one side before and said: 'Look, Muz, this is what I'm going to do – I'm going to bollock you at half-time, just to keep the lads on their toes. It's nothing personal, okay?' and I'd have nodded and that would have been fine. Instead, we didn't listen to Micky as he urged us to be cautious.

We ran out for the second half. And they ran out. They looked pissed off. They were shouting at each other. Pumped fists. Determination etched on their faces. And sure enough, they came out like a different team.

1-3.

Then 2-3.

And then the panic started to creep in.

'They can't do this, surely? We can't piss this away. Can we?'

Substitutions. Leicester City substitutions. Three of them. Strikers off. Midfielders on. Subconsciously, a message is picked up by the team. The boss is worried. We're hanging on.

3-3.

Shit.

Five minutes left and I could smell it. I could smell the looming disaster in the air. Defeat. Ignominy. Humiliation. And fear. I looked at my colleagues. They could smell it, too. They were choking on it.

"COME ON," I shouted. "COME ON. DON'T FUCKING DO THIS." But they couldn't hear me. They couldn't hear me for the crowd and an overwhelming, sickening sense that we were about to screw it up.

It was too late. I knew it was too late.

We were 11 dead men walking. Mortified. Riddled with doubt and fear. We could no longer string a pass together. The crowd sensed it. The Wolves fans, who'd been virtually mute in the first half, found their voice. The noise was deafening. It became the wind in the players' sails.

Wolves boss David Jones stood on the touchline, wafting his players forward. "Go on," he kept saying. "Go on," like he was urging on a boxer, a boxer who was nearly home, a round from the end. A horse in the National in the final furlong. And on they went, again and again, attack after attack. Relentless.

The 86th minute: 4-3. The record books tell me it was Henri Camara, their Senegalese forward. I can't remember the goal.

I just remember the feeling, the embarrassment. The last five minutes limped by. I looked at Peter Walton, the referee.

Just blow, ref. Just fucking blow.

Finally, he put the whistle to his lips.

Full time.

The final whistle.

Pandemonium. A celebration in gold and black. In a far corner of the ground, the blue corner, 3,000 travelling City fans sat in stunned silence.

It was the worst I have felt after a football game. Worse than losing at Wembley. Worse than being knocked out of a cup competition in the semi-final.

Saturday afternoon, October 25, 2003, 4.55pm, Molineux Stadium, Waterloo Road, Wolverhampton, WV1. Wolverhampton Wanderers 4, Leicester City 3.

Empty. Destroyed. Mugged. Mugs.

We trudged off in silence. There were mistakes, players who could have done better. No-one said anything. There was no point. They knew. They felt it.

I knew what was coming next, too. I was dreading it. Micky will be furious, I thought to myself as I walked off. We all knew it. And what was worse, he had every right to be furious because we had just thrown away a 3-0 lead.

We entered the tunnel, one by one, in silence, listening to the cheers and laughter and hearty back-slapping of the Wolves players. It was gut-wrenching. I was about to enter the dressing room when a man tapped me on my shoulder. He stopped me and Jamie Scowcroft. "Drugs test, lads. Sorry about this. We'll be as quick as possible," he said.

Usually, this is the last thing you want after a game. This time I remember feeling relieved.

Thank fuck for that.

He ushered us towards a small room. I remember sitting there, a plastic cup in my hand, looking at Scowy. He looked broken. Next door was our dressing room. All I could hear was shouting. A man bellowing. I didn't know who it was, his voice wasn't clear, but I could guess. He was incandescent with rage.

Scowcroft filled his plastic cup with piss and turned to leave.

"Not yet, son," I said. "Let's not go back yet."

A penny drops. Scowcroft nodded and returned to his seat.

And we sat there, in silence, me and Scowy, his cup full of piss, me holding mine, saying nothing, looking straight ahead, the sound of a man at the very end of his tether leaking in from next door. And still we sat, the man doing the drugs test standing by the door, wondering why it was taking so long.

"I think I'm dehydrated," I told him.

It was a feeble lie. The bollocking carried on.

Finally, it limped to a close. We headed for the door. The dressing room looked like a morgue.

If you're looking for one match to summarise that season, there it is, right there. Three-nil up. Lost 4-3. They say 'Foxes Never Quit'. It's the occasionally over-used motto at Leicester City. They did that day, and that season. We lost our resolve.

The summer before the season started was a good one for me on a personal level. I got married. Me and Carly, we'd been together since I was 15. She was my first girlfriend. Her cousin was in my class. She was from Canning Town. I was from Canning Town.

We went ten-pin bowling on our first date; me and Carly, my mate Ben Ferris and Kereen, one of Carly's friends. I remember Ben slipped me a token from the *Newham Recorder* newspaper, which gave me £3 off the admission price. "Here you go, Muz," he said. He had one, too. "Nice one, Ben," I said, tucking it into my wallet so Carly wouldn't see it.

I was shy and awkward. She was shy and quiet. I didn't know what I was going to say or talk about. But we just clicked. We got on. I liked her and we started going out. I can't make it sound romantic because it wasn't and I'm not in the slightest bit romantic. We went out and then we'd fall out. We'd perhaps arrange for me to come round at 5pm on Friday night and I'd forget and go out with my mates instead. Things like that happened a few times. They still do now. It infuriated Carly.

Then, when I moved up to Leicester and bought Spider Kalac's old house in Markfield, she came to live with me. That's when things changed and became more serious.

I was on holiday in Tenerife at the end of one season. I was living with Carly but we used to have time away with our mates, both of us. I remember sitting there one night, a bit drunk, missing home, missing her and I was thinking: 'What am I doing here without her?'

So I rang her. "When I get back," I slurred down the phone, "I'm going to marry you."

"All right, love" she said. "I'll see you when you get back."

But we did. We got married.

After a four-day stag party in Las Vegas – you don't need me to spell out the details, suffice to say I sat in my seat for the 11-hour journey home grey, broken, suffocated by this cloud that rained hangover and regret all over me, swearing I was

never going to drink again – we got married on June 7, 2003 at
The Queen's House, Greenwich, South East London.

I'm not very good at describing what our relationship is like. It
started slowly, kids' stuff really, but it grew from that into something. I couldn't imagine ever being without her. She's not just
my wife. She's everything. She keeps us all going. She's brilliant.

A newly-married man, I was happy. In that pre-season, after
that stag weekend and wedding, I needed to get back into shape.
Micky ran us and ran us. He ran us like dogs. We were a tight
unit under Micky Adams. A team again. Good lads. Close. We
looked out for one another. It wasn't quite what it had been
under Martin O'Neill – that would have been virtually impossible – but it was good.

Micky's task – and it's not easy, you see newly-promoted
Championship managers get this wrong every season, year
after year – was to make the squad stronger, without sapping
it of its spirit. It's a tricky thing to get right. Peter Taylor got it
wrong on both counts. He didn't buy quality and the tight unit
we were under Martin O'Neill evaporated. It killed us dead.

Micky had virtually no budget. The club had been in administration the season before. Prudence was the new watch-word.
But Micky acquired a dozen proven Premiership players who
would fit into the side, on and off the field. Fitting in off the field
is just as important as fitting in on it. Players like:

Ben Thatcher – Good lad, great left-back, hard as a rock, old-
fashioned footballer.

Ricky Scimeca – Quiet, nice chap, always gave his best.

Les Ferdinand – Les was 37, at the end of his career, but he
was still quality. Les was afforded special treatment by Micky
and Corky, which sometimes annoyed some of the already well-

established senior players at the club, but Les did the business. Decent bloke, too. Everyone liked Les.

Keith Gillespie – Mad as a march hare, properly loopy. His gambling was crazy, he really was that guy who would bet on two flies on the window. We knew he was in some financial difficulty because he'd talk about it as if it was nothing. But he couldn't stop betting. He was a lovely bloke, though and, on his day, still a great player.

Lilian Nalis – There's always a risk when you sign a foreign player. How will they adapt to life here? How will they fit into the club? There were no worries with Nalis. He spoke perfect English. He moved to Leicester, embraced the city, the club, the culture and slotted straight in.

Nicolas Priet – A fringe player. A centre-half. I think he was French too, wasn't he?

Craig Hignett – Higgy was hilarious and although he was perhaps reaching the end of his career, he was still a decent player, I thought. He was a big personality, too. The lads liked him. You need a few players like that in your team.

Peter Canero – Another fringe player, really. I can picture him. Dark-haired. Nice bloke. He didn't play much.

Steffen Freund – I hated playing against him when he was at Spurs. He was obnoxious, forever in your face, he never stopped working and if you were having an indifferent game, he'd delight in telling you. I feared the worst when he signed. I wasn't looking forward to playing with him. But he was all right. I liked him. He was surprisingly funny and self-deprecating.

Nikos Dabizas – On a free. At the end of that season, Nikos won the European Championship with Greece. He struggled with concentration at times but he was a decent centre-half.

Steve Guppy – Gupps came back from Celtic for a brief reprise of his City career. A diamond bloke.

Steve Howey and Marcus Bent – Both were established Premier League players. Howey was a top lad. I wasn't as close to Marcus.

Lee Morris – I think Lee spent more time on the treatment table than he did on the pitch.

On this shoe-string budget, Micky did well. The mood around the training ground was positive. We would compete. We might surprise a few people.

I was captain that season. I loved being the skipper. It came with more responsibility, pressing the flesh with the sponsors before kick-off, smiling for the camera, writing a column for the programme – which I did with the club's press officer – and a weekly column in the *Sporting Blue*, which I did with former *Leicester Mercury* journalist, Ken Widdows.

I had very little to do with journalists, really. I did the odd piece, here and there. And I didn't mind that. But I didn't want it every week. It wasn't me. I got to know a few of them, and some of them were all right, but I soon learned which ones were all right and which ones were always sniffing for a story.

Ken was one of the good guys. I liked Ken. He was an old school journalist and I'm sure I'm not betraying any confidences here when I say that Ken liked a drink. That was all right by me. So did I.

Ken had a sound knowledge of the game that went back years and a genuine love of football, the players, the clubs, the history. He would ring me every week and we'd decide what the column should be that week. He'd usually choose a topic – something that happened in the last game, a talking point, or a big game that was coming up and we'd just have a chat, me and Ken, like two old mates down the pub – and every week, without fail, Ken would turn it into something good.

I looked forward to Ken's calls, the same time every week, usually on a Wednesday night. He got to know my missus a bit. I got to know a bit more about him. He became more of a mate than a journalist I'd speak to every week to do my column. There were some nights when I knew Ken had, shall we say, enjoyed a drink, nights when he was refreshed.

"Yeah, I've been out Muz," he'd say, as if I couldn't tell and we'd chat and he'd laugh more than he would usually and it would all take twice as long – but then he'd ping me something over the next day and, somehow, I don't know how, he'd nail it. I never knew how he managed to do this. But he did.

Ken's columns were always better than the ones in the programme: more honest, straight-forward, better written. And then one Thursday he rang me in a panic.

"Muzzy, we haven't done your column, I was thinking…" and off he went on one. But we had done it. We'd done it the night before. He'd had a drink and he'd forgotten. I needn't have worried. Later that night – *ping* – he sent it over. He'd found the notes he'd forgotten he'd taken and knocked it into shape. Another column. Spot on. Good old Ken.

He retired a few years ago. I went to his leaving do. I bought him a drink and thanked him for always making me sound better than I was. Ken died in 2014. RIP, my old mate.

On the pitch, the bad run continued. Thirteen without a win from December to March. Then, a rare win, at Birmingham, before another eight without a victory.

And this feeling of anxiety – consciously and sub-consciously – started to creep in. The confidence of last season was replaced with fear. This is what happens when you lose. You lose more than points. You lose what you are, you lose your essence. Although Micky and Corky tried desperately to be positive, focused and upbeat, inadvertently, they fed our anxiety.

It happened like this: if a player was out injured and was 95 per cent fit and ready to come back for the next match but that next match was, say, Liverpool away, then Micky would put his arm round your shoulder and say: "Let's be careful, eh? Wait a week. See how you are in training. Let's aim for the next game…" because the next was Bolton at home, for example.

The unspoken subtext was simple: there's no point rushing you back for Liverpool away, a big game which we probably won't win. But 'COME ON – WE CAN BEAT BOLTON AT HOME, CAN'T WE, EH?' and then the stakes, the expectation, the pressure on that Bolton match would be subtly ratcheted up. It was an anxiety that fed into the whole squad.

There were all kinds of post-mortems and half-baked theories as to why we weren't performing. Were we fit enough? If we kept throwing leads away, were we lacking in stamina at the end of games? Lots of people, including Micky, seemed to think this was the case. So he ran us more, day after day in training.

Training would start with a run, we'd train and then we'd finish with a run. I did more running than Seb Coe that year. Did it help? We still went down. Make of that what you will. As the losing streaks grew longer, so did the running. We ran and ran, day after day. I think it was a bit more subtle than that.

We never had a settled side that year. Steve Howey, Taggs, Matty Elliott, Nikos Dabizas, Matt Heath and Frank Sinclair all played centre-half that season. We had an abundance of midfield players – me, Nalis, Scimeca, Impey, McKinlay, Guppy, Gillespie, Jordan Stewart, Steffen Freund – and, crucially, we weren't clinical enough.

We could be 1-0 up in a game, get a chance to make it 2-0 – and we'd miss. You couldn't miss at that level. Because if you missed, the other team wouldn't. That's the difference with the Premier League. It's an unforgiving place to play. That happened week after week. We were missing that bit of extra quality – not just up front, but all over the pitch, really. We felt the pressure and we lost our confidence. We lost our swagger.

Arsenal won the league that year. They didn't lose a game. We played them on the last day of the season. We were already relegated. We went 1-0 up, Paul Dickov in the first half. In the second half, they scored twice. We lost 2-1. Typical. We were relegated on 33 points. Played 38, won 6, drew 15, lost 17. Spurs ended up losing more games than us that season. They finished 14th. Other teams – Blackburn, Portsmouth, Everton – lost the same amount of games. They stayed up.

We took the lead in 12 games that season and either drew or lost. We worked it out one day – 28 points, squandered. That wasn't merely enough to save us from relegation – it was enough to finish fourth, one point ahead of Liverpool.

It's unrealistic, perhaps, to think we could've held on to every lead in 12 games – but 28 dropped points? I didn't expect us to finish a point ahead of Liverpool. But I thought we would compete.

Tactically, we were a bit naive for the Premiership, too. We played a brand of very direct football. It's what Micky and Corky have always done. It worked in the Championship. It's

234

served Micky well at most of the clubs where he has been. It served other teams well, too. We were hardly the only ones playing like that. But when teams turned on the style against us, we had no reply.

We went out, we still went out together and we drank. But we didn't go out as often because we didn't win as often. You can't go out, drinking, in a city full of football fans which you've let down, if you'd thrown away a match you should have won.

We'd have a drink midweek. We'd always done that. Martin never seemed to mind about that. And Micky didn't, at first, when we were winning and getting promoted. In the Premiership, and when we were losing, this became his thing. He would smell our breath at training.

One day, he brought a breathalyser in to the training ground. It all became a bit paranoid.

Then there was La Manga, Part 2...

15

LA MANGA – PART 2

These days, the players of Leicester City don't seem to head off for club sponsored four-day breaks in the Mediterranean. A chance to train with the sun on their backs, run on the beach, relax by the pool and *whisper it* perhaps even partake in a few beers in the evening. Or afternoon, even, leading into the evening. Sunshine trips in mid-season seem like a relic of another footballing age.

If Leicester City did decide to start this again, it's unlikely that they would be heading back to La Manga.

The club have a lifetime ban at the popular sports complex resort in Murcia, Spain: once because of the Stan Collymore fire extinguisher incident (we've covered that) and then again, just four years later, for what happened on a mysterious night starring a clutch of drunken Premiership footballers, some German models with a taste for the limelight all set against a backdrop of this Spanish sports complex.

I saw them as the coach pulled into the resort; two women by the entrance. Short skirts and high heels. Expensive handbags. Too much make-up. And that look. I didn't know what the look meant, exactly, only that it spelled trouble. I could see it. A few of the older lads recognised it, too.

"I'm sure we've all seen the young ladies by the entrance," manager Micky Adams said before we left the coach.

"I don't need to tell you what kind of women they are. I don't want to see or hear about any of you going within 100 yards of those women. Do you hear me?" No response.

Frankly, I thought they looked like a dog's dinner. Ropey old prostitutes, I thought. Some of the lads, though, well, you could put a short skirt and some high heels on a horse and they'd have been salivating and brushing up their lines. Micky knew. He could smell the trouble, too.

"Do you hear me?" he said, again. "They're bad news."

"Yes boss," came the half-hearted reply.

And that was it. I thought no more of it.

It was evening time when we arrived, dusk, getting dark. We booked into the hotel. I didn't see those girls again until two days later, when they – and us – were on the front pages of every newspaper in England and Spain. Here we go again.

The most surprising thing about arriving wasn't the girls or that no-one was really listening to Micky. It was that, when we landed, no-one wanted to go out. It was 2004. We didn't drink like we used to in the good old days of Martin O'Neill but we still went out. There was a bit of character in the squad again, a few boys, a few lads who liked a laugh and a night out.

I was waiting for someone to suggest a bar, a few beers. No-one did. Maybe all the pre-trip warnings from Micky, Corky and the chief executive, Tim Davies, had taken their toll. Perhaps, the lads who remembered what happened last time decided it was best to have a quiet night. I don't know. But no-one offered.

We booked into the hotel. We were doubling up. I was sharing with Ben Thatcher, or 'Snatch' as everyone called him. He was a London boy, a rock-hard defender and a good lad. I used to sit with him sometimes and say: "Are you sorting yourself out, son? Are you looking after your money? This won't last forever you know…" and he'd roll his eyes and shake his head.

One day, after another bout of unwanted advice, he turned to me with that look, that weary *don't-keep-on-at-me* expression and said: "Look, Muz, I don't fucking care about any of that. I just want to be the best dressed player in the Premier League. That's where I'm investing my money. The gear. Good clobber."

Snatch had 25 Prada suits. He had more shoes than Imelda Marcos. He was immaculate. I roomed with him a few times. I've never known anyone take so many showers. He smelled like the perfume counter in Debenhams.

And he was tidy – obsessively so. Everything in its right place. I don't think I'm the messiest – I know this because I roomed with Lenny for many years, which means I'm qualified to comment – but Snatch made me feel like a vagrant.

We had a room right at the end of the corridor. We sat on the bed, watching *EastEnders* and ordering room service. Club sandwich and chips. It took ages to arrive. We ate that, watched a bit more telly, Snatch did a bit more cleaning, he probably had another shower, then we called it a night. In bed by 10pm, like two good boys. I didn't hear a thing.

We went down for breakfast, not all of us, just me, Snatch and a few others, and then out onto the training pitch. A few warm ups. A jog. The rest came out in dribs and drabs, looking rough, I remember, folding into the back of the pack, bleary-eyed and blowing as we trotted around the perimetre of the pitch.

I smelled it first. A familiar stench, the aftermath of a good night out. It was the signature fragrance at Belvoir Drive for most of my time at City. Stale beer in the morning. *Eau D'onedayoldStella.* Hangover cologne.

"Oh yeah – who's been out then?"

It wasn't much, they said. Just a couple. A couple of quiet ones before bed. No big deal. It didn't smell like that. It smelled like a session, but I wasn't fussed. They had a few beers. So what? I remember feeling a bit pissed off that I'd missed out. I didn't feel like that for long.

We finished training and kicked back at the hotel. There was a Chinese restaurant on site. We went there. A big table, maybe 17 of us, sitting down, ready for a feast. We ordered the drinks.

I'd taken the top off my beer when my mobile rang. It was Alan Cork. He didn't sound pleased. "You better get yourself back to the hotel now. All of you. With your passports."

"But we're just about to eat, Al," I said. "We've ordered. The food is coming." He wasn't interested.

"Get your passports and meet in the boardroom. Ten minutes."

"What's happened?"

"I haven't got time to tell you now," he said.

"Is it bad?"

"Yeah. It's bad. It's about as fucking bad as it can be, son."

We met in the La Manga boardroom, the players, Micky, Corky, the Spanish police. We all had our passports. I remember looking around and some of the lads looked a bit sheepish. I still had absolutely no idea what had happened. I had even less idea that, in 24 hours, we'd be home and gracing every front page of the country's tabloid newspapers. Again. The reputation of Leicester City Football Club in tatters. Again, and again in La Manga, just four years after the last one.

Micky ran through what he'd been told. A drinking session, in the hotel last night. Leicester City players. Three women. The drinking that had carried on in their room, and then it all going wrong. Sexual assault. The girls are claiming members of the Leicester City Football Club raped them. *Raped them.*

I remember gulping hard, looking around the room. Everyone was looking at their shoes.

"But they don't know who," Micky added. "They don't know who did it. So hand your passports to the police," he said. "They're going to pick them out."

I looked at Snatch. He shrugged. We were in bed by 10, 10.30pm. I looked around at some of the others. They were white. This was serious. It was utter bollocks – I knew it was bollocks from the off – but it was serious.

You have to put this in context. At the time, the nation was being fed a constant diet of drunken, sex-mad footballers, going out, getting drunk, having orgies and 'roasting' girls.

We weren't angels at Leicester City. We liked a drink. I've known a few players at Leicester who liked the company of women, shall we say.

But we weren't rapists.

Corky collected our passports. The boardroom was silent. The police officers took them to a room nearby, where the three women would pick out the Leicester City players who drank with them the previous evening and then, they claimed, raped them.

It struck me as odd that if these girls had been sexually assaulted by players of Leicester City in the La Manga hotel then it would have been insensitive, at best, for them to be in a room next door, in the same hotel where they had allegedly been raped the night before, so they could pick out the guilty men.

It just didn't seem right.

Of course, two of the three women were the ones we saw by the hotel entrance the evening before, all hair and make-up, hips and lips, bad news waiting to be written.

They picked out virtually our entire first team: Keith Gillespie, Paul Dickov, Frank Sinclair, Matt Elliott, Lilian Nalis, Jamie Scowcroft, Nikos Dabizas, Danny Coyne and Steffen Freund. Nine players.

Lilian Nalis wasn't out that night. He was tucked up in bed. But because he had long hair, slightly similar to Ian Walker – who was out – he was picked. Walker wasn't identified. I doubt if there was a man as relieved as our goalkeeper in all of Spain. They were taken away and locked up in the Sangonera prison in Murcia. They shared the same cell for the next nine days.

So what happened? I'm still not entirely sure. I was in my room, watching *EastEnders* with the cleanest and smartest-dressed footballer in the English Premier League.

This is what I know. They were in the bar, having a few drinks. It wasn't a big night. They were keeping themselves to themselves but they were being pestered, constantly, by these three women, desperate to get in, to ingratiate themselves with them.

One of them said something about how small Paul Dickov was and Dickov said something about how big her arse was. This didn't go down very well, and she lunged at him.

Meanwhile, another one was trying to persuade Frank Sinclair to dance, and she was rubbing herself up and down his leg, while her friend was taking pictures. They leaked these pictures, these victims of sexual harassment, to the press.

The night culminated, the women claimed, with drinks in their room; drinks which got out of hand and led to sexual assault. They gave their clothes and knickers to the Spanish police for DNA analysis

'It's another black day for English football,' said Spanish paper, *El Pais.*

'Brainless, moronic and worse than hooligans,' said *El Mundo.*

Back home, the *Daily Mail* was predictably working itself up into a froth of righteous indignation.

'The Spanish forces of law and order are having to do our dirty work for us,' the paper bemoaned. 'If only a message this stern had been sent out sooner, then the English game might never have sunk this low.'

Even as the papers were hitting the streets, the case against the Leicester City Nine was unravelling. Elliott, Nalis and Scowie were released on bail. Dabizas and Coyne were provisionally released a few days later. Freund was released without charge.

It all seemed a bit ridiculous. Day after day, the papers were full of the girls' claims. People were asking me the same question. "You were there, Muzzy – what really went on...?"

Nothing went on. It was a tissue of lies. I thought that much seemed obvious. But when arrests are made, charges follow and you've got three of your best players in prison, then suddenly, people see the headlines and they forget people are innocent until they are proven guilty. They say shit like *'there's no smoke without fire'*. I know. I've done it myself. We all have.

We came home and tried to concentrate on our football. It wasn't easy. Our next game was Birmingham City away, Saturday, March 13, 2004. I was already aware of Steve Bruce's interest in me. Sav was ringing me every other week, asking me to come to Birmingham. That week, it seemed especially difficult to concentrate on the football.

What happens, though, in situations like this, if you have a canny manager, good people who know how to make the best of a bad situation, is that you develop a siege mentality. It galvanises you. We had reporters and camera men at the gates of the training ground every day. Questions on the way in, more on the way out. Micky made the most of that. He knew the lads were innocent. He knew the treatment we were getting was over the top. He turned that to our advantage.

Still, we were missing Gillespie, Dickov, Scowcroft and Frank Sinclair for the away trip to Birmingham. But I can't remember a game we were more pumped up for that season. With an understrength side – Micky even picked Peter Canero for that game, if he played again after that I can't remember it – we beat Birmingham 1-0. I ran out that afternoon and I was just relieved to be playing football. I put Les Ferdinand through. Les might have been 37, but he still knew where the goal was. He was brilliant for us that season. 1-0. Game over.

Dickov, Gillespie and Sinclair were eventually released on bail. In the weeks that followed, the case against them started to crumble. A reporter from the *News of the World* tracked the girls down. One of them offered to sleep with him for £500. The story was published that Sunday with her denials that she wasn't a prostitute, just an opportunist. I think people could make up their own minds about that.

Under further police scrutiny, their stories started to fall apart. Forensic analysis of their clothes and underwear showed nothing. Three months later, all the charges were dropped. The damage had been done by then.

Paul Dickov, a married father-of-three, called it the worst two months of his life.

Later, Keith Gillespie won substantial damages from the *Daily Star* and the *News of the World* for stories they ran which intimated he may have been guilty of the charges.

Frank Sinclair called it the grimmest period of his long career. "It made me a stronger person," he said. "Yet I know there will be some people who don't remember me as a player – just that I was locked up in a Spanish jail, accused of sexually assaulting a woman I didn't know."

We had night outs in Leicester far messier than what happened in La Manga in March 2004. Far messier. We did all this before mobile phones, before mobile phones with cameras on. All it would have taken was a person with a bit of a grudge, one person with a camera phone – *'Just look at the state of Leicester City's midfielder or defender on this night out'* – and, there you are. You're page 17 of a Sunday tabloid.

Still, both of those La Manga incidents had nothing to do with me. I'd bailed, drunk, before Stan let off the fire extinguisher. And I was in bed, eating sandwiches and watching *EastEnders* with Snatch, the most meticulous man in football, the second time around.

And yet the club is banned from La Manga for life.

Do you want to know a secret?

It's no big deal. It's really not that good.

COME IN NUMBER 6

Colin Tattum is the chief sports writer of the *Birmingham Mail*. A man not known for giddy excitement, in the summer of 2004, Colin was excited. Everyone in the blue side of Birmingham was excited. Here, he remembers Muzzy Izzet joining Birmingham, the fever that gripped England's second city that pre-season – and a new career at a new club which promised so much but was thwarted by injury.

We don't go a bundle on pre-season optimism at Birmingham. We've learned the hard way, more than once, that the heady sense of hope and excitement you have in August is usually all gone by October.
  But in summer 2004, I was excited. All Blues fans were excited. For once, it looked like we were going somewhere. I was the Blues

reporter for the Birmingham Mail but I was also a fan. I'd been a fan since the '70s. It was the most exciting summer for nearly 30 years.

We'd been promoted the year before under Steve Bruce. After one season in the Premier League – saved by the inspirational signing of Christophe Dugarry – Birmingham finished mid-table.

That summer, and with the full financial backing of the board – the Gold brothers and Sunday Sport owner David Sullivan – manager Steve Bruce went out and bought. And he bought big: Jesper Gronkjaer from Chelsea for £2.2m; Emile Heskey from Liverpool for £6.23m; Mikael Forssell on another season-long loan from Chelsea; Julian Gray from Palace; Mario Melchiot on a free; Darren Anderton; Dwight Yorke; David Dunn had been signed for £5.5m the season before; and then Muzzy Izzet.

Chairman David Gold called it "the finest squad of players at Birmingham City for 25 years." Robbie Savage predicted Blues would be bigger than Villa. It was typical Savage bluff and bluster, and yet few people were arguing. We were all swept along on this irresistible tide of optimism and euphoria.

I'd seen Muzzy a few times when he was at Leicester. I rated him. I liked his work-rate, his vision and I knew he was quick to get forward and that he liked to go on the attack. I knew he scored goals.

I thought – we all thought – it would be good for him to link up again with Savage and Heskey. I'd spoken to Bruce. I knew how much he rated him, too.

There was a fair amount of expectation on the lad's shoulders but, although I didn't interview him often, he seemed nice, quiet, decent. It didn't look like he would be bothered by it.

He started the first eight games that season. Bruce played him and Sav in the middle of the park. Sav did the donkey work, leaving Muzzy the freedom to play, to join the attack and have a more creative role. It was tailor-made for him, really.

Birmingham started slowly that season. Defeats against Chelsea, Spurs and Middlesbrough. Draws against Portsmouth and Bolton. A win at home against Man City. The team were finding their feet.

And then there was that Newcastle game at home. I don't remember what happened. I just remember them stretchering the lad off – and that was that. We never saw the real Muzzy Izzet again.

He came back occasionally that season and in the season that followed. You could tell Bruce desperately wanted him in the side. But you could also tell he wasn't right. I'm sure he'll tell you that.

We had so many injury problems that season and the next and the camaraderie was unsettled, I think, by so many new faces. Bruce admitted, later, that he tried to change too many things too quickly. They were a great squad on paper. You don't win football games on paper, though. They just didn't gel. At the end of the 2005/06 season, Birmingham were relegated.

It's hard to say how Muzzy is remembered by Birmingham fans. It's a case of what could have been, I think, rather than what was. We didn't see enough of the lad, although I do remember an away game at Spurs, I think it was, and he was class. He ran the show.

A shame, really. A genuine shame.

I made my Birmingham City debut on Saturday August 14, 2004. I know this because the record books say so. I don't remember it. I scored my only goal a month later; a neat pass by Jesper Gronkjaer, me moving inside the area, picking the ball up, a shot, in off the underside of the bar. That's what the record books say. I thought it was a tap-in. I can't remember.

I played 26 games for Birmingham. When I sat down to do this chapter, I was sure it was around 10. I remember a handful of them. I remember a couple of decent ones. I remember a couple more terrible ones; games where I played so badly I felt embarrassed walking from the pitch. There were games where I felt I had short-changed the people who bought tickets and Steve Bruce, the man who had brought me across the Midlands to play for his team. I didn't like feeling like that. My time at Birmingham wasn't great. I don't look back on it particularly fondly and I don't remember it well.

What I do remember is Sunday afternoon, October 3, 2004. St Andrew's, 29,021 people – a sell-out against Newcastle United. The 34th minute. A corner to Newcastle.

I don't remember if the ball was swung out directly from the corner or if it had been cleared. I was on the edge of the box. The ball came to me, high and out wide. I sprung, off my left foot, to bring the ball down with my outstretched right foot. I took the ball on the toe of my right boot. Out of the corner of my eye, I could see a blur of black and white heading my way. Black and white, closer and closer. And then... bang!

I'd played against Olivier Bernard the season before, when Newcastle came to Leicester in the Premier League. What did I think of him? Not much, really. I played against good full-backs. He wasn't one of those.

Bernard arrived like a steam train. He didn't get the ball. He got my left leg, the one I had planted on the ground. Crack.

I heard it before I felt it. And before I hit the ground, the pain. The overwhelming pain. The rest of it is a blur.

Grass. Cold, wet grass.

White light. White noise.

My fingers trying to grip the turf. Failing.

Sweating. Nausea.

Tears.

Crying.

So much pain, wave after wave of pain, so much fucking pain I thought I might pass out. Referee Howard Webb stopped the game. The physio came on.

"How bad is it, Muz?' he said.

I shook my head. I couldn't speak. I couldn't get my breath. My knee. *My fucking knee.*

It's hard to explain excruciating pain. It's beyond feeling, it transcends a sensation. It didn't feel like Bernard had tackled me, but that he'd slipped behind me with a Bowie knife and slashed every tendon and ligament in my knee. There's footage of that tackle. The match was shown live on Sky that night. I've never seen it again. I don't want to.

I knew, immediately, in that second, that things would never be the same again. I looked at the physio. I could see he was worried. "It's bad, isn't it?" I asked. He wouldn't look at me.

Bernard was still buzzing around, trying to pull me up, like I might play on. "Fuck off," I told him and, thankfully, he did.

The physio laid me on my back and pulled my knee one way, and then the other. I dug my fingers into the turf and I grimaced and shouted, begging him to stop.

"It's all right," he said. "It's all right."

I remember thinking to myself that it didn't feel all right. It felt anything *but* all right. I looked down at my leg, my knee. It was already starting to balloon.

"It's not your cruciate ligament," the physio said. "It's not that bad. Come on, let me help you up."

So, in front of nearly 30,000 people – 30,000 people I was utterly unaware of – and the Monday night Sky cameras, I ignored everything my knee and my brain was telling me and I tried to stand up.

"Put your arm round my shoulder," he said, "and put your left foot down." I put a small amount of weight on my left foot. The pain exploded through my leg, through my foot to the top of my thigh. I winced again. "This is ridiculous," I said. "Look at me. I can't play on like this."

The physio called for the stretcher. Stephen Clemence, son of former England keeper, Ray, stripped and prepared himself. The board came up. Come in number 6, your time is up.

In the 36th minute, they carried me off, down the tunnel and into the changing rooms. They put ice on my knee to stop the swelling. It didn't work. My knee swelled like a hot air balloon.

I had a box at St Andrew's, right next to Emile's, one along from David Dunn's. My mate, Steve Plews, a solid, Leicester lad, was watching in the box. He drove me home.

"Wait 'til tomorrow," everyone kept telling me. "It will feel better in the morning." But it wasn't better tomorrow. Or the next day. Or the next week. It was never the same again.

My knee is destroyed. I have something called a Chondral Defect – it's irreparable cartilage damage within the knee, basically a hole, a small void, in the bone that doesn't grow back.

It's not a common condition, but it's the same ailment that forced Ledley King, Jamie Redknapp and Darren Eadie to retire. I was another; another footballer finished before he was ready. I was 29 when I ran out for that Birmingham game. If I'd looked after myself, I had another six or seven years left.

I still run today. I turn out, occasionally, for a Leicester Legends side, playing gentle games for good causes. I'm fit but I'm not fit enough, but I still have enough to get by in these games. And yet every time, the morning after a run, the day after a charity game, my knee is shot.

I wake up the next day and the walk from the bedroom to the bathroom is excruciating. I take industrial strength Voltarol. I took it at Leicester, to help my back and I took it at Birmingham, to help my knee. I've got a drawer full of it still, to this day. It's strong stuff. I'd take it before a game on Saturday and I'd play and come through okay – but then I'd have stomach cramps all day Sunday.

Serge Pizzorno of Kasabian rang me a few days before he played in that Soccer Aid game a few years ago. He was in pain, he said. He didn't think he could play. Did I know anyone or did I have anything that might help? I had just the thing.

He came round and I gave him some Voltarol. Not the over-the-counter stuff, but the real deal, the accept-no-substitutes real McCoy. It takes all the pain away – and the lining of your stomach the next day. That's what it should say on the packets.

He scored a blinder in that charity game – lobbing David Seaman from outside the box – but the next day he called me at home. "My guts are rumbling and I've got stomach cramp."

"Yeah," I said. "I did warn you, didn't I?"

It had started well at Birmingham, even if, in that final season at Leicester, I'd had no plans to join them.

After Leicester were relegated, we had a meeting. I was fairly clear what I wanted. I wanted to stay. I didn't want to move house. My family were settled.

I'd only move, I decided, if one of the top clubs – Manchester United, Arsenal, Liverpool, maybe Chelsea, maybe Spurs or West Ham – came in for me. If not, then I'd stay in Leicestershire and I'd play for a Midlands club. My agent Jonathan Barnett thought I was being short-sighted and he told me so.

I went on holiday and we agreed to speak when I came back. "It's down to two clubs," Jonathan told me once I'd returned. "Birmingham or Villa."

Was I disappointed? I suppose I was. I was 29. I'd played in a World Cup. I thought I'd proved myself at the highest level for eight years. Birmingham and Villa. That was the choice.

I knew which one I fancied – or rather, which one I didn't fancy – before I met the managers. David O'Leary was the Villa manager. He came to my house one lunchtime that summer with his assistant, Roy Aitken.

He was pleasant and charming and we sat in the back room drinking cold juice and going through some small talk – which I've never been very good at – and all the time, before he's offered me a bean or started with his spiel, I'm looking at him and thinking: 'You led me a right song and dance when you were at Leeds, you bastard.'

He talked about Villa. He couldn't afford to sign new players. He had to get them on free transfers. He offered me good money, I can't remember how much, and I nodded along and I couldn't stop myself.

"What happened at Leeds then, David?" I said. "You said you wanted to sign me." He looked embarrassed.

Yeah, that was "unfortunate," he said. He was sorry about that. It shouldn't have happened. But when those two Leeds fans were stabbed in Turkey, you had to understand the sentiment around Elland Road at that time, he said. It wasn't good. It wasn't nice.

"I couldn't bring you to Leeds after that," he said, and I may have nodded and said the right things but, inside, I was thinking: 'You should have had the decency to tell me that at the time.'

He was there for about an hour. We shook hands, me, him, Roy Aitken, and they left. I watched as his Mercedes turned out of my drive and away into the Leicestershire countryside and I knew I would not sign for him.

An hour later, Steve Bruce arrived.

He's a lovely fella, Steve. He was full of infectious enthusiasm, about the club, me, who he was going to sign, where he was taking the club, where I'd fit in. He told me he was signing Emile Heskey, Mario Melchiot, Jesper Gronkjaer. They already had Mikael Forssell, Matthew Upson, Savage, David Dunn. They had a good team. Birmingham had lived for too long in the shadow of their near neighbours, Villa, he said. He was going to change that.

He asked me how much I wanted.

I shrugged my shoulders. I didn't know. I told him how much I was on at Leicester. He looked surprised, but not for long.

"It shouldn't be a problem," he said. "We want you at our club. I'll sort that out."

My wife came in and he smiled and said hello, and said charming things to her. Carly had made some cakes. "Would you like a cake, Mr Bruce?" she asked. He shook his head. Not for me, he said, and he turned it down. I don't think he's turned down many cakes since that day.

We shook hands and I said I would think about it, and he said that was fine, but I knew. I knew I would join Birmingham. Sav rang me the next day. "You've got to come," he said. I told him I thought I would.

A few days later, I went to see Steve at his house in Birmingham; a huge old place with enormous gardens and a river that ran through his back garden. "It's not mine," he said. "I'm just renting it." We signed the deal there. Three years, with an option for a fourth: £35,000 a week, exactly the same as I was on at Leicester. I was 29. My plan was simple: go to Birmingham, embrace it, play for three or possibly four years if it was good – and then return to Leicester and finish my career there, if they wanted me. That was the plan anyway…

We went to Scandinavia on our pre-season tour. There was no drinking. No parties. The players kept themselves pretty much to themselves. The one thing I remember during that tour was suffering from really bad hay fever and not being able to sleep. I asked the coach for a sleeping tablet and an anti-histamine tablet before a game. He put the sleeping tablet in my right hand and the anti-histamine in my left. "Don't get them mixed up, will you?" "Yeah, yeah," I said. "I'm not a kid."

As we sat down for our pre-match meal I took the tablet. Before the end of the meal, I was asleep in my chair. Eric Black had to shake me awake.

"What's wrong with you?"

"I don't know," I said. "I've come over all weird. I feel bad. I think I've got the flu."

"You can't have the flu, it's summer. You were fine this morning," and as he spoke to me, I fell asleep again in my chair. Yeah, I'd got them mixed up. I'd taken the sleeping tablet instead of the anti-histamine.

They had to drop me from the game. They perched me behind the dug-out in my Birmingham tracksuit. I think I was named as one of the subs. Eric told the press I had a tweak and they were just being careful. If they needed to give me a run-out, they would. I didn't see any of the game. I was sound asleep.

My injury was bad but what I did next, what I continued to do, didn't help. After a week or so, the swelling went down. So I carried on training. I knew it wasn't right but I knew it wasn't my cruciate ligament either.

"You'll be fine," everyone said. And I wanted to believe them so badly, I carried on. I wanted to be fine, even though my knee was telling me, constantly, that it wasn't.

A month later, I played for Birmingham against Liverpool at Anfield. I played for 88 minutes. I loved playing at Anfield but God knows how I managed to play for 88 minutes. We won 1-0.

A week later, we had Everton at home. I was still in the side. Still not right. In the 68th minute, Lee Carsley had a shot. I was on the goal line and I handled it. The ref had to send me off, the third red card of my career. I didn't play again that season.

For two years, I soldiered on. I trained when I shouldn't have trained. I lifted weights, cycled, ran and swam when I should have done none of those things. I took pain killers and vitamin shots and industrial amounts of anti-inflammatories. I played games I shouldn't have. None of this helped. It only made it worse.

"Keep going," they kept saying. "You'll be all right."

So I kept going. I trained and I ran and I swam and I popped the pills and all the time I wanted, so much, for it – for every-thing – to be right. But I was deluding myself. I walked up the stairs one night, and my knee went. It just went. Pop. Pain. Agony. Swelling all over again. And then, two years on, after two years of trying and failing, weighed down by this feeling of obligation – I felt I was letting people down – I couldn't take any more.

I quit.

It came after my final game for the club. April 8, 2006. Away to Wigan. Bruce picked me again. I was perhaps 60 per cent fit. Jarosik, Pennant, me and Damien Johnson in midfield. We needed to win. Birmingham were struggling.

Before the game, the physio spent an hour with me; a bit on my back, a bit on my knee, trying to get me right. I had probably my worst game as a professional footballer. Bruce took me off after 65 minutes.

I knew it was time.

I remember being interviewed by the club's PR man and approving the statement. *"It is with great sadness..."*

I drove home to south Leicestershire that evening and it felt like a huge weight had been lifted from my shoulders. At the age of 31, my career was over.

I had a year on my contract. I didn't get what I should have: 52 weeks multiplied by £35,000 a week = £1.82m. They offered me £500,000.

I accepted it. Frankly, I felt fraudulent taking that. Steve Bruce shook my hand and wished me well. That season, Birmingham were relegated.

After a lengthy wrangle with my insurance company – I should have expected this, but I didn't – they paid up. It took years. They gave me £350,000.

I played one more time after that. I turned out for Thurmaston Magpies in the Leicestershire leagues. The club was run by a local builder. He'd done up the house I'd bought for my mum and dad. They were short one week. 'Here, wouldn't it be funny if you played,' he said. So I did. I couldn't walk for two days after.

A few weeks after I'd quit Birmingham, I had a call.

I was in Asda at the time, doing the shopping with Carly. It was Tim Davies, the then-chief executive of Leicester City.

"I know you've been injured," he said, "but we think we can get you right."

"I'm not sure you can," I said. "I think it's gone beyond that."

He was unperturbed. He was sure the club could sort me out. "Why don't you come over? We'll have the physio take a look."

And, for a second, somewhere in the frozen food aisle of Asda in Fosse Park, Leicester, I wavered. I allowed myself to wonder. Running out at the Walkers Stadium, in the blue of Leicester City, the evocative strains of the Post Horn Gallop, the number 6 on the back of my blue shirt, my City shirt, back where I belonged.

My encore. It's what I had secretly planned.

I'd always wanted to end my career at Leicester. I wasn't born a Leicester fan. But I became one. They're my club.

But I couldn't do it. I was proud of the career I had at Leicester, what we achieved under Martin O'Neill and, to a lesser extent, with Micky Adams.

I'd have undone that legacy in a month.

"Thanks, Tim," I said. "But my career is over."

I put a bag of frozen peas in my trolley and I walked on.

LOUISE MOON

On the outskirts of the Thorpe Acre estate in Loughborough, north Leicestershire, sits All Saints Church, a small place of worship ill-equipped for big events.

It was where they came to say goodbye to Louise Moon, a 13-year-old school girl who died of cancer in August, 2007.

The church was too small to cater for all the people who wanted to pay their respects so a couple of hundred more stood outside with order of service cards, unable to get a pew but wanting to be there, nonetheless, to bid an emotional farewell to this popular young girl, taken too soon.

In the row behind the family, in a dark suit and sunglasses, stood Mustafa Izzet.

Louise's mum knew he was there. She could hear him fighting back the tears. Muzzy Izzet was Louise Moon's favourite footballer.

On the day Muzzy left Leicester for Birmingham in 2004, nine-year-old Louise Moon sobbed. He may have moved from Louise's club, but he didn't move from her heart. She left the posters of him on her wall. She didn't have the heart to take them down.

Three years later, as Louise lay dying from a cancer that had confounded all the specialists and experts, a member of local charity, Wishes4kids, visited her in hospital. Was there anyone she wanted to meet? She couldn't think much further than the former Leicester City midfielder whose pictures still adorned her bedroom wall.

"Muzzy Izzet," she said.

That night, after a phone call from the charity, Muzzy Izzet appeared at her hospital bedside. Originally, he asked if he could go later in the week. "There might not be a 'later-in-the-week'," he was told.

They chatted that night, Muzzy and Lou, for an hour-and-a-half. She seemed to rouse. He came back again, and again, as Louise clung on to life. She lived for another six months, which astounded her doctors, if not her family. "She was clinging on for Muzzy," says mum, Loraine. "He kept her going."

Muzzy Izzet played a big part in those final six months. He was so moved by Louise and her fight he became a patron of Wishes4kids. This is the story of a young girl and her final few months, told by her parents, Loraine and Jock.

Spring 2007. In a nice house in south Leicestershire, Muzzy Izzet is kicking his heels. It's three years since he left Leicester City, a year since he retired from Birmingham City and football. His career is over. He is looking for something to do, something good, something worthwhile.

Ten miles away, across the city of Leicester, in ward 10 of the Leicester Royal Infirmary, a 13-year-old girl is dying of cancer. Doctors had found Louise Moon's tumour four years earlier. It was a strange old thing, the doctors told her parents, Loraine and Jock; something they'd not seen before.

The tumour in her stomach had its own blood supply. It was a seething mass of twisted tissue which had somehow managed to entwine itself around Louise's liver, bowel, pancreas and kidney. It was so interwoven with all of Lou's internal organs that it was impossible to operate, said her consultant, Mr Nour.

That was the bad news. The good news, he said, was that it was benign. It wasn't cancerous.

"So what we'll do," he said, "is keep an eye on it. Monitor it. But as long as it's benign, we should be okay."

And that's what they did. Louise Moon left hospital and lived her life. And for four years, everything was as it should be. She ran and biked, laughed and loved and cried, living her life until, one day, there was an unexpected turn for the worse. The tumour stopped being benign and became malignant. It shouldn't have done this, the doctors said. This never happens. Yet in Louise's case, it had. Somehow, it had turned cancerous.

It was growing, too, rapidly, inside her stomach. They opened her up – a huge incision across the width of her stomach – and took a biopsy. It was sent off to be examined. It was cancer but a strange, new kind of cancer no-one had ever seen before.

The sample was sent to America, the Far East, to cancer specialists all over the globe. They all scratched their heads. It was cancer, they all agreed, but they didn't know exactly which kind or which strain. No-one had seen this cancer before.

For four years, it was something that they could live with,

something they could accept and elbow to the back of their minds and go out and do normal things like any other normal family. And now, for reasons that had even baffled the experts, it wasn't. Everything had changed.

"There's nothing we can do," said Mr Nour, as the family gathered in his consultant's room in early 2007. "It's terminal." And around that hospital bed in the Leicester Royal Infirmary, the Moon family gathered, waiting for their precious girl to die.

She was nice, Lou. Funny. Cheeky. Full of life and spirit, laughter and impudence. She was a character. She had a fully-formed personality, already, at the age of 13. She knew who she was, who she liked, who she didn't and she wasn't shy in telling you, either. She was a tom-boy, who played football with the boys and was happiest with her hands in her dad's tool-box.

"I used to bring home old computers from work," remembers Jock, "and she'd sit with her screwdrivers, taking them all apart, bit by bit, and then struggling to put them back together again." They called her Doris at home. There was no real reason for it, says Jock. "I called her Doris one day, she laughed, I laughed, and it stuck."

They remember the day everything changed. "We'd come to terms with her tumour. The doctors had said it was ok and we wanted to believe them. And, you know, she was ok. Louise lived her life."

It changed a few days before her 13th birthday, in March 2007. Lou was set to go to Tignes, France, skiing with the school. A few days before she left, she felt cramps in her stomach. There were tests and scans but the doctors said she should go on her skiing holiday. She would enjoy that. It would do her good.

"The doctor felt around and prodded her stomach and said

she should try to forget about it and enjoy her holiday," says Loraine. "I was a bit suspicious. Just the way he said it – *'go and enjoy your holiday'* – it sounded ominous."

Lou went on holiday. The pains didn't get better – they got worse. The school called them at home. "You better come and pick her up," a teacher said. "She's really not very well." Her stomach had swollen. The tumour was growing.

Dad Jock and a friend drove through the night from their home in Loughborough to Tignes, on the French/Swiss border. The car – a Vauxhall Astra, only a couple of years old – broke down a few hundred miles from their destination.

It was a Friday night. They couldn't get anyone to fix it. You can't leave it here, by the side of the road, said the French police. So Jock paid £150 to scrap his £5,000 Astra. They got a taxi to the hospital – another £500 – picked up Louise and booked three flights – £700 – home.

She spent Saturday night and Sunday at home, sedated with painkillers, and they went into the hospital on Monday. They weren't to know, but when they took her into the hospital on Monday morning, it was the last time Louise would see her home. Louise spent the rest of her days in hospital.

The Moon family had been City fans since Lou was a little girl. It started during the good times, the Martin O'Neill years, but they stuck with them through the Peter Taylor-era of relegation, then administration and Division One.

Her favourite player? Always, Muzzy. The number 6, Turkish international.

"Not only is Muzzy Izzet Leicester City's best player, he is also very handsome," Lou had written on a home-made poster she had created on her computer.

They went to all the home games and sat in the family stand, behind the goal, midway between the goal and the corner flag.

"Every time Muzzy came over to take a corner, Lou would stand on her chair and shout and wave," says Loraine. "She had one of those voices that carried, too. You could hear her above everyone else."

Her bedroom was covered in posters of her favourite band, Blue, and Leicester players, mainly Muzzy. Even when he left Leicester, Lou kept his posters on her wall. Her devotion to Muzzy transcended the team he played for.

When her condition deteriorated and local charity, Wishes4Kids, asked the family if there was anyone they could call, a pop star or sporting hero they could contact to speak to Lou, they said Patrick Kisnorbo, Leicester's Australian centre-half. The charity asked if he could make it. He couldn't. He lived too far away or something; something which made little sense to them. He couldn't make it.

Was there anyone else, they said. "Well, really, her all-time favourite player is Muzzy Izzet," said her mum. "But he doesn't play for Leicester any more. I bet he doesn't live round here any more. I don't know if you'll be able to get in contact with him."

He did, still, live in the area. The charity got in touch with him. They called him that afternoon. Muzzy turned up that night. He seemed a bit shy at first, remembers Loraine. Like he wasn't sure what to say and what to do.

"I think he was a bit overwhelmed – this young girl, in a hospital bed, all these tubes and machines. It wasn't a pleasant sight." Lou wasn't overwhelmed, though. She was delighted. "She made us leave her room, and she spent an hour with him – just him and her – on that first night."

They never knew what they talked about that first night, says Loraine. "We asked her. She wouldn't say. I know Muzzy was wearing a green hat and Lou asked if she could have it and he said she could.

"If I keep your cap, then I know you'll come back and see me," she said.

"I'll come back anyway," Muzzy replied.

He had tears in his eyes when he said goodbye to her after that first visit. It moved him. You could see it had, says Loraine. They just clicked. They got on. They liked each other. It was the start of a beautiful friendship.

Loraine would stay by her bed all day and then Jock would stay and sleep there at night.

Lou knew she had cancer. She just didn't know how bad it was, says Jock. "They said we should tell her. A very clever man who was a child psychologist at the hospital insisted we tell her what she had and how long she had left to live. I said to him: "You tell her that, son, and I'll thresh you. I'll thresh you to within an inch of your life."

He didn't tell her.

"She'd have given in if she knew that," says Jock. "And we didn't want that. It was best she didn't know."

It was hard on the Moon family. They dealt with it in different ways. Sister Kramie carried on going to work. It kept her sane. Loraine and Jock took it in turns to sit by her bed. They hardly spoke, says Jock. "We didn't talk about what was playing out right before our eyes. I don't think we had the words." It was awful, says Loraine. Bloody awful.

Several times Lou's health seemed to deteriorate. Doctors gathered and performed tests, stroked their chins and looked on, grim and concerned. Several times the family were told it *'wouldn't be long now.'*

Every time, every single time, Lou seemed to rally.

"You know why," says Jock. "She wasn't ready. She didn't want to go when she was having so much fun."

Muzzy came every week. Sometimes twice a week, sometimes three, sometimes four. "We turned up once and he was sitting there by her bed," says Loraine.

"Well, Carly [his wife] is having her pregnancy scan," he said. "So I thought I'd just come up and say hello."

"It got to the point where he'd just turn up. They loved him on the ward. He'd always go and introduce himself at the desk: 'Hi, I'm Muzzy Izzet, here to see Lou' – and then he'd go in.

"He brought a load of toys in one day – toys that his kids had outgrown – and they shared them among the kids on the ward. They all loved it when Muzzy turned up."

Louise asked him for a Leicester City shirt one day. Muzzy looked perplexed. He didn't have any. He didn't keep many. The ones he had kept he'd mainly given away.

He turned up the next day, though, with one of his Turkey shirts – from his World Cup semi-final appearance for Turkey versus Brazil in 2002 – and a signed shirt from Patrick Kisnorbo. He'd been to the training ground that morning and didn't leave until the Belvoir Drive staff had sorted one out for her.

Muzzy went on holiday that summer. "I won't be able to text you for the next week," he told Lou. "I leave my phone at home when I'm on holiday."

But that night, at 10pm, Lou's phone pinged into life. A message. 'Good night sweetheart,' the message said. 'I decided

I had to take my phone with me because I didn't want to miss saying goodnight to you.'

And you should have seen her face when that happened, says Loraine. "He made that little girl feel 10-feet-tall," she says.

Lou clung on to life for weeks, months longer than the doctors thought she would. They didn't know how she was doing it. But Loraine knew. In this hospital room, surrounded by beeping machines and white-coated doctors, she was having the time of her life. She clung on because of Muzzy.

Muzzy saw her for the final time on August 9, 2007. It was a Thursday. He stayed for an hour/an hour-and-a-half and they chatted and laughed and although she was weak from the cancer and the medication, she was buoyed, as ever, by his visit.

That night, while eating dinner, her head flopped. Her body was giving up. "She went into a semi-coma, really," says Jock. This time, it really did seem serious. This time, she didn't recover. She didn't rally.

Louise Kay Moon passed away in Ward 10 of the Leicester Royal Infimary, with her family by her side. Her funeral was held a week later.

At a small house off the Ashby Road in Loughborough, Louise Moon's memory lives on. It always will. She was too big a personality for it to fade away. The mantle-piece groans with pictures of her. Her work is still on the family computer. They don't have the heart to delete it. They miss her. They miss her every day. But when they talk of Lou, they smile. They remember who she was.

He's stayed in touch, says Loraine. He rings now and again. They see him, sometimes, down the KP Stadium with his son, shaking hands with well-wishers.

"He always hugs me," says Loraine. "I can't really put into words what he did for Lou. He helped her live when everyone else – all the doctors and specialists – were preparing for her to die. I'll always love him for that."

STARTING OVER

The alarm goes at 6am. The wife is up first, then me, then the kids and then it starts – the familiar hum of another day.

If it's a good day, nice weather, maybe I've not played the day before or been out on a five-mile run, then I won't feel the twinge in my back or the pain I've learned to ignore in my leg. If not, I feel it as soon as I walk from the bedroom and across the landing to the bathroom. Back first, then leg.

I was born with a back bone that doesn't quite fit into its socket, the Sacroiliac Joint. It was never a problem when I was a kid, and the physio at Leicester City always sorted me out when I was playing. "You'll have to watch this, you know," I remember him telling me once. "It may well get worse when you grow older."

It turns out he wasn't kidding, either. I have massages. Acupuncture. Physiotherapy. They glue it sometimes, to try to keep it in place, which works for a while, but not for long – or, at least, not long enough.

The knee I can manage. The knee is all right as long as I don't do too much on it. My problem is I don't always know when to stop. I run a lot. I like running. I like to keep fit, I like to stay in shape and I like the time by myself, just running, listening to my music. I don't want to be one of those blokes who lets himself go when he hits 40. I'm not as fit as I was when I was playing but I'm in decent shape.

I don't diet. I like a drink. And if I want a burger and chips, I'll have 'em. But when I feel my shirt getting a bit too tight, I pull back a bit. I'm more careful about what I eat then and I'll perhaps run a bit more.

I ran the London Marathon a few years ago for Wishes4Kids. I'm patron of the charity. I did it in 3 hours 22 minutes. Not bad, but I'd have pissed that when I was playing. Looking back, though, I think it was running that marathon that made my back worse.

Every day, after I've made breakfast and the kids have been packed off, I drive the 15 minutes from my house to Blaby and Whetstone Boys' Club where I meet up with my old mate/now business partner, Steve Walsh. Together, we run AFDA: the Advanced Football Development Academy.

By September 2015, we had 100 youngsters – aspiring sportsmen, footballers, PE teachers and coaches – enrolled on a government-funded BTEC course in sports studies. We have teachers, sports scientists and qualified physios who do all the technical stuff, and me and Wal coach them.

It's good. From nothing, we've created a worthwhile business which is giving a generation of young kids hope, a chance to make it in their chosen field. That's something.

When I finished playing football, I didn't have a plan, a definite idea of what I would do next. I wanted to stay in the game. It was all I knew, after all. But I wasn't sure how I would do that. And then one night in 2006, it all fell into place.

It was a Saturday night. Me and Carly were having a rare night out at a restaurant in Shearsby, north Leicestershire. As we walked in, Steve Walsh and his partner Sira followed.

I'd not seen him for years. He'd been living out in Spain and I didn't know he was back. We had a big hug and a chat.

"What are you doing, then?" he said. And I shrugged. I didn't really know, but I was toying with the idea of setting up my own football academy. He was thinking of doing the same.

"We should do it together," he said. And, right there, in a restaurant in Shearsby, north Leicestershire, an unplanned meeting between two old team-mates, a plan was born.

We met over a coffee a few days later and we put it all into place. Within months, we were off the ground: The Steve Walsh and Muzzy Izzet Soccer Academy.

We went into schools, trying to show kids through sport, about the values of determination and never giving up. Some of these kids were on the verge of being excluded. We were the last roll of the dice, sometimes. Maybe, the teachers, thought: 'Well, if they won't listen to us, maybe they'll listen to these two old Leicester City players.'

And, you know what, they did. They didn't see us as teachers, because we didn't act like teachers. They didn't call us Mr Izzet and Mr Walsh. The sessions were a bit more relaxed. Some of them were a handful, yeah, but they were just kids who had lost their way a bit. I think me and Wal could relate to that. We were hardly model kids at school.

It was our job, without them even realising it, to help steer them back on course. It was good and we enjoyed it. And then one day I received a call from my old team-mate, Steve Claridge.

Claridge runs an accredited BTEC sports studies course in Portsmouth. It was going well, he said, and the guys behind it wanted to bring it to Leicester. "I wondered if you and Walshy were up for it?" he said. We were.

And this is where we are now. We started with 38 students last year. There will be 100 this year, more again next year. Me, Walshy, Chris Tucker, who coached the City academy, Jon Stevenson, the ex-City player, a growing staff who cover everything, each of them experts in their field. It's going well and I'm proud of what we've built here – not just what we've achieved but what the kids have achieved.

I think back, sometimes, to that skinny kid I was at Chelsea, the early months of 1996, 21 years old, desperate to get into the first team, always overlooked, unable to get a game, beginning to think this was as good as it got – Chelsea reserves, a boss who didn't rate me, wondering whether I should jack it all in and go roofing with my dad...

And how that changed. From those early, desperate months of 1996, to Martin O'Neill signing me for Leicester and then playing at Wembley in the play-off final at the end of that season in front of 85,000 people. Unbelievable.

A World Cup semi-final, three more appearances at Wembley, twice League Cup winners, playing in Europe, the big domestic games, Anfield, Old Trafford, Upton Park.

But it's not just that, though. It's what happened every day, every week, behind the scenes at Leicester, which made my career special. It was who I did it with, not just colleagues but proper mates. Proper men. A proper team.

We didn't have sports science at Leicester City back then.

We didn't have the best equipment, or the best kits or the best facilities or the best stadium.

But we had something better than that.

I still think of those days and they still make me smile. I couldn't have asked for more. I was pleased I played for the team I did when I did.

The future?

I don't know.

I like what I'm doing now with Walshy. I didn't plan this. It just happened. The best things in life usually do.

I've got my coaching badges. But do I want to uproot my family and become a reserve-team coach at a struggling club in the Championship I have no connection with?

Nah. I don't want that. It wouldn't mean anything to me.

I see a lot of players from my generation putting themselves forward on Sky, doing interviews all the time, applying for every job going. I'm not like that. I'm happy as I am, thanks.

But then, you see, if someone I knew came forward and got the manager's job at Leicester City and they wanted me to go there as coach… I'd have to think about that, wouldn't I?

Because I'm not sure I could turn that one down.

Muzzy's Shoot Questionnaire

Full name: Mustafa Kemal Izzet

Birthplace: Mile End Hospital, Mile End, London

Birthdate: October 31, 1974

Height: 5ft 10ins

Weight: 10st 8lbs (around 11st 10lbs now)

Married: To Carly, June 2003

Children: Ella-Rose, Dylan, Lyla

Siblings: One brother, Kemal, six years younger

Car: Mercedes estate. I wish I still had my Jaguar XKR…

Favourite player: Of all time? Diego Maradona. At Leicester? Neil Lennon. At Chelsea? Ruud Gullit

Most hated player: For his skill and the fact he always seemed to do well against us, Thierry Henry. For general obnoxious mouthiness, Tim Sherwood

Favourite other team: West Ham

Worst other team: Millwall

Most difficult opponent: Zinedine Zidane

Player you always wanted to slap: There really weren't that many. Can I go for Tim Sherwood again?

Your boyhood heroes? Tony Cottee and Frank McAvennie

Which grounds did you enjoy playing at? Filbert Street and Anfield. Anfield was always special

And the worst? Kingstonian, where Chelsea reserves played

What were your pre-match rituals? I always used to put my right shin pad on first

Worst referee: I never took much notice, they generally do a difficult job pretty well. I wasn't a fan of Uriah Rennie, though.

273

Which team-mate was the worst dresser? Callum Davidson and Billy McKinlay. Although I remember we were on a club break in Tenerife once and Arnar Gunlaugsson turned up one night in a white suit and a black shirt. He got so much stick but, in a way, though, he looked so bad, he looked good

Best country visited: Bahamas

Favourite food: Pie and mash/Dolma

Miscellaneous likes: A few pints in a pub with my mates (Carling if it's a big drink; Peroni if it isn't). A lie-in, a full English breakfast, playing with my kids, putting my boots on, watching boxing. I'd rather watch a good bout now than a football match

Miscellaneous dislikes: Rude people, hangovers, bullshitters and liars, Brussels sprouts, night clubs. I never really liked night clubs. I'm glad I don't have to go to any now

Favourite TV show: *Only Fools and Horses*

Favourite bands: Rolling Stones, The Beatles, Oasis, Kasabian, The Who, Led Zeppelin, Guns N' Roses, Springsteen, early Bee Gees

Favourite actor/actress: Daniel Day Lewis, Robert De Niro, Helen Mirren

Best friend: I have three – Stuart Hibberd, Danny Youles and Ben Ferris. They were all in my class at school

Biggest influence on my career: My dad and my mum

Biggest drag in football: Pre-season. Always pre-season

Personal ambition: As a player, it was to play well enough and be consistent and to be recognised as a decent player. Now, I just want to bring up my kids right

If you weren't a footballer what would you be? I'd maybe have been a roofer with my dad. Or sign-writing. Art and graphic design was the only lesson I enjoyed at school

Which person would you most like to meet? I'd liked to have known my grandma, my mum's mum, Vera. I knew all my other grandparents. She died before I was born. I've heard all sorts of good stories about her. I often wondered what she was like

Who would you never want to meet again – outside of football? There were a few so-called investors – leeches – who latched on to me and took me for a few quid when I was a footballer

Did you read your match reports? Yes, in *The Sun* and the *Leicester Mercury*. They were never right

What was the worst thing you ever read about yourself – football and non-football? I had some death threats once. It was not long after that Leeds fan was stabbed in Turkey. That wasn't very nice. The police got involved

How would you like to be remembered? As a decent bloke who had time for people. And a good dad.

Muzzy's best ever LCFC team:

Flowers
Kamark Elliott Taggart Walsh Guppy
Parker Lennon Izzet
Heskey Collymore
Subs: Walker, Savage, Cottee, Claridge, Marshall, Sinclair

Muzzy's worst ever LCFC team:
Kalac
Willis Carey Dabizas N Lewis
Delaney Freund J Lewis Ellison
Benjamin Gunnlaugsson
("Sorry lads. I didn't enjoy that...")

1. Chelsea reserves v Wycombe Wanderers, 1995/1996

It was a friendly, to give some first-teamers a run-out. Mid-way through the second half, Hoddle pinged a beautiful 40-yard-pass to me. I was making a run into the opposition's half. Without the ball touching the floor I flicked it, with my right boot, over the defender. I was still a good 30 yards out. The ball looped over him. I carried on running. The ball still hadn't touched the floor. As it came down, over the defender's head, I hit it, with my left foot and it flew into the top corner. It was a bit like Gazza's Euro '96 goal for England v Scotland – but better. Michael Duberry was playing in that game. I read an interview with Doobs once and he said it was the best goal he had ever seen. He was right, too, I reckon. Hoddle then took me off: "Go on. You're not going to top that." And yet he still wouldn't pick me, the bastard.

2. Grimsby Town v Leicester City, November 30, 2002

I'm still asked about this one. Andy Impey slipped past their left-back and knocked a hopeful cross in behind me. I had a go at an overhead kick more in hope than expectation. It was a nice goal, I enjoyed it – and it's still regularly voted the best ever Leicester goal. I can't tell you how proud that makes me feel.

3. Leicester City v Tottenham Hotspur, October 19, 1998

It was the night when the speculation about Martin possibly leaving reached fever pitch. There was always a great atmosphere at the midweek games, but I preferred playing Saturdays

276

as there was too much hanging around. Some preferred night games, and would have a nap in the afternoon. I could never do that. I was usually so excited that by kick-off I was knackered.

In this game, the ball came out to me and I think Stephen Clemence came charging out. I had no time to consider my options. I just hit it, on the volley, bang. It flew into the corner.

4. Leicester City v Leeds United, League Cup, November 11, 1998

Another night game – maybe I liked them more than I thought… There was a punt into Nigel Martyn's box. He came out, came too far and couldn't handle the ball so headed it – straight to me. I side-foot volleyed it back over him and the defenders, and it went in without bouncing. I was happy with that one.

5. Leicester City v Crystal Palace, December 6, 1997

Lenny took a short corner and there didn't seem to be much on but I dinked it past one player, which opened up their defence. I could see their keeper, Kevin Miller, slightly out of position. It was late on, we were 1-0 down and the pressure was on, but it was a great chance and I bent it into the top right-hand corner.

6. Chelsea v Leicester City, September 17, 2000

This was the only win against what you might call decent opposition early in Peter Taylor's reign. The game had barely started when Steve Guppy danced down the left and floated a deep cross into the box, behind the penalty spot. I launched myself at it and met it nicely. The ball seemed to fly off my head, past Carlo Cudicini and into the Chelsea goal. I missed an easier header later but we still won 2-0. I always enjoyed scoring v Chelsea – especially when we won.

7. Leeds United v Leicester City, April 5, 2004

We lost this, 3-2. Another late goal which left us with nothing, the story of that season under Micky Adams. This was a genuinely great game, both sides attacking freely, lots of chances.

It was the second half. I got the ball inside their area. No-one tackled me. I got nearer and nearer until, about 25 yards out, I had a dig. It flew past Paul Robinson. It was a nice goal.

8. Leicester City v Blackburn Rovers, September 24, 1997

Another night game, just before the end of the first half. We were attacking, one of their players cleared and it came to me on the edge of the box. I had one touch, which flicked the ball into the air and I volleyed it in. That one was all right, too.

9. Leicester City v Liverpool, September 18, 1999

We always did all right against Liverpool. We went 1-0 up when I set Tony Cottee up, putting him through one-on-one. Michael Owen then scored twice, but O'Neill threw Matt Elliott forward, as he did late on if he thought we could still win.

Usually, this meant we'd play to Matty's strengths in the air, but the ball came to him outside the box. Matty looked up and saw me running in from the left. He played a little deft lob to me, I chested it down and slotted it in, 2-2 in the 88th minute.

10. West Ham United v Leicester City, November 14, 1998

It felt strange to score against West Ham, the team I supported as a lad. I remember it because I froze. I was struck by the enormity of it. *Shit, I'm going to score against West Ham.* It's deadly, allowing yourself to lose concentration, even for a second. Luckily, I regained my composure and passed it into the net.

DO THEY MEAN ME?

A selection of former players, friends, family members and a former manager tell their Muzzy Izzet stories...

Steve Guppy

"When I joined Leicester in March 1997, I didn't know Muz. But he seemed friendly, decent – all the players were. They were a welcoming bunch. No prima donnas.

"I was staying at a local hotel when I signed and the night before my first training session Muzzy called me. 'That's nice,' I thought. 'What a top bloke.' He was helpful, welcoming me to the club. He said they were a good bunch of lads and how I'd fit straight in. Nice touch. I really appreciated it.

"'We've got a late one, tomorrow, saaahn,' he said. 'You don't have to be at the training ground 'til 11.30am.'

'Great', I thought. 'I'll have a lie in'.

"I still got in early, about 11am – just as all the lads were coming in from the training pitch. I looked over and there was Muzzy and Lenny and a few others and they were pissing themselves. They'd done me, good and proper.

"Martin O'Neill fined me £800 for that – £800! I can laugh about it now. I don't think I was laughing then. I vowed I'd get him back. I don't think I ever did."

Neil Lennon

"There's a photo of me and Muz, naked – for some reason it was on the wall of the City stadium for years afterwards, it still might be – with just the League Cup protecting our modesty.

"It was taken after the League Cup final replay in 1997 and we had a few that night! That picture doesn't just sum up that night, but those City years. It was a magical time.

"I remember Muzzy turning up, this scrawny kid from Chelsea reserves no-one had heard of. He was there two days and Martin put him on the bench for that Sheffield United game. I was injured and watched from the stands. We weren't great – and the fans let Martin know it – but that was a turning point. We went on a great run after that, culminating in the win at Watford when Muzzy scored the winner.

"We hit it off straight away. He was a tremendous player. He had a superb first touch, great vision and he had a great engine, too. He was such a naturally fit lad. He could run all day.

"He soon developed into a first-class, all-round midfielder. I loved playing with him. He was deceptively tough. He had great stamina, a real will-to-win. He also had a knack for making late runs into the box – and he could finish. I'm often asked who were the best players I played with. He'd be in my 11. He'd be one of the first names on the list.

"More than that, though, he was a lovely, laid-back lad. There was no edge to Muzzy at all. I'm sure there were times when I drove him mad. We roomed together for most of my time at City. He used to say I snored. It drove him mad. We had to sort that, so we ended up getting suites or single rooms.

"There was this thing when one of the papers photographed us as The Kray Twins – probably because Muz is from the East End – and they had us looking all menacing and tough. What a load of bollocks. We were pussy cats, really.

"We got up to all sorts, I can't tell you half the things we did. Going out, drinking 'til all hours, playing cards at Willie Thorne's on a Tuesday after training. It was just great craic.

"Muzzy was the sensible one. At La Manga, he was calming us down, shushing us in the bar when we were getting too loud. Always smiling and laughing. And then – bam – he'd disappear. His David Copperfield act. He'd be there, laughing and drinking – and then he was gone.

"If he says that I was Martin's favourite, you can discount that. It's utter bollocks. Martin was always having a go at me. But never him. Muzzy was his favourite. He loved Muzzy."

Steve Walsh

"When he turned up, I thought he was a school kid, he was so small. My hopes weren't high! But in those first few days, he showed us what he was made of. There was just something about him. It wasn't just his talent. It was his charisma.

"I was worried about him being so thin — but I needn't have been. He was brave, determined, he had massive stamina. The times he tracked back, making tackles on the edge of our box. Him and Lenny and the shifts they put in — they kept me going for another five years. They saved my career. He had the skills to wriggle out of the tightest places — and he could finish, too. His all-round game was magnificent.

"People ask me who was the best player I played with, and it was Muzzy. I say Matt Elliott for his defensive ability and his spirit — but Muzzy for his skills. In the dressing room, when the piss was flying around, he stood up for himself from day one. He had an answer for everything.

"In one training session Martin O'Neill made us form a circle and, one by one, we had to do something. Muz did this ridiculous Turkish dance, gyrating and limbo-ing, going down on one leg. It was hilarious.

"Then Martin said: 'Right — now you all do it' and we were falling down and laughing. We couldn't do it.

"I met him by chance at a restaurant after I'd returned to England after a short time in Spain. I was thinking about putting a football school together. So was he. So that was it. We joined forces. It's been brilliant, really. We've built it and built it and we've taken it somewhere we didn't expect it to go.

"He's been a really good friend to me over the years. He's helped me in so many ways and I'd like to thank him for that. I appreciate it.

"I look forward to the future. I hope we've got another 10, 15 years working together. It's been great."

Ian Marshall

"Martin signed me that first year in the Prem. It was a good team, and good camaraderie. We got on well but Muzzy was the stand-out quality player. He'd do flicks and keep-ups in training, stuff we couldn't do, and we'd laugh and jeer at him, and say: 'You can do all that – but I can still elbow you in the nose, son' but Muzzy took that skill and used it on the pitch. If you were in a hole, lay it off to Muz. That's what we'd do. And you knew he'd hold it up. He wouldn't lose it.

"Him and Lenny in midfield… brilliant. Lenny holding, Muz going forward. He set up a few goals for me. Nothing we ever worked on. We never worked on anything at Leicester. We just played five-a-sides. We knew what we were doing. But he could tackle, too. He got stuck in and never shirked a challenge.

"We had some great nights out… We were playing snooker at Willie Thorne's one Tuesday night and then we moved over to the dart board. We'd been drinking all afternoon and someone decided to throw a dart at someone. Well, that was it, it kicked off. There we were – the players of Leicester City Football Club, throwing darts at each other in Willie Thorne's snooker club. There was one in someone's shoulder. I had one in my hand. It was fucking stupid, but funny.

"I played for a few clubs but the four years I had at Leicester were the happiest of my career. I still live here. Quite a few of us – Walshy, Muz, Elliott – none of us are from Leicester, but we settled – it's where we feel at home."

Frank Sinclair

"I knew Muz at Chelsea. He was a bit younger than me, but I knew him. I played with him. I knew what kind of player he was. Funny, really, because you'd think a player like Muzzy, with his touch and his vision, his work-rate and his feet, you'd think Glenn Hoddle would be all over him but he wasn't. I never understood that. But Chelsea's loss was Leicester's gain.

"I'd been at Chelsea, where I thought we all got on and had a good team spirit. But it was even better at Leicester. There were no big time Charlies at Leicester. It wasn't allowed.

"I remember on my first day, Garry Parker came over as we walked out on the training ground and he patted me on the back. 'Great to have you here, Frank,' he said. And he kept patting my back. I felt something slide down my back. 'He's put some wet grass down my shirt,' I thought to myself. It wasn't. It was a toad. A fucking massive toad. That's what it was like.

"There were a lot of pranks. Muzzy was always in the thick of that – but he always passed the buck if there was any trouble, ha, ha, oh yeah, he was quick at doing that.

"We had a Sunday Club, a drinking club where we'd meet at 2pm at the Soar Point, near the River Soar, just down from Filbert Street.

"So at 2pm, get the drinks in, watch the game on TV. Sometimes, if we'd done well the day before, it would go from Sunday afternoon, to Sunday evening, to 2am Monday.

"There was me, Lenny, Muzzy, Walshy, Taggs, Elliott, Marshy. They could drink. They made me drink pints. I liked shorts, Southern Comfort. But they made me drink pints. You should see them drink pints. I couldn't drink pints like them – but I was lucky. I never got hangovers.

"He liked his clobber, too. Muz thought he was the best dressed player. He loved all that. What he usually did, though, was clock what I'd bought and go out and get that, but in small…"

Emile Heskey

"Full credit to Martin O'Neill. He spotted Muzzy's potential. He came from Chelsea reserves but, within weeks, he became Leicester's talisman. He was a massively important player for us, a big part of that promotion drive in that 1995/96 season.

"I remember the penalty he won against Palace at Wembley. He should never have got that far, really. But that's what he was like. When he had the ball at his feet, you couldn't stop him.

"I could race him and beat him over 50 metres. But put a ball at his feet it gave him an extra momentum. You couldn't stop him. I was lucky to play with some top players in my career. He was right up there. He had the skills of Joe Cole – but he had this brilliant strength and stamina, too. No-one covered as much ground in that Leicester team as Muzzy.

"You'd see him time after time, surrounded by two, three, maybe four players – and he'd wriggle out of it. It wasn't a fluke. He did that in training. I remember the goal he set up for me at Old Trafford, the first game of the 1997/98 season – he beat Gary Neville and then Ronnie Johnsen in the tightest of spaces, chipped the ball over to me – and that was it, 1-0.

"Best of all, though, he was just a great lad to have at the club, a great lad to play with. I don't think you'll find many people in football who have a bad word to say about Muzzy."

Matt Elliott

"Muzzy Izzet was not only one of the best players I ever played with – him, Lenny, John Collins and Gary McAllister were the best, I think – but he was also one of the most underrated. Not by us, the Leicester players, or by the fans. We knew what he could do. But by other teams, journalists, pundits.

"He had all that brilliant technical ability, but he was fit, too. He had great stamina. He was box-to-box – and he scored goals, double figures, or near to double figures, every season.

"The fans loved him not just for his goals – and he scored some spectacular ones, too – but because of his commitment. He was a whole-hearted, committed player. He had a great work ethic. He could have gone on and played for a bigger club, definitely. Their loss was our gain, really.

"That year in the Championship under Micky Adams – he was the best player in that division by a country mile. The gulf in class some weeks, watching him strolling around in the middle of the park... well, it was embarrassing.

"After Martin left and Lenny, Peter Taylor seemed to play him in a deeper role. We played a straight 4-4-2 under Taylor, which hampered his natural game – he liked to bomb on, join the attack. Also, because we missed the void left by Neil Lennon, Muzzy – because he could play anywhere – was detailed to do a bit of that. He did it, but it was a waste of his talent.

"I remember one game against Arsenal. Robbie Savage received the ball from Gerry Taggart. Sav was in a tight space, a couple of players on him. He lost the ball and threw his hands up in the air, gesticulating as if it was Taggs' fault. Gerry wasn't having that. They were still rowing and bickering at half-time.

"'What's going on?' said Martin. They blamed each other.

"'Right,' said Martin. 'Shut the fuck up. Both of you.' And then he pointed at Taggs. 'I've decided you're to blame, Gerry. Never, ever pass the ball to Sav when he has a man on him. It's okay to do it if it's Muzzy. He won't lose it. But not Sav.' It was true, too. That's what he was like. We all knew: if you were in trouble, lay it off to Muzzy. He'll get you out of it.

"We were in a hotel, rooming somewhere before a game. I'd grown my hair a bit – nothing like his. He had all sorts of haircuts – long, short, shaved, blond, Alice bands. He fancied himself as a style icon, Muzzy. I didn't like having hair, really – but I'd grown it a bit. And I thought: 'Well, he'll know about what to do with this…' so I asked Muz.

"He got all of his gels and pastes out. And he styled my hair, bending it this way and that. I couldn't see what he was doing but he was was making the right noises. 'Looks *magniff*, mate,' he kept saying. We went down for dinner and the lads pissed themselves. They hammered me. I looked at Muz. He was laughing his head off. It wasn't that it was that bad. It just wasn't me. He made me look like a member of fucking Boyzone.

"I washed it out that night. I had my hair shaved the day after the game. That was it for me and hair – and I certainly never took any more fashion tips from Muzzy."

Andy Impey

"You saw what he did in games, but I saw what he did in training. He was brilliant. He'd do some outlandish stuff and we'd stand back and say: 'For fuck's sake, Turk – how'd you do that?'

"He's a special player. I wouldn't say he carried our team – we had other players, too – but he was the main man. I remember one game, a pre-season match at Northampton. I passed the ball to him and I could see their full-back pounding in. He flew in at Muz, but Muz did this thing where he controlled the ball, flicked it over the defender and turned, all in one movement. He was away and this big full-back was on his arse. I was laughing my head off – but he did something like that all the time.

"I knocked the cross in for him for that overhead kick at

Grimsby. I'd just come on. It was freezing cold, windy and raining. I beat their left-back and crossed the ball in. It wasn't a great ball. It was behind him. He made it look good.

"As a bloke, he's like that comedian, Micky Flanagan. Always chirping. Always on. Cheeky Cockney chappy. That's Muz. Although he wasn't quite so chipper when I reversed my car into his Jag in the car park at Leicester one afternoon.

"I just meant to wheel-spin away and leave him in dust. It didn't quite work – I reversed straight into his XKR in my Porsche. It looked horrendous. I remember him saying, almost crying: *'Look what you've done to my facking car.'*

"Cost me £4,000 to put that right."

Tony Cottee

"When I first joined, he came round to my house in Chigwell. He'd been to see his folks in the East End and I said I'd give him a lift up to training.

"So we met each other, shook hands, and I drove us up the M1 to Leicester. He was telling me what it was like, what the lads were like – and then he sheepishly confessed that I was his boyhood hero. He was a West Ham fan and he had posters of me on his wall. Ha, ha, ha, ha. I was like: 'Cheers mate – make me feel ancient, why don't you?'

"I had three great years at Leicester. I was lucky in my career. We had good characters at West Ham, good people at Everton – there were a few issues, but nothing major – and a dressing room full of jokers at Leicester.

"The camaraderie there was brilliant. I know why – Martin had rescued us, each one of us, from somewhere. We were, all of us, grateful to him. We had a great balance, especially in midfield. Lenny was a great player, Sav was busy, Parker was still a classy midfield player, Guppy was putting great crosses in – but the best player, the most skilful player, was Muzzy. He had the best technique.

"We had a good chemistry. I made runs and Muzzy was so intelligent that he'd find me. I loved playing with him."

Gerry Taggart

"One of my fondest memories was on the coach back from Wembley, the League Cup final, after beating Tranmere.

"We were heading back up the M1. The beers were out. We were laughing and drinking, waving at all the other City fans coming back. It was always a great place to be, that City coach after a big win. We were heading to Sketchley Grange, the hotel in Hinckley. It was going to be a grand night.

"Then, from somewhere, a bottle of Jack Daniels appeared. Muzzy leaned over and said: 'I'm having that.' He downed that bottle more or less single-handedly. We got back to the hotel and there was nothing left. He'd drunk it all.

"We looked at him and you could tell he was gone. He stood up from his seat – and fell forward and landed on his face. He was paralytic. We had to carry him in. I think he spent most of that night in a dark corner, drinking coke.

"And then there was the time, when we landed at the airport after La Manga, that we got on the bus to come home and all the photographers were waiting for us, taking our pictures.

"I was sitting at the window, he was next to me. As the photographers were taking these pics, he leaned over and put his Vs up. I thought no more – until the next day and it was all over *The Sun*, my face, his V-sign. It looked like it was me.

289

"When I got into training Martin called me into his office. He was always bollocking me. I was used to it.

"'I suppose you're going to tell me this is not you?' he said.

"'It's not me, boss.'

"'And I suppose you're not going to tell me you don't know who it is?'

"'I don't know who it is.'

"I knew who it was, alright. It was Muzzy. Martin threatened to fine me a week's wages. But he never did.

"I'm told Muzzy later coughed up to it. I'm not surprised. He was always an honest lad. He was a great bloke to have around and a brilliant player. He's remembered for his goals. But people overlook all his other attributes – stamina, vision, passing, two good feet, good in the air, a proper box-to-box midfielder. He was never any bother, either. No ego. Just a good lad."

Micky Adams

"Muzzy would come into work, happy, smiling, joking with everyone, and get on with his job. He was an all-round good guy.

"There were some forceful characters in that dressing room. It wasn't always an easy team to manage. But Muzzy just got on with the job – no drama, very low maintenance. If I had a team of Muzzy Izzets at every side I've managed I'd be a happy man.

"My biggest memory is that overhead kick at Grimsby. We got battered and then Muzzy scores that goal. He had that bit of skill, that extra bit of quality that can turn games around.

"He was my captain for a while. He wasn't always the most vocal, perhaps, but he led by example. I'm surprised to hear him say he was in the comfort zone for a while. He's doing himself a disservice there. The truth is, we weren't doing very well and it wasn't a great team. Comfort zone or not, I remember him as the shining light in that team.

"When I first took over, it was the first day back after we'd been relegated, and I told them: 'If anyone wants to go, you're free to leave.' Quite a few were surprised to find that other teams didn't want them. I think what Muzzy did was galvanise them a bit; bring them together, bring a bit of camaraderie back. We needed that. That promotion season was a good season.

"I was disappointed when he left Leicester. I knew it was coming but, still. It was a shame to see him go. I remember reading about his injury. That was a shame, too. He was never injured much during his time at Leicester."

Richard Broadbent, ex-Leicester Mercury, now *The Times*

"I went to interview Neil Lennon at his house and there was one of those nice, arty black and white photographs that new parents get done of their kids on the wall in the front room. Only this portrait was of Lennon with his other half – Muzzy.

"They had a thing going. Find an Izzet goal on YouTube and the chances are the first player on hand to hug him was Lennon. They were Starsky and Hutch in shin-pads. They might be the best thing that ever happened to Leicester City. Izzet's underrated flair and Lennon's beautifully-controlled belligerence were a match made in Filbert Street heaven. They were soul-mates. Garry Parker had more skill than both and Robbie Savage played like a man in desperate search of his limitations, but Izzet and Lennon were the heartbeat of the glory years. That bond was real and, in a sport where players come and go, and often could not give a fig about anything much beyond a new tattoo, they were loved by the fans, too.

"Look at the Leicester midfield today, any day, really. It does not compare. How City, how any team, could use an Izzet and a Lennon debunking expectations and playing and flirting with the air of players who knew they were in on something special.

"They were heady, strange times. As a reporter on the *Mercury*, you would ring O'Neill for team news and then, at 2am, the phone would go and a slightly menacing voice would say: 'Spencer Prior's got a groin.' And although we did not know it at the time, we would never have it so good again."

Eddie Niedzwiecki, former reserve coach at Chelsea

"I had a lot of time for Muzzy; he was a good kid, full of enthusiasm, brimming with talent, a great family, too. I liked his dad, Mehmet, and his mum, Jackie. He could handle a ball in a telephone box. He had such a great technique and a deft touch, with both feet, that he was very skilful in the tightest areas.

"Chelsea let him out on loan. I was there when he made his debut against Sheffield United. He played well, too. And that was that. He made that attacking midfield position his own. It was a good move for him and it worked out well. I followed his career closely. I was delighted to see him do so well, to see Leicester do so well. The fans took him to their hearts.

"Why did he never get that chance at Chelsea? I don't know. I wish I did. He always impressed me. Chelsea missed a trick."

Alan Birchenall, ex-Leicester midfielder, now club ambassador

"I've been at Leicester City since 1971, with a couple of years off for good behaviour. In that time, I've played with or seen about 500 players – from Shilton to Worthington, Weller, Lineker, McAllister, the present lot and a few the club historian ran through with me who, I have to admit, I couldn't remember. Muzzy was in the top 11. He could have played in any Leicester team. That Bloomfield side of the '70s, the team I played in, if he'd taken my place, we'd have been unstoppable, ha, ha.

"How can I describe him? Well, there was only one George Best – but I used to watch Muzzy some games, the way the ball stuck to his feet, how he wouldn't give it away, how opposing defenders would tackle him yet he'd shrug them off, he'd bounce off them, even though he looked like he was seven stone wet through, and he reminded me of Best. He had that balance.

"When Martin signed him, I hadn't heard of him. I thought he was one of those players managers buy 'for the future.' But Martin put him straight in. What a player he was over the next eight years – and a lovely, decent, unassuming lad, too. I knew I could always call on him to help with community stuff – he never shied away from that – and I remember him with Macca, our kit man, at Baffone's, on a Saturday night, worse for wear, on the karaoke as if they could really sing, murdering every tune. Terrible singer – great player."

Matt Piper

"People ask me who were the best players I played with. There's Niall Quinn, Kevin Phillips, Neil Lennon – but *the* best, for me, was Muzzy.

"I looked up to Muzzy when I made it into the first team. He looked after me, too. He gave me good advice on all sorts of things – money, interviews, going out. I appreciated that.

"I still play for the Leicester Legends team. Muzzy doesn't play every game – but when he does, I can guarantee he'll do something which will make me think: 'Shit, how did he do that?'

"We played against the Forest Legends once in Quorn. The ball went out for a corner. I went to take it and the big lads – Taggs, Walshy – came up. It was like 1999 all over again.

"Muzzy put his arm round my shoulder as I went to take the kick. 'I'll be on the far edge of the box.' he said. 'Try and float one over – I'll volley it in.'

"I didn't rate his chances but I knocked a great ball to him (!) and he smacked it, on the volley, with his right foot. *Boom*. It crashed against the bar. It would have been a brilliant goal.

"Taggs and Walshy jogged back, moaning about what a waste of their time it was going up for the corner. Ha ha ha. Class."

Stuart Hibberd, childhood friend

"We go all the way back, second year at primary school, I think. We were seven, maybe eight years old. He came to our school and said his name was Christopher. He was so wary of standing out, this little Turkish kid in the East End, that he started telling people his name wasn't Mustafa, it was Christopher.

"He was tiny – but he could handle himself. He was popular, too. Everyone liked him. There were always scraps and fights at school but, you know, I can't remember Muz ever being in one.

"I played Sunday football with him and was at Charlton with him. There were probably better footballers around aged nine or 10. But Muz always had this brilliant technical ability. He always had a ball at his feet, and he was always playing. As we grew up, and age and size became less important, that's when he shone. That's when his technical ability came to the fore.

"We played against each other in the final of the London Cup. I was the goalkeeper. His team won 2-0. He scored them both. One of the goals was a cross that floated over my head and somehow went in. To this day, he'll say: 'Yeah, I meant that.' He didn't. He fluked it, the jammy bastard.

"He should have made it at Chelsea. I was there that night when he was on the bench for them, against West Ham, and Eddie Newton broke his leg. Hoddle wouldn't put him on. I was glad when he left. He was a legend for Leicester City.

"He's still the same person today as he was at school – he's loyal, decent, funny, down to earth. There's not a bad bone in his body. He's got some money, but good luck to him. He's not flash with it. It didn't change him. We'll go out and, to this day, he doesn't like anywhere swanky. He loves a shit pub, Muz."

Danny Youles, childhood friend

"Christopher. That's what he told me, as well. It must have lasted for a few weeks that, *Christopher*, until we found out the truth. I don't know what he was worried about, really. Within a week, maybe two weeks, we'd all started calling him Muzzie.

"And that was how we spelled it, too – Muzzie, with an 'ie' rather than a 'y'. It only became Muzzy when he went to Leicester and I guess Muzzy was shorter for the headline writers. The only time I remember him being called Mustafa was when the 2002 World Cup was on and every time he was featured, they always called him Mustafa Izzet.

"As a kid, all he wanted to do was play football. I was pleased for him when he came to Leicester. I saw a lot of games. I'd go up to watch him and Muz would say: 'Come on – come out for a drink with us after.' I wasn't sure if that would be okay but they were lovely blokes, those Leicester players. Neil Lennon, Scott Taylor, Steve Walsh – a really good bunch.

"I'm a West Ham fan, but I saw more Leicester games than

West Ham between '96 and 2004. Even now, even though he stopped playing for them, I still look for Leicester's results.

"I've known Muzzy for more than 30 years. There are no bad stories to tell about Muz. He's just a decent bloke, a good mate, one of us, still. He hasn't changed."

Terry Skiverton, former Chelsea reserve defender
"We played together; Under-11s and Under-12s at Senrab, and then all the way through the Chelsea youth team and reserves.

"There's a picture of me, Muzzy and Andy Grant, three of us from Senrab, signing for Chelsea at 14 and Muzzy looks about six! He was a skinny kid, but no pushover. And he was so skilful. He could create something out of nothing.

"I usually played centre-half, but for one season at Senrab they played me in midfield. It was my job to nobble people, win the ball and give it to Muz, who'd create something. I remember the coach saying: 'Terry, you'll never be a midfielder – but you can learn from Muz and it'll be good for you.' It was, too.

"My dad died when I was a lad. But Muzzy's dad, Mehmet, was like a surrogate father to me. He was good, too – he'd tell both of us if we played well and he'd tell us if we played badly.

"We came up the hard way. Those games in East London were brutal – dads shouting, fighting on the touchlines. Fouling. Swearing. Racism. Violence.

"If you can prosper in that, you can play anywhere. It's where Muzzy earned his stripes.

"I remember, as lads, on the way home on the Tube, we'd practise doing interviews. He was always better than me at that, too. I'd stutter occasionally and he'd say: 'You can't fucking stutter on telly, Skivo' and we'd laugh and laugh and laugh.

"I don't see him as often as I'd like but when we do, we pick it straight up. There's no edge to Muzzy. He's always been a funny, easy going, down-to-earth kid – and he still is."

Tim Flowers

"When I signed for Leicester, Martin O'Neill told me straight: 'I'm taking a chance on you, pal, so don't let me down.' I promised him I wouldn't. I don't think I did, either.

"The lads were in Athens, Greece, on a pre-season tour. I flew out the next day with Martin and John Robertson. I knew a few of them, I'd played against them. I knew they were tight. I could tell from their work ethic. It was a fantastic changing room. They welcomed me straight away. They were friendly, decent, the piss-taking was ferocious.

"It was a man's club, Leicester. You look at that back line – Walsh, Taggart, Elliott – you knew where you stood there. But then you go from defence to midfield and there was quality there, too. Lenny was a great player, Garry Parker was a great player, Savage, too. But Muzzy was quality.

"I remember the season we beat Tranmere to win the League Cup. Muzzy had this awful leopard skin thong. He wore it as a joke in one of the early rounds, and then for every round from then on. He'd walk around the changing room in it looking ridiculous, and we slaughtered him for it – but it did the trick!"

Kem Izzet, brother

"There are six years between us – it's a lot when you're kids. By the time I wanted to do stuff, he'd already done it. I spent a lot of my childhood travelling to Kingstonian watching him play for Chelsea reserves. He'd be 18-19. I'd be 12-13. We'd get back at 10.30pm. School the next day. I'd be asleep in the back of the car. I loved it. When I got older, Dad took me everywhere, too.

"Mum and Dad forced him to take me places. He'd meet Carly – but he had to take me with him, too. I can just imagine how much he loved that!

"We played football. He always put me in goal and then he'd just fire shots at me. I'd moan and then he'd go in – but that only seemed to last two or three minutes and he'd feign an injury or nip off for a piss or something – and then I'd be back in again. Great! I don't want to sound like I'm moaning, though. I loved our childhood. I loved tagging along with my big brother. He was my idol growing up. And when he made it at Leicester I'd tell people: 'That's my brother playing for Leicester in the Premier League.' I saw every game for the first three or four years. I loved watching that team – and I was super proud. Me and Dad loved it. Mum didn't go – she'd get too nervous.

"My favourite game? That Watford game is up there, when he scored to put Leicester in the play-offs. We were in the away end. That whole end was whammo! I still think that's one of the best atmospheres I've ever witnessed at a football game.

"But my favourite was the play-off final against Palace. I was two seats away from the Wembley steps. When he made that climb to get his medal, I leaned in and gave him a hug. That was a special moment. I'll never forget that.

"He was always a great player – but playing at Leicester gave him a confidence. The success didn't change him. He has a pretty tight group of friends. He gives people the time of day and he's decent – but he doesn't let people in very easily.

"How was my football career? Well, when I was at Colchester, we'd play away from home and there'd be a small write-up in the programme and when it came to me, I swear, every single time, it said: 'Younger brother of Muzzy Izzet, Kem Izzet...' and then they'd say I was a tenacious midfield player or whatever.

"Later in my career, the 'younger-brother-of-Muzzy-Izzet' bit was relegated further down the page. It never disappeared, but it went further down. I understood. I'm proud to be his brother. He's a good bloke and, as a footballer, massively under-rated."

Jackie Izzet, Muzzy's mum

"He was always a good kid. I don't think he was ever in any kind of trouble all through his childhood. Canning Town was like anywhere. There were some rough kids around – but Muzzy steered away from that. It was always football with him. He was the sort of lad who liked being at home. He didn't have sleepovers or stay anywhere else. He liked being at home.

"There's six years between Muzzy and Kem. They're quite different people. Muzzy is very diplomatic, very easy going. Kem is a bit more outspoken, a bit more straightforward. Now they're older and that six-year gap isn't so pronounced, they get on well.

"I used to watch him play but it made me feel ill. If it was tense and they were losing 1-0 or 2-1, and the clock was ticking down, I'd have to keep walking out to stand in the concourse. I couldn't bear it. Even watching it at home, on the telly, if it gets tense, I can't stand it. I have to go in the kitchen.

"I don't watch it now. I've spent enough time watching football, with him and then Kem. I'm so very proud of him, I'm very proud of both of them. They've both done well.

"Muzzy is still a good kid. He's still grounded, down to earth. He was fortunate to have the career he had, but it didn't change him. He's very family-orientated, and it's lovely to see him now, as a father, with his children. He's a good dad. I love that.

"He's so forgetful, though. We had a Staffie dog called Bonnie when we lived in Canning Town. He took her for a walk once. He was 14 or 15. He was only supposed to take her to the green, near our flat. He was gone for about two hours.

"He came back without her. He took her for a walk – and then got involved in a football match. He forgot about Bonnie. She was lost. We searched everywhere for her – Battersea dogs home, all the dog pounds – she was gone.

"And then, two months later, we saw her being walked by this chap. 'Oi, that's our dog,' we said. He wouldn't have it. So we had to follow him home, argue with him and, in the end, pay him to get our own dog back – because Muzzy lost her. But that's Muzzy. He loses everything."

Mehmet Izzet, Muzzy's dad

"I arrived as a three-year-old at the end of the 1950s. I knew no English, I didn't know what we were doing. My mum was sick on the boat all the way from Cyprus. We came from Larnaca, by the beach – nice weather – to live in the slums in north London. It wasn't a great start.

"At school, me and my two brothers had to learn quickly how to look after ourselves. We got some stick – so you learned to put a marker down. But we were raised as English. We embraced the country while remembering, always, our Turkish roots.

"I met Jackie when I was 16. She was beautiful. She still is now. I got her pregnant, and I remember having to tell her old dad, old Georgie Newman. I thought: 'He'll be bloody furious with me' but he was all right. We got married and lived with him for a bit. I didn't marry in haste. I knew she was the one. I worked as a shoe-maker, but Georgie said: 'Why don't you come with me, roofing – you'll earn more money.' So I did, and that became my job. It was hard work, but honest work.

"Muzzy was a lovely little lad. I loved being around him. Kem was the same, too. They've both been good kids. I'm a lucky man. It was all football with Muzzy. He trained five days a week, then played games the other two. Everything I taught him, he got straight away. He picked things up so quick. I thought all kids were like that. It was only later, when I saw him in other teams with older kids, that I realised that wasn't always the case.

"The technique side of his game, the skills, that was never a problem. It was his size. Muzzy is 5ft 10ins now – but I remember Terry Skiverton was that size when he was 16. Muzzy was 5ft then. But it was playing those games, against kids twice his size, that toughened him up. We tried everything with him, though. Pasta, milk puddings, Mackeson Stout. None of it worked.

"I remember Chelsea stiffing him, going back on their agreement. They changed their mind when I showed them the contract, but still. It left a nasty taste. I remember saying: 'Look, son, we can try somewhere else' but he stuck at it.

"We went to Florida that year for our holiday. He didn't go. He stayed so he could go to Chelsea. He showed balls as a kid. I was so proud of him. I thought that was fantastic.

"I was there with Kem when he made his debut at Leicester. It was atrocious. So much booing. When they brought him on, I remember everyone around us was going: 'Muzzy who?' And then he picked the ball up and went past three players. That shut them up. The highlight for me was that Palace play-off win. He had to get 100 tickets for that one. We were ALL there!

"I was a West Ham supporter, growing up. But I don't bother about them now. Leicester are my team now. We have had so many good times following Leicester. We moved up here in 2010. We live in the neighbouring village. I see him most days. I come over, do his garden, bits and pieces. He's looked after us. I want to help."

Carly Izzet, Muzzy's wife – the final word...

"I saw him for the first time walking home from Woodside School in Canning Town. Summer 1987, a few months after Mum and Dad split up. He was small and thin and went to the school opposite, which somehow made him more unobtainable.

"I wasn't the only one who liked him. All the girls at his school did and a good number at my school, too. He was skinny and small but funny, charming and handsome, too.

"It was months before we spoke. We became friends and I fancied him, not realising he fancied me, too. He was even more shy than I was! Nothing happened for a couple of years and then one day he came to my house and asked if I'd go to the late night pictures at Barking with him.

"I was thrilled – but couldn't. My mum wouldn't let me stay out until past 7.30pm. But it made me like him even more – it seemed so grown up that he could stay out until past 9pm.

"He came back and suggested a night at the bowling alley in Beckton with his mate Ben and my friend, Kereen. I was so delighted that even when I spotted him paying with coupons from the *Newham Recorder* I didn't mind, I thought it was funny.

"We fell out sometimes. He'd say he was coming round and then play football, so I'd get the hump and that would be it, and we split up for about a year when we were maybe 17. I went out with someone else. I think he went out with a few girls. All it did was make me realise how much I liked Muzzy.

"He wasn't like the other East End boys. He was kind. He had old-fashioned manners. My mum thought he was lovely. He had a nice way about him. You go to school in East London and there aren't many boys like that. Muzzy stood out.

"I knew he played football but I didn't have any interest. I never asked him about it, and he never told me, really. When he was a kid, at school and we were going out, I thought he wanted to be a sign-writer. That's what he used to tell me.

"We were going out when he was at Charlton. I know he went to train with others, but I thought all boys who played did that. It didn't seem a big deal and he never made it sound like one. I only knew what he was doing, really, when he joined Chelsea.

"I was a PA at *OK!* magazine and one of the blokes was a fan. He knew I was going out with Muzzy and he said one day: 'I see your bloke's on the bench tonight…' and I didn't even know.

"Muzzy used to moan about Glenn Hoddle, going on about the lack of opportunity, how he wasn't getting a proper chance. I kept saying to him: 'If it's that bad then go somewhere else.' But he wouldn't. He wouldn't quit. It's not in his nature.

"I was on holiday when he signed for Leicester. I rang him from Tenerife and he wasn't there. 'He's gone,' his mum said. 'Gone where?' I asked. 'To Leicester. He signed today.'

"People next to me in the hotel were from Leicester. I didn't tell them I was his girlfriend. I said one day: 'My boyfriend has a chance to move to Leicester with his job – I might go with him' and they pulled a face. 'Don't do it, love. 'It's a shit-hole!'

"Two months later, I quit my job and moved up, into a detached house on a newish estate in Markfield next to the motorway. It was nice. Quiet. The people were friendly. The club's old goalkeeper had lived there before us. He was 6ft 8ins and had altered the doors so he didn't have to dip under them. We had the tallest doors in Leicestershire. The only downside was that it was colder than London; when it snowed, it settled for days. It was like living on the side of a mountain.

"We always talked marriage but I didn't want the aggravation. We'd mention kids – I wanted four, he wanted one. We got engaged when I came up and that would have done. But after we had Ella, I wanted us to have the same name. He agreed. He was on holiday and rang me from a bar. He sounded drunk. He said he loved me and that we should get married.

"We were married on Saturday, June 7, 2003, and now live in south Leicestershire with our children Ella, Dylan and Lyla. We love it. We moved in the summer of 2000. This is our home now. We're settled. I love London and I miss Canning Town – well, what it used to be – but this is our home.

"We've never had a big argument. Muzzy's too laid back. I still love him. He's a brilliant dad to our children and he has time for them. They adore him. His worst faults? He's more miserable than he used to be – but that's his age! And he forgets everything. I blame football for that. He never had to do anything. He never had to think for himself. The club did it all for him.

"We have an old-fashioned division of labour. He can't cook. He can't do a thing. I don't think he's ever ironed. But he's funny. He still makes me laugh. He's kind and generous, honest and loyal. A good man. A good dad. A good partner.

"I can't imagine being without him."